MARBURG REVISITED

MARBURG REVISITED

A REEXAMINATION OF LUTHERAN
AND REFORMED TRADITIONS
EDITORS,
PAUL C. EMPIE & JAMES I. McCORD

AUGSBURG PUBLISHING HOUSE
Minneapolis, Minnesota

MARBURG REVISITED
A Reexamination of Lutheran and Reformed Traditions

Library of Congress Catalog Card No. 67-11715

Preface

EARLY in this decade the desirability of theological conversations between members of the Lutheran and the Reformed traditions was discussed informally. In the spring of 1961 sponsorship of such conversations was approved by the North American Area of the World Alliance of Reformed Churches Holding the Presbyterian Order and the U.S.A. National Committee of the Lutheran World Federation. A preliminary meeting was held in New York in February, 1962; annual consultations thereafter culminated in a meeting at Princeton, New Jersey in February, 1966, when the sessions were given over chiefly to summarizing and evaluating the previous discussions.

It was agreed that the objective would be "to explore the theological relations between the Lutheran and Reformed churches to discover to what extent the differences which have divided these communions in the past still constitute obstacles to mutual understanding." In order to encompass the concerns of groups within the two traditions not related to the two sponsoring organizations, invitations were extended to and accepted by the Orthodox Presbyterian Church, the Christian Reformed Church, and the Lutheran Church-Missouri Synod to take part. It was clear from the start that the individuals named to participate would speak for themselves, their conclusions neither necessarily representing nor binding the respective churches which appointed them.

The papers and summaries prepared in connection with each annual consultation were printed in pamphlet form and given wide distribution among the clergy of the related church bodies in this country and Canada. The recommendation that this material be made available for use in theological seminaries led to the decision to have them printed together in a single volume.

The statement drawn up and unanimously approved at the final session is ample evidence that these theological conversations were fruitful. Although all discussions were "off the record" and it is not always easy to relate the summary statements to the papers discussed prior to their formulation, it can be said that as the participants became better acquainted and more effective in communication, caricatures disappeared and misunderstandings were rectified. Most important of all, distinctions were made between differences which were matters of relative emphases rather than contradictions in substance. Not all controversial points were touched upon nor were all differences resolved. However, the conclusion that each group recognized in the other a true understanding of the Gospel is significant and the implications of this fact are inescapable.

We suggest that the materials in this book be read in the light of the following statement adopted by participants in their final session:

During these four meetings we have examined carefully the major issues which have aroused theological controversy between our traditions for generations past. At some points we have discovered that our respective views of each other have been inherited caricatures initially caused by misunderstanding or polemical zeal.

In other instances it has become apparent that efforts to guard against possible distortions of truth have resulted in varying emphases in related doctrines which are not in themselves contradictory and in fact are complementary, and which are viewed in a more proper balance in our contemporary theological formulations.

A number of differing views and emphases remain to be resolved, but we are encouraged to believe that further contacts will lead to further agreement between the churches here represented. We regard none of these remaining differences to be of sufficient consequence to prevent fellowship. We have recognized in each other's teachings a common understanding of the Gospel and have concluded that the issues which divided the two major branches of the Reformation can no longer be regarded as constituting obstacles to mutual understanding and fellowship.

We are grateful to God that he brought us together for these discussions, acknowledging that such confrontation under the guidance of the Holy Spirit was long overdue. Although we can speak only for ourselves, we express our conviction that the work begun in this way must not be permitted to lapse, but should be carried on to fruition by the churches we represent.

We who have had the privilege during the course of these conversations of strengthening the bonds of Christian unity and brotherly affection thank God for the evident working of his spirit in our midst and pray that what was begun in this way will be carried on to a successful conclusion with all "deliberate speed."

James I. McCord, *President*
Princeton Theological Seminary

Paul C. Empie, *Executive Director*
National Lutheran Council

CONTENTS

PART III

PART IV

PART V

Chapter One

GOSPEL, CONFESSION AND SCRIPTURE
by Warren A. Quanbeck

THE Reformation of the sixteenth century, in its initial period, was not a movement of rebellion against Catholic authority or doctrine. Luther's Ninety Five Theses were the work of a loyal Catholic and intended no break with the church. He was rather asserting the catholic and apostolic tradition against dangerous innovations in the preaching and sale of indulgences. In his monkish sincerity and innocence Luther was surprised that Rome did not support his gesture. He never quite overcame his disappointment that the hierarchy of the church supported manifest error and repressed a biblical understanding of the church's doctrine and practice.

The Augsburg Confession of 1530 is similarly not the manifesto of a rebellious or separatist group, but is intended as the confession of the true catholic faith in opposition to questionable late medieval traditions. A doctrine or practice is catholic not because it occurs within the catholic church, but because it is an expression of, and consonant with, the apostolic gospel witnessed to in the Scriptures. The purpose of the Reformers is the plain and clear exposition of the good news by which the church lives, so that the church may be reformed and renewed by the proclamation and apprehension of the gospel.

The church of the Reformation is therefore not a theological or ecclesiastical innovation, but an assertion of the true apostolic and catholic tradition in a day of theological confusion and corrupt practice. It finds its roots not in ideas originating in the sixteenth century but in the Scriptures, the prophetic and apostolic witness to Jesus Christ. It looks for its origin not to Reformation Day 1517, but to the events of Good Friday, Easter and Pentecost, when God's redemptive love for mankind achieved its climactic expression. It accepts the centuries of the church's life as the story of God's redemptive deeds among a disobedient and refractory people. It sees the theological, liturgical and disciplinary heritage of the church as evidence of the Spirit's working among men. But the Reformers perceived very early in the struggle that traditions cannot be accepted uncritically. The measuring rod of the apostolic tra-

1

dition in Scripture must be set over against all of the other traditions to assess their truth, soundness and validity. The Word of God gives life to the church, and also judges the church. God is no departed benefactor whose heirs may make free with His treasure. He is the living Lord who rules His church by His activity in the Holy Spirit. When church leaders rule the church as if it were their own property, then God is barred from His own household and His treasures are ransacked by pirates.

Whatever the Protestant Reformation has become, in its different aspects and emphases, under a variety of historical circumstances and social situations, its initial impulse was the assertion of the apostolic gospel against all other traditions, however august or distinguished their spiritual pedigree. The Lutheran and Reformed churches, have, moreover, maintained through the centuries a common emphasis upon the centrality of the gospel as the life-giving and renewing power in the church. The true church is to be found where the gospel is proclaimed and the evangelical sacraments administered. There God meets sinners with His grace and acts redemptively in their midst with word and sacrament.

I. THE GOSPEL

THE Reformation may be described from one point of view as the rediscovery of the strangeness, offense and glory of the gospel. This is not to suggest that the gospel was unknown during the middle ages, but that it had been domesticated and made manageable through theological, liturgical and administrative devices. The Reformers had a vivid sense of the otherness of God and His sovereignty over church as well as the world. They recognized that God is the living God who exercises His kingly rule, and not a retired chairman of the board who has relinquished the administration of His church to others. Their awareness of the sovereign presence of God finds eloquent expression in their doctrine of the gospel. The gospel is not common human property, discerned by all men in the structure of the universe, or deduced from human experience. It has not been invented or discovered by men, but is a message from a realm beyond man's reach, a word accessible to men only because God has broken into human affairs and startled man to awareness with His speech to them.

The Reformers' understanding of the gospel has received dramatic reinforcement in the literary and historical studies of the Bible in the last century. This did not seem to be the case at first, and most churchmen reacted against the historical study of the Bible, as a movement subversive of faith and morals. But while some theologies of their period have had their relevance questioned, the Reformers, and especially Luther and Calvin, have emerged from the process of historical study with more impressive stature than before. It is particularly their exposition of the Scriptures which commends them to the twentieth century student. But the problems of the twentieth century differ greatly from those of the sixteenth. We cannot stand pat on quotations from the Reformers or the confessions, but must speak to the questions that are being raised today. The following statement is an attempt to speak to the questions raised by historical-critical study of the Bible and the church's tradition from the theological viewpoint of Luther and the Lutheran Confessions.

The good news which calls the church into being and by which it lives is the message which comes from God Himself, the good news of His love for sinners and of His redemptive intervention in human history. This saving purpose of God is not a sudden and capricious act bursting forth without notice to the apostolic community, but is prepared in the history of Israel in the covenant of promise. The Christian church knows itself as continuous with Israel, accepts the Old Testament as its authoritative Scriptures, knows its Messiah as the revelation of the Covenant God and sees the history of the covenant people as the preparation for His coming. The New Testament Gospel is fulfilment, a development out of God's earlier dealings with Israel. The coming of Messiah is not the rejection of Israel's history, but its consummation.

Prophecy As the Word of God

Studies in Old Testament theology in our time have given us the materials for a richer and deeper apprehension of the gospel. The gospel proclaimed by the apostles is seen against the background of God's message through His prophets. The prophetic message is not simply a restating of the content of natural human religion. It is, to be sure, historically conditioned, and grows out of concrete human situations. But its distinctive quality is that it transcends the human situation and points the way to a new relationship, the covenant, a new obedience, the life of God's people, and a new destiny, life with God who gives Himself in a unique way through the prophetic message. Unlike the vegetation religions which surrounded Israel, and whose attractions were a perennial problem, the knowledge of God in Israel is not natural, achieved through fulfilment of ritual. No Israelite knows God simply because he has been born in a certain territory. Knowledge of

3

God is granted in the covenant, which stands because of God's gracious initiative in making Himself known to His chosen people. And within the covenant God speaks through His prophets to give the knowledge of His will. He differs from the gods of the nations in that He is a God who speaks. He does not wait for men to attend to Him, but takes the initiative and seeks them out. And He seeks to draw them to the service of His purpose as He shows them His love and favor within the covenant, and He guides them to the knowledge of His purpose for their salvation and the salvation of mankind.

The Old Testament teaching concerning the Word of God would be unique among the religions of the Middle East even if this were the whole story. But there is more. As Israel grows in understanding of its covenant relationship to God it comes to recognize that the word spoken through the prophet is also the word by which the world has been created and is sustained. The God of Israel is not one among the gods, one of the more influential and certainly the most eloquent. He is the only God, the maker of the worlds. All things come from Him, and of His power and goodness all things subsist. Israel finds its own place in the world of nations and of created things in its awareness that the God whose word called the universe into being, also called Israel to be His servant, and entrusted to it the task of bringing the knowledge of His glory and love to all the world. Israel's destiny is not simply to bask in the status of most favored nation, but to devote itself to the honor of the divine name.

Because the Word of God is not only the prophetic word, but the creative word as well, it can be recognized as the word of *power*. God's speech is not simply divine talkativeness and certainly not merely human chatter. It is the way God chooses to relate Himself to His world and His creatures. His word is the vehicle of His action. When He speaks the universe comes into being. His address calls Israel to be His servant. His word delivers a helpless band of slaves from their bondage and ushers them into the land of promise. His word speaks judgment upon a complacent and disobedient nation and sends them off into captivity to learn their lessons the hard way.

In the New Testament the prophetic word returns to Israel in the ministry of John the Baptist. After two centuries' dearth of the word of prophecy, God speaks again to His people. The Jewish people throng to the Jordan valley to hear John's preaching, agog with excitement as they hear his call to repentance and his promise of the Messiah's imminent coming. The Jewish authorities find his ministry more disquieting, because he not only preaches but administers a baptism conveying forgiveness of sins. As custodians of the institutions of Israel's religion they find this rite a disturbing new rival to the temple cultus, and inquire at once about his authority to baptize. But what disturbs the Jewish authorities comes to us as a reminder of the event character of the prophetic word. God's address is a word with power, not only generating sound waves in the atmosphere but accomplishing the divine purpose.

Jesus of Nazareth also appears to Israel as a prophet. He speaks the Word of God and the word is with power. By His word He casts out demons, heals the sick, gives sight to the blind, cleansing to lepers, hearing to the deaf, and life to the dead. His miracles manifest the power of the divine word on His lips. He invites His contemporaries to see in His works the manifestation of the powers of the new age foretold generations before by the prophets. He suggests that He is the stronger one come to bind the adversary and despoil his possessions. He makes claims to authority over law, Sabbath, temple and tradition which shock His theologically trained contemporaries. He sets aside the tradition of the elders, assumes an authoritative posture in the interpretation of the law, and astonishes ordinary people to remark about His new teaching with authority, not at all like the scribes.

But Jesus' claims of authority go beyond anything in Israel's experience with the prophets. He dismays the rabbis by disregarding the "hedge about the law": healing on the sabbath, sharing meal fellowship with sinners, choosing a tax collector as a disciple. He sets aside the exegetical proprieties and speaks an authoritative word about the law, dropping a remark that He has not come to destroy the law but to fulfil it. He assumes authority as Lord of the Sabbath and seems to seek out occasions to demonstrate it. When questioned about His disciples' neglect of fasting, He uses the occasion to intimate that He is the bridegroom of Israel, to His contemporaries a frightening appropriation of a title belonging to the Covenant God. He claims authority to forgive sin, an authority which every pious Jew knows belongs to God alone. He ignores the proper temple authorities and proceeds to reorder the temple by force, the act either of a revolutionary or one with quite exceptional authority. When the Jewish authorities show their resentment of His program, He affronts them the more by selecting from among His disciples a band of twelve, a public gesture of reconstituting the twelve tribes of Israel.

Even for His disciples He remains an enigmatic figure. While His claims to authority seem to include Messiahship and more, He deliberately eschews the title of the common expectation, Son of David,

5

and uses instead the ambiguous self designation Son of Man. He puzzles His followers by references to betrayal, ignominious treatment by Jewish authorities, death by crucifixion and a resurrection. He emulates the prophets of ancient times by symbolic actions in the ceremonial entry to Jerusalem or the cursing of a fig tree. But whereas the symbolic actions of the prophets point to the activities and judgments of God, Jesus interprets His symbolic actions in terms of His own significance. At times He seems the humblest man of His age, playing with children, risking gossip by speaking to a strange woman, accepting ceremonial contamination by touching a leper, washing His disciples' feet as though He were a household servant. At other times He arrogates to Himself passages of Scripture that seem the sole property of the Covenant God, and interprets His own career in terms that embrace not only Israel but the entire world. When we read the synoptic Gospels in the light of modern studies in the rabbinic or apocalyptic traditions the Jesus who emerges from their pages has no resemblance to the gentle Jesus of popular religious art or of some alleged educational aids. He can be approached by the humblest of creatures but at the same time estimates His own person and career in cosmic and eternal terms.

The Apostolic Preaching As the Word of God

The crucifixion of Jesus shatters the Messianic expectations of His disciples. Their theology has no place for a disgraceful death, nor for the unexpected and inexplicable fact of resurrection. The Fourth Gospel suggests that they tried to return to old vocations and patch up the tatters of disappointed hopes. But after Pentecost, perhaps to their own surprise, they find themselves only a little better off theologically, but possessed of new and unexpected resources of power. When they testify to Jesus, His ministry, death and resurrection, as the act of God for the redemption of Israel, they discover that their words are words of power and are the Word of God. Through their preaching new followers are won, the young community is encouraged and strengthened. The power of the word is manifest in acts of healing and restoration. New and strange manifestations of the Spirit accompany their simple and humble proclamation. Just as the ministry of Jesus added new and surprising dimensions to the prophetic word, the word concerning Jesus Christ is now manifest as a new aspect of the Word of God. In Israel the words of exposition attending the reading of Scripture are only the words of men, not of God, and are scrupulously kept in their place. In the new Israel the witness to Jesus Christ as God's redemptive deed is more than the word of man—it becomes the instrument of the Holy Spirit. It is taken up into the divine purpose and becomes itself one of the acts of God in the history of salvation. But where the apostle witnesses to Christ as Messiah and Lord, where the praises of God's redemptive deeds are sounded, there God acts anew to bring to present reality the benefits of Christ's life and death for mankind. The gift of prophecy was a sporadic thing in the old Israel; in the new messianic community the Spirit is present as power. The risen and exalted Christ continues to live His redemptive life in the community which is His Body through the presence of His Spirit. The apostolic preaching is the renewed offer of Christ and life in Him, as the congregation responds to God's address it experiences anew His presence and power.

Jesus Christ the Word of God

As the apostolic community carries out its mission in the world it comes to recognize yet another aspect of the Word of God. What is implicit in the earlier tradition becomes explicit in the teaching of the Epistle to the Hebrews and the Gospel of John: Jesus Himself is recognized as the content of the divine message, the Word of God. The Johannine tradition presents Christ to the hellenistic world as the Logos of God. The author of the Letter to the Hebrews also points to Jesus Christ as the culmination of divine revelation. "God has spoken to our fathers in many and various ways, but in these last days He has spoken to us by a Son." In these formulations the church recognizes the creative and transforming newness of Jesus the Lord. He is a prophet, indeed the greatest of the prophets, yet more than a prophet. He is Messiah, but one quite unlike the common expectation, strange, enigmatic and awesome. He cannot be contained within traditional categories. He is a teacher, but one whose originality does not consist only in new ethical insight. In a bold and magisterial way He points to Himself as the fulfilment of the divine purpose and as one with the God of the Covenant. To do justice to these claims one is pushed either into scandalized opposition or to a loyal search for categories adequate to the truth about Jesus. The early church intends to maintain biblical monotheism. But in view of what Jesus said and did and was, they are compelled to construct new theologies which climax in trinitarian doctrine. Anything less tries to domesticate Jesus within the framework of the old Israel or some hellenistic religion or syncretism. But the old wineskins cannot hold the new wine. Jesus cannot be applied like a new patch on old clothing. He shatters all the contemporary theologies and demands bold and creative thinking to deal adequately with what God has brought to pass in Him.

The experience of the apostolic age recurs in the history of the church. We try to receive Jesus as Messiah, and then try to fit Him into the categories in which we live. We do so because we have not grasped the dimensions of the biblical witness to Him, or because we desire insulation against the terror of the divine presence, or because we are managing His church as efficiently as possible. But Jesus will not be domesticated, however ingenious our attempt or sincere our motives. He will not be managed but wills to be the Lord, and shatters our theologies and piety, just as He did those of His disciples.

As heirs of the Reformation we see in the turmoil and tragedy of the period one of these painful but salutary experiences of Christ asserting His sovereignty. Luther summed it up in such terms when in 1538, comparing Rome and Reformation, he remarked: "We have no differences on the deity of Christ, nor on His humanity. The difference lies here: they will not let the Holy Spirit do His work." In this devastating understatement Luther reminds us that apparently small differences can be tremendously significant. The divine address gives us a new understanding of who God is, of what our world is, and of what we are and are intended to be. The message of the Reformation is that we seek to do justice to this transforming encounter in our theology, our churchmanship, and our relation to the world.

Law and Gospel

The realization that Jesus Christ the Redeemer is also the Son through whom the universe was created has creative theological power in the church. Creation and redemption are held in close connection as the acts of the one God. Dualistic solutions of the human dilemma, such as Zoroastrianism or Marcionitism, have always been attractive to the ethically serious thinker, and were tried on for size by some theologians in sub-apostolic times. But the church resolutely rejected dualism, maintaining a biblical evaluation of the world as God's creation. The obedience of the Christian is to be worked out in the world, not in flight from it. At the same time the church recognizes that the world suffers from the consequences of the Fall, and that as a result the Christian affirmation of the world cannot be an unqualified one. Christian theology, especially in the Lutheran church, has sought to express the unity and tension of this relationship by using the language of law and gospel.

When the Christian has met God in Christ through faith he learns

8

that his previous sinful existence, and the world in which he lives, are to be understood in theological terms. His total environment, though ambiguous as a result of sin, is a creation of God, and basically good. To the man who lives without Christ these ambiguities, combined with his own sinful self assertion, become opportunities for idolatry. Man seeks to be god in his own life and to exploit the world of nature, of history and of human society to his own advantage. But his natural life is not without the presence of God, who has structured His creation in accordance with His will. Even in the fallen world sinful man meets God behind masks, which conceal His presence, but at the same time exercise His preserving grace and judgment. Man's sinfulness is curbed by the political authority, which punishes evil doers and rewards those who practice civil righteousness. It is curbed also by the family, where limits are set to human freedom and the benefits of life in community meted out. It is curbed by man's social and economic interdependence, where anti-social behavior is repressed and at least a minimum of cooperation worked out. These structures of the created world are at work even after the Fall, and manifest the preserving goodness of God as well as His judgment upon sin. Here the same love, which in the fulness of time chose the way of the cross, operates to limit the exercise of sin and to preserve the world for the coming of the gospel.

Thus in the natural world man meets God, but meets Him not as God of love but as providence and judgment. Here God meets man with His law, to require that he be responsible, to prod him when he sins. Man is surrounded by God in every moment of his life, but his encounter with God is not "saving" but an occasion for frustration and judgment. This is especially so because the natural realm is not one of reason and freedom, but of irrationality and ambiguity. The criminal occasionally goes unpunished and the comparatively righteous man suffers. Reward does not always accrue to the deserving and the fool is often accounted noble.

The natural realm is a realm of paradox. Here man meets God **9** in the experiences of daily life, but he encounters not the God of grace but the God of wrath. He is constantly in the divine presence, but God remains hidden. His meeting with the hidden God is at once an experience of judgment, and at the same time reception of God's mercy in preservation. The realm is one of ambiguity, inequity and injustice, but in the shadows stands God keeping watch over His creation, and guiding it toward the accomplishment of His loving purpose.

Where the law gives an encounter with the God of judgment, the gospel gives a knowledge of the God of love. Where law demands, insists on responsibility, and threatens with death, the gospel offers the love of God in Christ, creates freedom and promises life. The law meets man in his self-assertion and unbelief; the gospel is received only in faith and self-surrender. The law challenges man to keep its demands and then mocks him with a reminder of his failures; the gospel invites him to put his trust in God's love and faithfulness, and leads him into God's household, and not just as a servant or suppliant but as a son. The law meets man in every circumstance of life, although man may run away from its demands; the gospel meets him only in the word concerning Jesus Christ, in the church's announcement of God's great act for the world's salvation.

In the gospel God offers man in Christ the gift He offered first in the creation of the world. What man lost through his grasping, is given him anew in Christ's self-giving. In sin man has lost the image of God in the sense of a life which reflects God's love. In Christ the image is being restored in him, and with it authentic human existence is recovered. In Adam man seeks life, but seeks it by self-assertion. In Christ man receives the gift of life, and lives in it as he dies and rises anew each day with Christ. Where sin afflicted man as guilt, bondage and rebellion, in Christ he lives in forgiveness, freedom and sonship. Thus redemption in Christ is God's recapitulation, His way of returning to the beginning.

The gospel is not only fulfilment of law, it is its transformation. The man in Christ has received forgiveness, freedom, adoption; he also recovers his life in the world in a new dimension. In Christ he has both redeemer and creator, salvation from sin and death, and also the recovery of the natural, the worldly, the secular. He is now enabled to go into the world as God's man, a free man. Formerly he lived in the world as idolater, aggressor, exploiter. Now he has recovered his true identity and knows his place in the world. He no longer strives to be the *"Übermensch,"* even of the junior grade or garden variety. He accepts his status as a creation of God, lives by the grace of God, and seeks to be a Christ to his neighbor. By submitting to the sovereignty of God in Christ, he discovers the true freedom, and is delivered from the demand, the power and condemnation of law. To be sure, whenever he fails to respond to God's invitation to live in Christ, he asserts himself anew, and comes once again under the judging action of the law. Luther's phrase "simul justus et peccator" does not suggest that nothing real has happened in faith, but that the believer finds himself struggling with the old nature, and tempted to live his own way rather than God's. The righteous man is the new man in Christ; the sinner is the old man in Adam, who must daily be put to death.

The question of the third use of the law has been a vexing one in Lutheran theology. For Luther the law always condemns. Its function in the life of the Christian is to rebuke him when he forgets that he has put on Christ. When he lives by the Spirit he is free of the law, but when he yields to the persuasions of the flesh, the law seeks to drive him again to Christ. The Formula of Concord in its discussion of the third use of the law makes the same point. For although Christians "are indeed reborn and have been renewed in the spirit of their mind, such regeneration and renewal is incomplete in this life. In fact, it has only begun, and in the spirit of their mind, the believers are in a constant war against their flesh (that is, their corrupt nature . . .), which clings to them until death" (Formula of Concord, Epitome, Article VI, 4).

The life of the Christian in the world is a free and willing submission to the conditions God has given him. He accepts himself, his family, his work, friends, neighbors and community, not as blind fate but as the will of a loving Father. These are the opportunities God gives him to share Christ with his neighbor. He serves God in his neighbor, not to the dictation of the law, but as a free child of God. He seeks to be Christ to his neighbor, not by attempting a carbon copy of the days of His flesh, but by becoming conformed to Christ who is the image of God. He does not seek to make his life a museum of relics of the apostolic age, but seeks the mind and spirit of Jesus Christ as his own, so that he may do "what love requires" in the quite new and original situation in his life. It is as he lives in Christ in the concreteness and realism of His body the church that he hears anew the liberating word of the gospel, meets the risen and regnant Christ at His table, and thus grasps some of the meaning of his incorporation into Christ in baptism. As he shares the joys and sorrows of God's people, he is built up as a living stone in the temple of God's presence. As he joins with God's family in their worship of adoration, thanksgiving and intercession, he becomes a living branch of the true vine, and bears fruit. It is in the common life of God's ordinary people, in the indwelling of the Holy Spirit, that he is equipped for his Christian warfare.

This is not to be understood as antinomianism, the use of discipleship as a cloak for hypocrisy, but as an insistence that man becomes God's man only in the freedom of faith and in the fellowship of God's

11

household. Both are necessary. Freedom apart from the community of faith may become religious titanism or bourgeois conformity. Where God's people do not enjoy open freedom in the gospel they may settle for the pettiness of moralism and legalism.

II. CONFESSION

Confession As Doxology

T HE term confession derives from a variety of Old Testament and New Testament expressions whose central thrust is the praise and glorification of God. To confess is to herald forth the mighty acts of God by which He has delivered His people, as in the Exodus. It is to hymn the praises of the God of the Covenant whose glory it is to show mercy to the afflicted, to heal the broken hearted, and to deliver the captives.

A subsidiary usage, "to confess one's sin" seems to be a different category, but in reality is not. For the biblical tradition, confession of sin is a form of the praise of God. By acknowledging his transgressions, man recognizes that God is justified in His sentence and blameless in His judgment (Ps. 51:4). Confession is not man's dismal savoring of his wickedness and perversion, as though in the absence of virtuous acts and achievements he accumulated spiritual capital by dwelling on his transgressions. This is simply the way western religious man seeks to assert his ego even in the presence of God. For prophetic religion the accent is on the praise of God, and confession of sin by man is tributary to this doxological function.

The early Christian community focused its praise of God in the confessional formula "Jesus is Messiah." This is to affirm that God has wrought another and greater Exodus in His Messiah, and it praises Him for His redemptive deed. The church accepts the ignominy of the cross in spite of its offence to Jews and its foolishness to Gentiles, because in the light of the resurrection it discloses both God's judgment on sin and His mercy to sinners. The proper response to God's deed of redemption is worship and praise, the faith-full acceptance of God's gift of life and the adoration and thanksgiving of the Redeemer.

When the church began its missionary work on hellenistic soil it faced the problem of translation. To a Greek speaking community the expression "Jesus is the Anointed-One" had too little specific content to be religiously or theologically serviceable. Without an understanding of the Old Testament, and the prophetic interpretation of its vocabulary, the hellenist was cut off from the meaning of the church's confession. Missionary preachers confessed their faith in the Messiah in the phrase "Jesus is Lord," making use of another title of Jesus current in the Palestinian church, and relating to the vocabulary of the Septuagint where *Kurios* renders both "Adonai" and the tetragrammaton, the ineffable name of God.

This venture in translation, the first of many made by the Christian church in its missionary work, helped hellenists understand the religious vocabulary of the church, but still left many problems. For while to the Jew schooled in the Old Testament there is only one *Kurios,* the living God of Israel, to Gentiles there were many *kurioi,* each of them contending for the religious loyalties of the ancient world. The danger was that Jesus should be understood as one of these lords. This would indeed give Him a place, and perhaps an honored one, among the generously hospitable religions of the time. But it offended the monotheistic convictions of Christians that Jesus should be patronized by false religions by being admitted to the Pantheon. To avoid syncretistic appropriation of the church's treasure, the church had to learn to maneuver defensively. And with this struggle against misunderstanding and syncretism the early church developed another function for its confession, the confession as hermeneutical guide.

Confession As Hermeneutics

During the apostolic period the church waged a defensive battle on two fronts. It had to contend with the syncretistic tendencies of the ancient world, but it had to struggle also with the synagogue. To the old Israel the Christians were an increasingly vexatious problem. In the earliest days of the church, Christians were mainly Jews, and remained within the fellowship and religious practice of Israel. At first they appeared to be simply another party or sect within the nation, a sect maintaining that Messiah had come, and was to be identified with the crucified and risen Jesus Christ. Christians continued to live within the covenant, observing the law, taking part in worship, although with certain additions of their own, such as the celebration of the Lord's Supper. But as time passed the confession of Jesus as Messiah began to transform the religious thinking and practices of the Christian community. When the mission among Gentiles got under way, and Paul began to receive Gentiles into the fellowship without circumcision or the keeping of the Mosaic law, tensions began to increase. Synagogues in the Dispersion received the first Christian missionaries cordially and listened attentively to their witness. But when the missionaries made converts to the new fellowship, many of them the fruit of missionary

13

activity by the synagogue, hospitality turned into hostility. When Gentile converts became numerous the whole question of "covenant succession" became critical. Where is the true Israel to be found? In the synagogue, which has all the marks of the covenant: the Torah, circumcision, the Sabbath, the tradition of the elders, the cultus?—or in the new fellowship which claims to be continuous with the old Israel but has abandoned Torah, circumcision, sabbath observance and cultus and rejected the tradition of the elders?

To us who have known only contemporary Judaism in its cultural isolation this problem seems remote and unreal. Furthermore, the Old Testament plays so small a part in our theology and piety that we find it difficult to imagine it as a critical hermeneutical problem. But to the early church which had only the Old Testament as its Scriptures, this problem was crucial. It was especially troublesome because not all Christians were of one mind in the understanding of the Old Testament and the relation of Jesus Christ to it. In Israel there had been a variety of interpretations of the messianic hope, and this variety was reflected in the early Christian community. But since Jesus was proclaimed as Messiah of Israel, and the Christian community knew itself as the true Israel, a persuasive Christological interpretation of the Old Testament was of great importance.

Within the pages of the New Testament we find the documents of this encounter. The Epistle to the Galatians shows us Paul's radical Christological interpretation of the Old Testament as against that of the Pharisaic party in the church. The Gospel of Matthew and the Epistle to the Hebrews lead us into the debate between church and synagogue, showing the intensity of the struggle and the argumentation employed. The church utilized the doctrine of the Virgin Birth to support its claim to be the true and legitimate Israel. The Messiah is at once continuous with the old Israel, a Jew born under the law, and at the same time God's new man, a new beginning, the breaking in of the eschatological dimension. The church differs from the old Israel in its practice because it is the new community, the fellowship of the Spirit. Because God has entered upon a new stage in His dealings with men, therefore the church differs in structure from the synagogue. When the new age has dawned, the shadow is replaced by substance and the prophetic gives way to fulfilment.

The New Testament also shows us some aspects of the confessional development of the church against hellenistic syncretism. In Ephesians, Colossians, the Pastorals and the Johannine literature we can observe the Christian community under the guidance of the Spirit striving to express its witness to Jesus as Messiah and Lord. Against tendencies to dilute the Christian message into either a philosophy of religion or a legalistic ritualism the apostolic writers stress the event character of the Messiah's coming and the significance of the church as the Body of Christ, the organism in which God's redemptive realism finds continuing expression.

The hermeneutical function of confession is apparent also in the growth of the church's confessional formula. The simple confession of the hellenistic church "Jesus is Lord" has by the early second century taken a form approximating that of the Apostle's Creed. Harnack regarded this development as the influence of hellenistic speculation upon the basically ethical religion of earlier times, a shift completed in the Trinitarian and Christological speculation of the third and later centuries. More recent studies in the history of the creeds lean toward another interpretation.

The addition of the first article to the creed is now seen not as a speculative interest in theology or cosmology but as Christological statement. It affirms that the One whom we encounter in Jesus the Christ is the Lord of the covenant, the same God who created the world. Against either gnostic speculation or the distorted Paulinism of Marcion, the church asserts the continuity of the covenants, affirms the Old Testament as its authoritative Scripture, and insists that Jesus is to be understood only against the background of the prophetic witness of the Old Testament. The proper setting for the understanding of the church's proclamation is the prophetic scriptures of the Old Testament and the community of Israel as God's people. The gospel must not be extracted from this context and placed in the setting of syncretistic religion or that of the mystery cults.

Similarly, the addition of historical clauses to the basic Christological affirmation—suffered under Pontius Pilate, crucified, dead and buried, descended into Hades—does not represent the work of a church historian who has strayed into a class in systematic theology. Against all docetism whether of Hebraic or Hellenistic origin, the church asserts the historical character of God's address in Christ. The docetists seek to protect God from contaminating associations with a material and sinful world. The church insists that God is not embarrassed by the material, for He made it, and that incomprehensibly enough, He has chosen the way of incarnation for the assertion of His redeeming love for sinners. The clauses added to the Christological confession summarize the apostolic proclamation, furnishing the setting apart from which Jesus the Christ cannot be properly understood. He belongs in

15

the context of Israel, of the Old Testament, of a God who speaks and acts in history, of the activity of the prophets, and of the common life of God's people in the Christian community. The God and Father of Jesus Christ is not an aristocrat, a philosopher, or a country gentleman. He is a God who works, and His creative activity endows with dignity the world that He has made and all human toil and activity within it. This is the apostolic proclamation, reasserted and reinforced in the creeds.

Similarly, the Nicene creed does not seek to add to our store of information about the household affairs of heaven, but to give the proper hermeneutical approach to the act of God in Jesus Christ. In Jesus the Lord we encounter the God of the Covenant, the creator of all things. In Him we meet, not just the highest of the creatures, but One who is consubstantial with the Father. He is begotten, not in the sense that He is the biological generation of the Father, but in the sense that what is begotten is of the same kind as the begetter, while what is made is qualitatively different from the maker. So the church affirms her conviction that in Jesus Christ the believer meets not only a man, nor a great prophet. He is the Messiah of Israel, and a greater Messiah than had been expected; He is Very God.

The Augsburg Confession performs the same kind of interpretative function. The medieval church assumed that Scripture, the church's tradition, and scholastic theology were identical in content. Any tensions between Scripture and tradition were resolved by use of the Quadriga, the medieval system of biblical interpretation which recognized four levels to the truth of Scripture: literal, tropological, allegorical and anagogical. Great respect for the authority and content of the Scriptures could thus coexist with a theology and practice quite different from the Scriptures. Intentions were doubtless commendably good, but where a semi-pelagian or pelagian estimate of man was operative, other areas of theological thought were skewed, resulting in unbiblical teachings in soteriology, ecclesiology and pneumatology. Luther in his monastic innocence and sincerity thought to do the church a service by calling attention to the threat to Christian faith and life implicit in the preaching and sale of indulgences. When the authorities refused to acknowledge the authority of the apostolic tradition in Scripture over the ecclesiastical tradition, the Reformers loyally continued to assert the apostolic tradition against those who claimed the apostolic succession. As the fourth century tested catholic teaching on the doctrine of the Person of Christ, the sixteenth century assesses the truth of the church's proclamation on the issue of justification. If any merit can be ascribed to man in his justification before God, then the glory of Christ is diminished and obscured. For if man is able to accomplish his own salvation, then Christ died for nothing.

But the assertion of the apostolic tradition on the doctrine of justification involves more than an editing of a chapter of dogmatics. God's act in justifying the sinner through faith in Jesus Christ is so central that the recovery of evangelical perspective here calls for correction of emphases in all dogmatic and ethical topics, the whole understanding of the life with God and in the world. The Augustana accordingly does not break off with article four, but proceeds to delineate the biblical perspective in the doctrines of the church, the sacraments, the new obedience, church government and discipline, and relation to civil government. The article on justification is the point at which Christ *the* light of the world has broken through the clouds which obscured Him, and gives new illumination to the understanding of all of life.

The other confessions in the Book of Concord share the hermeneutical function. This is quite explicit in the case of the two catechisms. Luther's visitation of congregations in 1528 and 1529 left him horrified at how little understanding of the Christian faith and life was manifest among the people. The small catechism was written to provide a household manual for plain people, an introduction to the meaning of the Christian faith. The "large" catechism is addressed to pastors, and offers them an evangelical interpretation of their tasks and responsibilities.

This understanding of the significance of the confession is also stated explicitly in the introduction to the Epitome of the Formula of Concord. "In this way the distinction between the Holy Scripture of the Old and New Testaments and all other writings is maintained, and Holy Scripture remains the only judge, rule, and norm, according to which as the only touchstone all doctrines should and must be understood and judged as good or evil, right or wrong."

"Other symbols and other writings are not judges like Holy Scripture, but merely witnesses and expositions of the faith, setting forth how at various times the Holy Scriptures were understood in the church of God by contemporaries with reference to controverted articles and how contrary teachings were rejected and condemned." (Formula of Concord, Epitome, Introduction, 7, 8.)

Confession As Formulation of Truth

Ever since the Christian mission entered the hellenistic world, influences have been at work to produce another understanding of confession, as the definitive formulation of the truth. For the biblical tradition truth belongs to God and is accessible to man only as God chooses to reveal it to him. The apostolic witness points to the disclosure of truth in Jesus Christ, who is Himself the truth. This truth of "being" is apprehended by faith in Christ, so that man "knows" the truth (in the biblical sense of knowing) and abides in the truth as he lives in Jesus Christ in His Body the Christian church. Language has an instrumental function in relation to truth, pointing to the Person in whom truth is to be known, and offering, in the proclamation of the gospel, the encounter with the living God who is the truth.

For the hellenistic world truth is usually assumed to be accessible to man, capable of expression in propositional form, and to be apprehended by man's intellect or reason. Where this hellenistic attitude toward truth becomes predominant in the Christian church the vocabulary of the Bible is understood in hellenistic categories, with a resultant distortion in the understanding of the biblical message. Truth becomes accessible in the form of theological propositions, faith is altered to mean the acceptance of the truth of statements, theology becomes a shrine for the truth rather than a tool for witnessing to the truth in Christ. The theologian acquires unique status in the church, as the one who by his conceptual precision and dialectical agility is master of the truth. Dogmatic statements become repositories for the truth and are to be defended with all energy, because truth stands or falls with them. And from this arises the *"rabies theologorum"* of which Melanchthon complained so poignantly. From this follows also the somber history of theologians and church groups engaged in bitter struggle for the truth, each persuaded that the formulation of his tradition is the truth, and that those who resist or deny it are not merely opposing men, but denying the Holy Spirit.

Twentieth century theological scholarship has at its disposal a perspective which should overcome the distortions of this over-intellectualized view of confession and theology. Comparative studies in philosophy, history, religion and linguistics, the work of various schools of analytical philosophers, and penetrating studies in the theology of the Bible should provide the equipment to enable us to take truth seriously without idolizing the symbols that point to it. We can recognize that God's disclosure of Himself to man has taken place in the context of history, taking the risk of exposure to the relativity and contingency of the historical process, but yet offering to the believer knowledge of the truth and a share in the life that is really life. As we have come to see the historical and human character of the Bible, so we can perceive the historical conditioning of the theological process. No theological concept can be absolutized, for only God in Christ is absolute. This is, of course, not to abandon the theological enterprise, which still keeps its highly important function of examining the proclamation, teaching and practice of the church to see that Christ is heralded forth as God's offer of life to sinners. Neither does it propose a plunge into mysticism or a theology of irrationalism. God addresses man in His *Word;* He speaks to the whole man, body, soul, mind, will, emotions. But it does suggest that those who aspire to theological understanding need a proper humility as well as a disciplined ability to distinguish between the categories of the Scriptures and those of the theological traditions.

III. THE SCRIPTURES

THE Christian church knows God through His address in history. He revealed Himself to Israel in the Exodus, the judgment of the exile, and the restoration. By His grace Israel was able to live by knowledge of Him through the institutions of the covenant: He revealed Himself to the disciples in the Jew of Nazareth in Galilee, Jesus the Messiah of Israel. He continues to reveal Himself to the Christian church in the proclamation of the gospel and the administration of the sacraments. Here the risen and exalted Jesus Christ is the present and effectual action of God through His servants in the ministry of the church. It is Christ who is the true preacher of the gospel, the true minister of God to unite men to Himself in baptism, the true host at the feast.

Because God has chosen to make Himself known in the contingency of the historical process, the events which reveal Him are limited in time and place. Not all cultures or ages can be contemporary with Jesus the Christ. But the knowledge of God is not therefore at the mercy of human forgetfulness or mystical notions of spirituality. God has given Scripture and the church to connect the once-for-all act in Jesus Christ with the present act of the Holy Spirit, who is the presence and power of the risen Lord. God calls His church into being by the word of the gospel and by His presence as Holy Spirit equips and empowers His people for His service. To His church He entrusts the Scriptures, the prophetic and apostolic witness to Jesus Christ, the bearer of His word.

In her confession that the Bible is the word of God the church states her conviction that the Bible is also an act of God in the history of salvation. The Spirit has moved His servants to write; He has given them understanding of the redemptive significance of His historic deeds; He has led His people to preserve and treasure the testimony of His servants; He has guided the church in the selection of a library of books which serve as effective witness to His self-disclosure in Christ, the prophetic witness in the Old Testament, the apostolic witness in the New Testament. The detailed study of the Bible in modern times has made it plain that He has not done this by a stenographic process, by suspending the human consciousness of His servants. He has used men in their human limitations of language, style, and knowledge, has accepted the natural and historical limitations of the created world, and has yet so guided the process that the resultant collection of books serves His salvatory purposes. The Bible is from one point of view a completely human book, and demands for its proper understanding the detailed study of language, literary and historical context, authorship and date. But it is at the same time a unique book, because in the providence of God it serves His redemptive purpose. The church has learned in its Christological reflection to reject all Ebionite, Docetic, Appollinarian, Nestorian and Eutychian misunderstandings. In the present century it is learning that each of these Christological errors has a parallel in the approach to Scripture. Any doctrine of Scripture which denies or abridges the fully human character of the Bible is a danger to the gospel and the church, even though it may be motivated by opposition to liberal theology. For just as the revelation of God is given in the human being Jesus of Nazareth, so also the Word of God is given through the historical witness of men in the Bible.

Since God's revelation takes place in events it is necessary that the revelatory event be preserved in the memory of God's people. In the Bible we have the recollection of God's redemptive deeds, culminating in Jesus Christ the crucified, risen, and exalted Lord, in the sending forth of the Spirit and the establishment of the apostolic community, the church. The history of Israel is not only a matter of archaeological interest for specialists in middle Eastern civilization and religion. It is the history of God's people, and is thus the family history of us who live by God's grace in the church. If we would know who Christ is, we must know Israel's history and theology, for He discloses His identity and mission by relating Himself to that history.

The career of Jesus Christ is, moreover, not a matter only of biographical curiosity, as though we were seeking by psychological penetration to detect the secrets of human greatness. The gospels are not written as biographies but as proclamation: they offer us the life of Christ, lived once in the days of His flesh and now lived anew in the Christian community. The Evangelist proffers not merely a satisfaction for our historical or biographical curiosity, but the overwhelming gift of God in Christ.

The history is in the service of God, a bearer of revelation. But the events are capable of more than one interpretation. The Exodus can be explained as a series of coincidences in political, social and natural affairs. But the Scripture records the prophetic interpretation of these events as the unfolding of God's purpose for Israel's redemption. Jesus of Nazareth has also been interpreted in many ways. He can be seen as a great teacher, the greatest of the prophets, a good man victimized by the scheming of His enemies, an apocalyptic visionary, or a religious reformer trapped by the ecclesiastical machine. But the New Testament writings present Him as Messiah of Israel, Son of God, Saviour, Redeemer, Judge. They do not provide demonstration of the truth of their claims, but present the challenge to faith. In Jesus Christ God offers us life. Choose life!

The Spirit of God uses the Scriptures as the instrument to make the saving events contemporary with sinners of all times. As the Scriptures are read, studied, proclaimed within the fellowship of faith the word spoken in Jesus Christ is spoken once again, re-presenting God's saving act in the proclamation of the church. The revelatory event of the past becomes a living reality in the present. This takes place through the working of the Holy Spirit in the context of the Christian congregation. Through the exposition of Scripture, God speaks His creative and liberating word, bringing men under His judgment, offering sinners His grace.

The authority of Scripture is the authority of the *deus loquens,* the God who speaks in Scripture. He gives us not only historical information and theological interpretation, He offers us Himself. In the Scriptures we hear the address of the living God, whose word is also deed. There is no way to demonstrate *a priori* the authority of the Scriptures. Traditional arguments based on the Bible's realism and honesty, the beauty of its language, the inner harmony and consistency of its teachings and its numerous other excellences speak persuasively to those who have already experienced its power, or are by acculturation inclined to accept such claims. But to those outside the household of faith such arguments have little force. The Christian conviction that the Bible is the Word of God rests upon the experience that God the Holy Spirit has spoken authoritatively from its pages. The literary and historical study of the Bible has emphasized the human aspect of the sacred writings and has thus lessened the dangers of bibliolatry, of making the Bible an end in itself rather than an instrument of the

21

Spirit. By doing so it has also renewed our appreciation of the Reformers' stress upon the *testimonium spiritus sancti internum*. The Bible is God's instrument prior to, and independent of, its impact upon men, but its proper function is performed when it confronts men effectively with God's judgment on sin and His offer of forgiveness.

Christ As the Content of Scripture

The initial impact of historical studies in the Bible seemed inimical to a Christian use of the Old Testament. The correlation of prophesy and fulfilment was threatened by the new insistence upon the historical meaning of every Old Testament passage. But while some interpretations of Old Testament prophecy have been casualties of historical scholarship, the Christological dimension of Old Testament interpretation has been recovered in a richer and fuller way. The Old Testament contains a number of theologies, but from these our Lord selects one and gives it His sanction. It is entirely possible to derive a theology of achievement from the Old Testament, and insist that religion at its best is character development. It is also possible to insist that the servant songs of Isaiah are to be understood as referring to the nation, and not to any individual. There is nothing in the Old Testament itself which compels a scholar to come to a Christological interpretation, as the flourishing Jewish biblical interpretation today shows. That men perceive Christ in the Old Testament remains a miracle of the Holy Spirit, who alone gives understanding of the divine purpose. But Jesus interprets the Old Testament as a message of God's gift of life, a gift, moreover, offered in His person. He who accepts Jesus as Messiah and Lord accedes to the claims that Jesus made for Himself, and these involve a comprehensive Christological interpretation of the Old Testament. This interpretation is not, however, a jerry-built allegorical construction, but is oriented to the history of Israel and to its historical institutions of king, priest, temple, cultus, sabbath, covenant and law.

The historical studies have also questioned the unity of the Bible, even of the New Testament. The scholars of the sixteenth century took the unity of the Bible for granted, and assumed a common vocabulary and theology. We still tend to read the synoptic Gospels as though they were written by Paul, and find the vocabulary of Reformation theology throughout the New Testament. But what historical scholarship in its earlier stages took away, it has in more developed forms given back in enriched and revitalized condition. We now see the New Testament as a unity in diversity. The diversity is not a chaos of unrelated and competing theologies, nor is the unity a lifeless and artificial fabrication. The unity is the *kerygma,* the word concerning Jesus Christ, and is richer and deeper for the various vocabularies which develop to expound the relevance of the gospel. The diversity is the range of different theological interpretations within the pages of the New Testament, which do not threaten the unity of the testimony but rather show how comprehensive and far reaching the good news really is. God's address to mankind is not limited in its application to the Jewish people and to Palestinian soil, but relates to all sorts and conditions of men, and hence has the possibility of being meaningful for us today.

The Bible presents formidable problems of interpretation. Because it is composed of many books, written over a period of several centuries, out of different cultural situations, it requires the services of many specialists in order to apprehend its message. Apart from the problem of establishing the text, which is in itself a major undertaking, biblical interpretation requires specialists in language, literary forms and style, archaeology and cultural influences. It demands knowledge of the history, customs, ways of thinking of the people who produced and read it, an understanding of the historical situation in which the book was written and of the author's purpose.

There are those, of course, who have no patience with this exacting task of critical interpretation and prefer to deal with the Bible as though it had no relationships to its times, a timeless book untouched by human hand. Their motives are not always questionable or vicious; they are frequently reacting against what they regard as a relativizing of the biblical message. They fear that once the critical process is under way it will be impossible to point to a sure message from God. But it is important to recognize that the historical character of the Bible makes the critical process not only permissible but necessary. The gospel is not present in the Bible like precious metal in unprocessed ore, gold amid dross. We cannot print certain passages in red letters as the divine message and dismiss all others as merely human verbiage. Because God manifests Himself in history, every part of the Bible has its proper place in the unfolding of the divine purpose, though not every passage has the same function. The theological insights of the book of Joshua are not on the same level as those of the Fourth Gospel, but Joshua has nevertheless its proper place in relation to the coming of the Christ. The message of the Bible comes to its focus in the person of Him who is the Word of God. The relationship of each part of the Bible to its total message can be determined by its relationship to Christ, and what it contributes to our understanding of God's purpose in Him.

23

Biblical interpretation requires therefore not only literary and historical principles but a theological principle as well. God's message to us in Christ varies with our relationship to Him. He whose relationship to God in Christ is evasion or rebellion will hear God's address to him as a demand for responsibility. When he heeds this message and comes to know himself as God's creature, he can listen comprehendingly to the offer of life in Christ. At its deepest level, biblical interpretation demands not only sound critical judgment but an existential relation to the God who speaks in Scripture. For only the Holy Spirit can give understanding of the realities of God's redemptive purpose, which is the content and unifying principle of Scripture.

It is wrong to make law into gospel, to interpret the message of the Scriptures as a demand for character development. It is also wrong to turn gospel into law, to assume that the authority of the Scripture is a legal authority. The Lordship of Christ is perceived only in the experience of repentance and faith. This happens most commonly, not to an individual reading his Bible in isolation from the Christian tradition, but in the setting of the church's worship and proclamation. The interpretative context for the understanding of the Scripture is provided by the testimony of the church given in sermon, song, visitation of the sick and needy, and in Christian fellowship. Wherever the church shows forth the love of Christ in word and work, the living context for the understanding of the Scriptures is present, and the Spirit acts anew to proclaim the saving word.

Chapter Two

GOSPEL, CONFESSION AND SCRIPTURE

by George S. Hendry

O F all the names which have been borne by the churches of the Reformation none is more descriptive of what is essential in their faith than the name "evangelical"; for the Reformation originated in the recovery, or rediscovery, of the gospel in the midst of a church in which it had been largely transformed into a law. "The Reformation of the sixteenth century," wrote Philip Schaff, "is, next to the introduction of Christianity, the greatest event in history . . . It was a deeper plunge into the meaning of the gospel than even St. Augustine had made."[1] The churches of the Reformation are those which live by and proclaim the message of salvation as the gift of God's free grace through Christ, to be received by faith alone, and are therefore properly called evangelical. It is a matter for regret that this beautiful name, which has adhered to the churches in Germany and other parts of Europe, has now disappeared from the scene in the United States in the recent realignment of Lutheran and Reformed churches there. Nothing can ever be so important to the Lutheran and Reformed churches as to be evangelical, i.e., to hold firm to the gospel and to maintain the integrity of their testimony to it.

The Reformation may be said to have been accomplished in the the church when the church was moved to confess its faith in the gospel which had been restored to it. It has often been remarked that the confession of faith is, historically, a phenomenon of the Reformation. It was not known in the unreformed church, and the confessional documents which now exist in the Roman Catholic Church originated in opposition to those of the Reformation. It is the church of the Reformation that is the confessing church.[2]

---

[1]Schaff, Creeds of Christendom, 1931, I, p. 204.

[2]The question has been raised whether the churches of the "catholic" type, which adhere to the ancient creeds and use them in the liturgy and in catechetical instruction, are not equally entitled to be called confessional or confessing churches. In principle, there is no reason why they should not. The issue that was raised at the Reformation, however, was whether the ancient creeds, which were accepted as authoritative state-

25

This is no mere historical accident. There is an intrinsic connection between Reformation and confession. One of the basic elements in the recovery of the gospel, in which the Reformation originated, was the realization that the gospel is not a word *of* the church, but, by its very nature, the word of God *to* the church.[3] The church cannot handle this word as if it had it under its own management and control. Whenever the word is made an instrument in the hands of the church, it loses both its credibility and its efficacy. The word retains its veracity as the power of God unto salvation when it comes *to* the church and the church receives it by faith as not its own.

The gospel, then, is not a word which the church speaks. But it is a word to the church which constrains the church to respond. The word which the church speaks in response to the gospel is its confession, and so responsive in character is the confession that, though it is something the church truly speaks, it may also be said to have been "composed" by God (as the German text of the Preface to the Book of Concord says of the Augsburg Confession).

This is the basic sense of confession in the New Testament. It is the first word which faith speaks in response to the gospel, and it takes the brief and highly concentrated form of an acknowledgement that "Jesus is Lord" (Rom.10:9, I Cor.12:3; cf. Jn.20:28).[4] The AC with its concentration on the gospel of Christ comes close to this model.

In the churches of the Reformation, however, the term was extended to embrace documents of three different types which serve three more or less distinct purposes in the church. All three are represented in the official collection of Lutheranism, two among the Reformed:

(1) The first type is represented uniquely by the AC. There is no Reformed confession which resembles the AC in its concentration on the gospel. Its nearest counterpart on the Reformed side is the first edition of Calvin's *Institutio,* which he presented to the King of France as a "confession" in 1536.[5] The *Institutio* of 1536 exhibits a similar concen-

---

ments of the confessional tradition in which the whole church stood, were adequate to confess the faith in relation to the specific questions that divided the church at the time; whether, therefore, the ancient creeds should be regarded as an incentive to contemporary confession, as is stated in the Preface to the Epitome of the Lutheran Formula of Concord, or whether they are held to preclude it. There is a difference between a church which *has* a confession (Bekenntniskirche) and a confessing church (Bekennende Kirche). The Church of England, for example, has a confession in the Thirty-Nine Articles, but it could hardly be said that this is how the Church of England confesses its faith.

[3] Cf. H. Diem, *Theologie als kirchliche Wissenschaft,* 1951, p. 19; L. Newbigin, *The Reunion of the Church,* 1948, p. 61.

[4] Cf. E. Schlink, "Die Struktur der dogmatischen Aussage als oekumenisches Problem" in *Der kommende Christus und die kirchlichen Traditionen,* 1961, pp. 33ff.

[5] Library of Christian Classics, Vol. XX, p. 9.

tration on the gospel. Calvin employs the term frequently in his letter to the King; sometimes he varies it for "Christ" or "Christ and his gospel." Calvin also resembles the AC in his concern to rebut the charge of innovation and his stress on the catholicity and antiquity of the evangelical faith: "he who knows that this preaching of Paul is ancient, that 'Jesus Christ died for our sins and rose again for our justification' will find nothing new among us. That it has lain long unknown and buried is the fault of man's impiety. Now when it is restored to us by God's goodness, its claim to antiquity ought to be admitted."[1]

(2) There are the writings which were designed for the instruction of the people in the evangelical faith which they confessed. These had antecedents in the pre-Reformation church and tacitly followed their pattern. Luther's Catechisms expounded the Ten Commandments, the Creed and the Lord's Prayer in succession, and Calvin followed his example in the first edition of the *Institutio,* which, though it was used to make confession before the King, was written primarily for the instruction of his French compatriots who were "hungering and thirsting for Christ."[2] The Geneva Catechism of 1543 contains the same three ingredients—but with a significant change: the Creed is expounded before the Law. Calvin's Catechism also differs from Luther's in its much greater elaboration: it has 373 questions and answers, some of which make considerable demands on the child's intelligence. In this respect it sets a pattern which was followed by most of the Reformed Catechisms, the Heidelberg, the Westminster, etc., and which tends to assimilate them to the third type.

(3) The third tpye of confessional document is that which is designed for the clarification of the church's mind concerning the faith which it confesses and the definition of its position on questions in dispute. It is represented in the Lutheran collection by the Formula of Concord, which is not strictly a confession, but rather an authoritative interpretation of the Augsburg Confession (which some Lutherans regard as the only true confession). The FC is related to the AC much as the Definition of Chalcedon is related to the Niceno-Constantinopolitan Creed. The difference between them may be expressed in this way: The AC answers the question, What is evangelical? the FC answers the question, What is Lutheran? The Reformed confessions for the most part fall into the latter category. This is not to say that they lack the note of confession in the basic, evangelical sense; for this note is present in all of them, and occasionally it is sounded like a

27

---

[1]op. cit., p. 16.
[2]op. cit., p. 9.

clarion, as in the Scots Confession of 1560. But it remains true that the Reformed confessions have more the character of constitutional documents, by which the confessional position of the churches is defined, than instruments with which they actually confess their faith. The crowning example of this type of document is the Westminster Confession of Faith, which originated, not in a confessional situation at all, but in the context of a politico-ecclesiastical scheme which was the price of a military alliance. It is a miracle of grace that the Westminster Confession, considering the circumstances of its origin, is not a great deal worse than it is.

The varied character of the confessional documents points to some of the difficulties which underlie the confessional relations of Lutheran and Reformed churches. Both are avowedly confessional churches, and they have this in common over against churches which profess, or pretend, to be non-confessional. But in view of the wide range of meanings which the term "confession" covers, the churches may be confessional in widely different ways, depending upon the point in the spectrum at which each has its confessional focus. And when they are focussed at opposite ends of the confessional spectrum, as is the case with most of the churches represented in these conversations, the common title may conceal the extent of the distance between them. For, apart from the common name, what has the Augsburg Confession in common with the Westminster? (The question almost sounds like an echo of Tertullian's, What has Athens in common with Jerusalem?) It is clear that not only a hundred years of history lie between them, but such vastly different conceptions of the nature of a confession, that it is a question whether the term has not been stretched beyond the limits of its natural resilience. And how does subscription to the AC compare with subscription to the WCF? It would be easy for any evangelical Christian to subscribe the AC (as Calvin did); for it is little more than an acknowledgement of the gospel. But subscription to the WCF has long been a problem in the churches which hold to it.

The problem is intensified by the fact that the WCF fills a role which is primarily constitutional rather than confessional, and this tends to assimilate it to analogous political models. To swear allegiance to the constitution of the United States, for example, means to bind oneself to every article and every amendment in it. And it seems natural to assume that subscription to the Confession of Faith should be understood in an analogous way as acceptance of every article it contains. There have been groups and individuals in the Presbyterian Churches— and still are—who would have the meaning of subscription to the Confession of Faith understood in this way and who would question the orthodoxy of any one who takes exception to any single proposition in it. Yet the Presbyterian Church has from its first organization in this country employed formulas of subscription which certainly did not require this interpretation and may have been intended to exclude it. The Adopting Act of 1729 required all ministers to accept the Confession of Faith and the Larger and Shorter Catechisms by declaring their "agreement in and approbation of" them "as being in all the essential and necessary articles, good forms of sound words and systems of Christian doctrine."[1] At the reorganization of the Church in 1788, after the Revolutionary War, this was replaced by the formula which (with some modifications) is still in use and which prescribes two questions: "Do you believe the Scriptures of the Old and New Testaments to be the Word of God, the only infallible rule of faith and practice?" Then, "Do you sincerely receive and adopt the confession of faith of this church as containing the system of doctrine taught in the Holy Scriptures?" There has been considerable discussion as to the precise meaning of this formula, and particularly of the reference to the system of doctrine. Is it logically—or theologically—possible to distinguish the system from the sum of its component parts? There has been fairly general agreement with the position taken by Charles Hodge one hundred years ago (to the consternation of many in the church at that time) that adoption of the system does not commit the subscriber to acceptance of every proposition contained in the Confession as a part of his own faith, but rather to some selection of doctrines which have been historically designated "fundamental"; the Church at a later date took the hazardous step of identifying five such doctrines as "essential and necessary" (though it balked at the logical implication that other doctrines were not essential or necessary).[2] On the other hand, when the Church adopted a Declaratory Statement in 1902/3 defining the interpretation of certain propositions in the Confession of Faith, this would seem to presuppose a view of subscription as connoting acceptance of every proposition in the Confession: and, as was said above, there are still some in the Church who take this view (in theory, if not in practice)—as recently as last year (1962) an attempt by a small but determined minority to have a minister excluded from membership of presbytery, because he refused to affirm his belief (or disbelief) in a doctrine contained in the CF, was carried to the supreme judicatory, where it was defeated—but (characteristically) on a point of order.

29

[1]Lefferts A. Loetscher, *The Broadening Church*, University of Pennsylvania Press, 1954, p. 2.
[2]A. A. Hodge, *Life of Charles Hodge*, Scribners, 1880, pp. 406ff. Loetscher, op. cit., p. 98.

The position of the Church of Scotland in the matter of subscription is defined more clearly—but at the cost of claiming for the Church a degree of doctrinal authority, which is barely compatible with the position of the WCF, to say nothing of the Scots Confession of 1560. The Form and Order for Ordination includes this statement: "The Church of Scotland holds as its subordinate standard the Westminster Confession of Faith, recognizing liberty of opinion on such points of doctrine as do not enter into the substance of the Faith, and claiming the right, in dependence on the promised guidance of the Holy Spirit, to formulate, interpret, or modify its subordinate standards: always in agreement with the Word of God and the fundamental doctrines of the Christian Faith contained in the said Confession—of which agreement the Church itself shall be sole judge."

II

THE second problem that has to be discussed is that of the relation of the confession to the Scriptures. In both Lutheran and Reformed churches the authority of the confession is subordinate to that of Scripture. The difference is underscored by the difference in the verbs employed in the Presbyterian formula quoted above: the Scriptures are "believed," the Confession is "received and adopted."[1] In fact, the primary function of the confession is to affirm the supreme and sole authority of Scripture in the Church, and it has done this so effectively that, despite the suggestion in the Formula of Concord that Luther's Catechisms might substitute for Holy Scripture as "the laymen's Bible," its authority has to a large extent disappeared behind that of Scripture, and the confession itself has become a dead letter in the church. There are, of course, differences between the Lutheran and Reformed Churches in this respect, and differences also between both of them as they exist in Europe and in America. There is less confessional consciousness in the Reformed churches than in the Lutheran,[2] and less in both churches in Europe than in America.[3]

30

[1] The Formula of Concord uses the verb amplecti of the ancient Creeds (Intro., #3), so also Melanchthon (CR 9,279; 23,195, cited by Elert, Morphologie des Luthertums, I, Page 183).

[2] Unless it has escaped my notice, no article on the confessions has appeared in either of the two leading journals of Reformed theology in the English-speaking world since its inception (Theology Today, 1944; Scottish Journal of Theology, 1948). By contrast, The Lutheran Quarterly, The Lutheran Church Quarterly, The Lutheran World, and The Concordia Theological Monthly have carried a large number in recent years; and one appeared in the first number of Dialog, the latest to be founded.

[3] Cf. Tappert in Essays on the Lutheran Confessions etc., 1961, p. 27. No doubt part of the reason is that the Churches in America required the confessions to identify themselves over against the state and other churches. Interest in the confessions appears

The function of the confession, however, is not merely to assert the supreme authority of Scripture; it is to provide authoritative guidance and direction in the interpretation of Scripture. When the confession is virtually allowed to disappear behind Scripture, the result tends to be a kind of Biblicism, which deviates from the hermeneutical direction of the confession. Here we have to note one of the basic differences between the confessions, to which reference has already been made. If we may disregard for the present the catechetical documents, the remaining two types may be characterized as the evangelical and the constitutional respectively. The Lutheran confessions belong for the most part to the former category, the Reformed to the latter. The difference reflects the different stages at which they originated; the Lutheran confessions, with the exception of the Formula of Concord, were all in existence by 1537, the Reformed originated after that date—the seven most important of them in the two decades between 1543 and 1563, "when the age of the Reformation was already beginning to pass over into the age of Orthodoxy."[4] To use a military metaphor, if the Lutheran confessions, with the AC as their spearhead, represent the initial breakthrough of the Reformation, those of the Reformed churches, with the WCF as their rear-guard, represent the consolidation of the position gained.

The evangelical type of confession I have so named because it is concerned primarily to assert the efficacy of the gospel, i.e., the evangelical message of salvation by grace through faith in Christ. No formal statement of the authority of Scripture appears in any of the Lutheran confessions prior to the Formula of Concord, and there only in the form of an affirmation of its superiority to that of all other writings. It has often been said in explanation of this silence that the authority of Scripture is presupposed, and that it could be left that way because there was no controversy between the Reformers and their opponents on the point.[5] No doubt there is truth in this. The question is, however, whether the doctrine of the authority of Scripture, when it was made explicit in the Reformed Confessions and in the Lutheran dogmatics of the post-Reformation period, corresponds to the form in

31

---

to have been at a relatively low level in the Lutheran Church in Germany until it was stimulated by the theological quickening of the 1920's and, more especially, by the church sthuggle under the Third Reich. Cf. Schlink, *Theology of the Lutheran Confessions*, p.v.

[4] Paul Jacobs, *Theologie Reformierter Bekenntnisschriften* (Neukirchener Verlag, 1959), p. 11.

[5] Cf. Elert, *op. cit.*, I, p. 159: "The authority of Scripture was a commonplace, not only to Luther, but also to all his opponents, to Thomas, and above all, to the school of Occam"; Althaus, *Die Theologie Martin Luthers* (Gütersloh, 1962), p. 17: "The authority of Scripture is the premise of all theological thinking for Luther."

which it was implicit in the primitive evangelical testimony. Three features of the evangelical confession point up the relevance of the question.

(1) The AC, which is the classic example of the evangelical type, is not interested in any form of the written word (scripture), but solely in the preached word. It is not through revelation or the inspiration of Scripture that we obtain faith, but through the divinely instituted office of preaching (AC, Art. V). The AC here reflects an emphasis, frequently expressed by Luther, on oral proclamation as the proper form of the gospel, the *viva vox evangelii,* which corresponds to the *kerygma* of the New Testament, although the significance of this NT term does not appear to have been perceived by any of the Reformers. Luther sometimes contrasts the *viva vox evangelii* with writing, which he regarded as the proper form of the law: "For in the New Testament the preaching must be done orally, with the living voice, publicly. . . . Christ himself did not write his doctrine, as Moses did his, but gave it orally; he also commanded that it be done orally and gave no command to write it. . . . It is not neo-testamental to write books of Christian doctrine . . . Before they (the apostles) wrote, they first bepreached and converted the people with the bodily voice, and this was their real apostolic and neo-testamental work."[1]

(2) It is saying virtually the same thing when we say that the evangelical confession is interested in the word that is efficacious rather than in the word that is authoritative, i.e., the word that has *dynamis* rather than the word that has *exousia.* Of course, the efficacious word must be authoritative; but, on the other hand, the authoritative word is not necessarily efficacious. The efficacious word is the word that has the character of address, the word that is directed to a hearer and strikes home to him in such a way that he feels himself personally addressed and "put on the spot."[2] It is this kind of experience of the word that brings forth evangelical faith. But there are words in Scripture which, however authoritative, do not have this character and cannot be so experienced. "Therefore," says Luther, "We must use Scripture with discrimination. The Word came in a variety of ways from the beginning. It is not sufficient to observe whether it is God's word, whether God spoke it, but rather, to whom it is spoken, whether it concerns you or another. It is as different as summer from winter . . .

32

[1] WA,10,I,1, 625f. Further passages to the same effect in Althaus, TML, p. 72. It is interesting (and surprising?) to catch a distant echo of this Lutheran emphasis on the priority of the preached word a full one hundred years later in the Westminster Shorter Catechism: "The Spirit of God maketh the reading, but especially the preaching, of the word an effectual means of convincing and converting sinners, and of building them up in holiness and comfort, through faith unto salvation" (A. to Q. 89).

[2] My rendering of Elert's word, *gestellt* (ML,I, p. 60)

There are two kinds of words in Scripture: one does not apply to me and does not concern me, the other does. On the word that does apply to me I may boldly venture and rely as on a firm rock. . . . The false prophets come and say, 'Dear people, that is the word of God,' and it is true, we cannot deny it. But we are not the people to whom he is speaking."[1]

(3) The efficacious (and orally proclaimed) word, which generates evangelical faith, is the word of the gospel. But this word cannot be heard unless it is rightly distinguished from other words, especially the word of the law. It is a primary purpose of the evangelical confession to draw this distinction. Thus it is the interpretation of Scripture, rather than its authority, with which the evangelical confession is concerned; it defines the perspective from which the two principal components of Scripture, the gospel and the law, can be correctly "divided" from each other.[2]

These features of the evangelical confession seem to me to set a question mark against the traditional view that the evangelical confession of the gospel presupposes the inherited doctrine of the authority of Scripture and does not materially affect it (except for isolating it from Tradition). Two facts lend support to the traditional view. The first is the impressive example of Luther, who combined his evangelical testimony to the gospel with frequent and vigorous assertion of the authority of canonical Scripture as a whole. It is well known that the (later?) writings of Luther provide copious material in support of the "conservative" view of Scripture.[3] The second is the fact that the authority of Scripture, when it becomes explicit in the later Confessions, is affirmed substantially in traditional terms; the only difference—and this comes out much more clearly in the Reformed Confessions—is that it is separated from the authority of the church and established on the intrinsic ground of divine inspiration.[4]

Nevertheless, there is a certain tension between the evangelical confession of the gospel and the traditional doctrine of Biblical authority, and it has been questioned whether the Reformers and the authors

33

---

[1]WA,24,12 (cited by Elert, ML.I, p. 160)

[2]The Lutheran confessions more than once invoke this traditional (but erroneous) translation of 2 Tim. 2:15.

[3]Cf. B. A. Gerrish, "Biblical Authority and the Continental Reformation" in *Scottish Journal of Theology*, 10,4, pp. 342ff. Elert suggests that the hardening of Luther's view into a formalistic Biblicism was strengthened by his emphasis on the external word in opposition to the Enthusiasts. (ML I, p. 162).

[4]Cf. WCF I.

of the Confessions were altogether consistent, or successful, in combining them. The former is concerned with a principle of Scriptural interpretation, which is discriminative in effect; it affirms that a certain specific content of Scripture is decisive for faith and constitutes a norm for the interpretation of the whole. But such a principle of interpretation cannot be derived from a doctrine which ascribes authority to Scripture on the basis of its divine origin and which is essentially indiscriminate.[1] Moreover, it is not Scripture, the written word, to which evangelical faith responds, but the preached word, as was already noted; and these are not merely two different "forms" of the word, they point to two different roles or functions of the word, the word as source of faith ("means of grace") and the word as norm of doctrine ("rule of faith"). It is an over-simplification to relate the latter to the former in terms of presupposition or implication; the relation between them is more complex and stands in need of further clarification.

The question may also be presented from the angle of the implied concept of faith. Is the faith by which we respond to the gospel and accept Christ identical with the faith by which we accept the authority of canonical Scripture? The Reformers strove to maintain the equation by relating both to the inner witness of the Holy Spirit, which, according to Calvin, who develops this doctrine most fully, serves not only to produce faith in the saving word of the gospel but also to establish our conviction of the divine origin and authority of Scripture as a whole; "For as God alone is a fit witness of himself in his Word, so also the Word will not find acceptance in men's hearts before it is sealed by the inward testimony of the Spirit. The same Spirit, therefore, who has spoken through the mouths of the prophets must penetrate into our hearts to persuade us that they faithfully proclaim what had been divinely commanded. . . . Therefore, illumined by his power, we believe neither by our own nor by anyone else's judgment that Scripture is from God; but above all human judgment we affirm with utter certainty (just as if we were gazing upon the majesty of God himself) that it has flowed to us from the very mouth of God by the ministry of men."[2] In contrast to Luther, who ascribed our assurance of the specific word of the gospel to the testimony of the Holy Spirit, who says to us in our hearts, "That is God's word,"[3] Calvin ascribed to it also the authentication of Scripture as a whole. He saw this as the

34

---

[1]Elert says that the distinction between the gospel and the law (though "it raises a host of problems") shows that there can be no question of "an indiscriminate authority of Scripture, completely uniform in all details." (ML, I, p. 159).
[2]Inst. I, 7, 4f.
[3]Weimarer Ausgabe 10, 1, 2, p. 335.

only way in which he could effectively oppose the contention of the Romanists that the authority of Scripture was derived from that of the church. He argued, rightly, that the canonization of holy Scripture by the church was not an act of conferring authority on it but rather an act of acknowledging its intrinsic divine authority, the criterion of which was divine inspiration. Calvin implies, however, that the test of divine inspiration must be repeated in all of us before we can accept the divine authority of canonical Scripture, and that we may not rely on the church's historical application of the test. This interpretation is made explicit in the statement of the Gallican Confession: "We know these books to be canonical and the very sure rule of our faith, not so much by the common accord and consent of the church, as by the inner testimony and persuasion of the Holy Spirit, who enables us to distinguish them from other ecclesiastical books, on which, though they may be useful, no article of faith may be founded."[1] Similarly, the WCF traces the distinction between canonical and apocryphal books solely to the presence or absence of divine inspiration, and declares that the authority of the former "dependeth not upon the testimony of any man or church, but wholly upon God."[2] Is this not *Schwärmerei?*[3]

When Calvin returns to the subject in his great chapter on faith, the stress is now on the gospel or the promise of mercy in Christ as the "proper" object of faith, but this presupposes a more general concept of faith as acceptance of the authority of Scripture as a whole: "When we say that faith must rest upon a freely given promise, we do not deny that believers embrace and grasp the Word of God in every respect."[4] Calvin is at pains to refute those who "unjustly charge us with denying, as it were, that faith has regard to all parts of the Word of God,"[5] but at the same times he maintains that the kind of faith which "holds the Word of God to be an indisputable oracle,"[6] even though it may respond in some degree to the precepts, the threats and the promises, still falls short of true faith, which he defines as "a firm and certain knowledge of God's benevolence towards us, founded upon the truth of the freely given promise in Christ, both revealed to our minds and

35

---

[1] Art. 4 (Niesel, *Bekenntnisscriften und Kirchenordnungen der nach Gottes Wort reformierten Kirche,* 1938, p. 67.)

[2] WCF, I, 2-3.

[3] How is the test of inspiration applied to determine canonicity? And can we assume that the result of the test will always coincide with the historical judgment of the church?

[4] *Inst.* III, 2, 29.

[5] loc. cit., #30.

[6] loc. cit. #9.

sealed upon our hearts through the Holy Spirit."[1] The conception is formalized in the WCF in which faith is depicted, so to speak, in the shape of a three-tiered pyramid, in which it ascends (like providence in orthodox dogmatics) from a general form as faith in the Word as a whole, through a special form in which it responds appropriately to specific contents of the Word, to the most special form as faith in Christ: "By this faith, a Christian believeth to be true, whatsoever is revealed in the Word, for the authority of God himself speaking therein: and acteth differently, upon that which each particular passage thereof containeth; yielding obedience to the commands, trembling at the threatenings, and embracing the promises of God for this life, and that which is to come. But the principal acts of saving faith are accepting, receiving, and resting upon Christ alone for justification, sanctification, and eternal life, by virtue of the covenant of grace."[2]

The relation between these various concepts of "faith," more especially between evangelical faith and Biblical faith, is a problem that requires clarification. Divergent views on the problem are found within both Lutheran and Reformed Churches. There are those in both churches who hold to the traditional or "orthodox" view that evangelical faith presupposes and implies Biblical faith, and who contend that the former cannot stand without the latter. They can claim the support of statements in the Confession and in the writings of the Reformers. On the other hand, there are those in both churches—and they form the majority in each—who have difficulty with the equation and who feel that if Christ is the "proper" object of faith (to use Calvin's phrase), this is so different from acceptance of the divine inspiration and authority of Scripture that it is misleading to apply the same term to both. It would be manifestly absurd, for example, to equate *hanc fidem* of AC V with the belief that "Scripture is from God." Nevertheless, they do not deny that Scripture is from God or that this rests ultimately on faith, but they would argue that the Scriptural principle of the Reformation churches is a product of reflection on faith rather than an immediate deliverance of faith, and they would agree with Elert that "in the believing subject as such . . . there is no room for reflections on the literary origins of the records."[3] There is need for clarification of the status of the Scriptural principle in relation to evangelical faith.

36

---

[1] loc. cit. #7.
[2] WCF, XIV, 2.
[3] ML. I, p. 172f.

SUMMARY STATEMENT

Gospel, Confession and Scripture

1. Both Lutheran and Reformed churches are evangelical in the sense that they are rooted in, live by, proclaim and confess the gospel of the saving act of God in Jesus Christ. They receive it as it is revealed in the prophetic and apostolic scriptures, attested through the witness of the Holy Spirit, and preserved in the tradition of the catholic faith as expressed in the commonly accepted creeds of the ancient church.

2. The churches of the Reformation confessed this gospel by means of the biblical concept of justification by grace through faith alone. The scriptures also present the same gospel in other concepts, such as reconciliation, regeneration, and redemption. An evangelical confession accordingly may be, and has been, framed in terms of one or more of these.

3. We are agreed that the new life of faith in Christ involves obedience, but there is some question concerning the place and meaning of law in the new life.

4. The Church is constrained by the gospel to confess its faith. Such confession takes the primary form of praise to God. It must also take the form of confession before man, testimony to and defense of the gospel in various historical situations.

5. Confession takes a variety of forms both in scripture and in the Church. The history of the Church exhibits such types as the doxological confession which celebrates the glory of the gospel, the kerygmatic which identifies and declares the gospel, the catechetical which serves for the instruction of believers, and the critical which distinguishes the gospel from errors and misunderstandings.

6. The confessions originated in different geographical and historical situations and they use different vocabularies. These differences do not of themselves preclude unity in the faith which is confessed in them.

7. Credal and confessional subscription is regarded seriously in both Lutheran and Reformed churches, but there is some diversity of opinion concerning its meaning.

8. We are agreed that in the canonical scriptures of the Old and New Testaments the acts of God which culminate in the revelation of Himself in Jesus Christ, His Son our Lord, are set forth by chosen witnesses under the leading of the Holy Spirit.

9. The confessions affirm the supreme authority of scripture as the norm for the proclamation of the gospel and provide authoritative guidance and direction in the interpretation of this normative scripture.

Chapter Three

LUTHERAN-REFORMED DEBATE ON THE EUCHARIST AND CHRISTOLOGY

by Joseph McLelland

O UR task is to approach the historical controversies of our two communions, in Christology and Eucharist, from the point of view called "historical-critical." First let us state certain axioms of our approach.

Was it Santayana who first said, "Those who fail to comprehend their histories are doomed to re-enact them"? The problem is, that when one tries to comprehend one's history, one is tempted to select certain historical weapons, to clean and oil them and so to re-enact old battles with the zeal of certain Americans during this continuing centenary of the Civil War! The temptation or the question has been put well quite recently, at Faith and Order in Montreal, 1963: "We still find it hard to know what God calls us to keep or to abandon what He calls us to venture."

Part of the answer to this question might lie in the new understanding of dialogue. We may contrast the mood of *debate* with that of *dialogue*. Debate is by definition an argument about the positive and negative answers to a thesis, answers which cannot coexist. With some justification, therefore, debate could be defined as the exchange of mutually exclusive errors. Dialogue, on the other hand, consists in a new polarizing of the answers, so that they are open to a new element, to what Skydsgaard calls "the third party in the conversation—the truth itself." Now in the Reformation, the moods of debate and dialogue are not always clearly distinguishable. Ernst Bizer finds dialogue present, in his fine study of "The Problem of Intercommunion in the Reformation": "It is a false historical perspective to see the Reformation as time of division and opposition, and to overlook this striving for unity. That they did not attain their end detracts nothing from their impressiveness, though it faces us with the question why they failed . . . Even Calvin's writings against Westphal are to be understood in this way" (*Intercommunion,* ed. D. M. Baillie, 1952, p. 59). I should think that this view is too optimistic to suit all the Reformers equally well. From the dialogical point of view (the assumption that truth includes both sides of the question at issue) one should have to describe a sort of spiral, with irenical types like Bucer and Melanchthon at the center, Oecolampad and Peter Martyr farther out, then Brenz and Calvin and finally Luther, Zwingli and Beza. That is, the posture of the various Reformers varies with their assumption about the area of truth, about the way theological truth was present in the discussion. At least, our critical survey of their debates must have before it this question of their intention, and of the extent to which it informed their answers positively or negatively.

Finally, the question of limits for discussion in this paper presents a problem. I suggest that we may consider the essential ground as that between Marburg, 1529 and Montbéliard, 1586. After that the long period of cold war set in, marked with certain signs of thaw to be sure, but not really changing until the "German Evangelical Theology" of the nineteenth century, and the various conversations leading up to the present situation of dialogue in this ecumenical age. (I am somewhat hesitant of saying too much on this point, lest Herman Sasse be quoted against me—he regards these historical conversations as examples of the Reformed error of supposing that the Reformation produced one "evangelical" church, to which both Lutheran and Reformed belong— it is an "utter impossibility" to reconcile "two fundamentally different conceptions of Revelation and Gospel" (*Here We Stand,* pp. 100, 146)). These later developments more properly belong to the second paper, therefore here we shall concentrate on the period 1529-1586, assuming that the general history is in mind, and that we may select persons and subjects to illustrate our critique.

Luther and Zwingli

The accidents of history are not always kind. Marburg was the end of the beginning but also the beginning of the end. It was the conclusion of a series of skirmishes, in which (following Köhler, Pelikan, Fischer) we may say that Zwingli had been the aggressor, Luther the defendant and Bucer somewhere between a referee and a second to Zwingli. The tragedy of Marburg was that it gave Luther a fixed idea of all Southern gentlemen as "Zwinglian." He never quite shook this image of the Reformed party, except in relation to Calvin and then it was too late. Even if we note that agreement on so many points was reached, with only the Eucharist outstanding, and moreover that Zwingli himself was probably moving toward a more positive theology, still for Luther Zwingli was typical. Indeed, Luther believed that the "sacramentarian" position had three heads—Carlstadt, Schwenkfeld and Zwingli. As late as the Formula of Concord this grouping seems hard to shake off, and sacramentarian-spiritualist-symbolist appears to be the Lutheran idea of the Reformed theology. The background to Marburg therefore is not just the medieval debate of modernism against the *via antiqua,* but also this emergent debate precipitated by the Radical Reformation. (When Luther met Schwenkfeld at Wittenberg as early as 1525, he already associated his teaching with the Swiss, and in conversation could not resist once replying to him with, "Yes, Zwingli"!)

The Radical Reformers, as they are now called, interpreted the Lord's Supper in terms of the presence of Christ's "celestial flesh," and used especially John 6 to support their doctrine. The concept derives most likely from medieval eucharistic piety, although originally associated with Gnostic and Monophysite christology, and with the Cathars. The Radicals used this to develop their teaching that in the sacrament, only believers eat Christ's flesh, but what they eat is Christ's true flesh. They thought they had the best of both worlds—Servetus criticized both Lutheran and Reformed doctrine, identifying the former with transsubstantiation and the latter with symbolism. In John chapter 6 they found the "standard" for "the proper order of the words of the Supper . . . the words of the Dominical Supper must be weighed and compared with John 6: My flesh *est* flesh indeed: and that the words This *est* my body are the same as: My flesh *est* food indeed" (Schwenkfeld—in Williams, *The Radical Reformation,* p. 112). Apparently Luther did not take their concept of *Geistesfleisch* seriously enough; certainly he felt that it raised no question about his own doctrine of the special nature of Christ's glorified humanity and its presence in the Sacrament.

As to the medieval debate, one is always tempted to proceed from generalizations to conclusions that are deductively neat but misleading. How simple, for example, if Luther were the realist and Zwingli the nominalist! The matter of symbols and names would be quite manageable then—in modern terms indeed! (C. C. Richardson treats Zwingli like this, and so his influence on Cranmer is handily explained). But in fact it is Luther who is the nominalist and Occamist, open to an authoritative scripture as Zwingli was really not, for Zwingli represented the philosophical scholasticism somewhat closer to moderate realism than one might expect. Thus had Seeberg interpreted the two, and the

41

classic and exhaustive analysis of Köhler agrees: "Hier stehen sich in Zwingli und Luther Humanismus und massiver Biblizismus, Thomas von Aquino und Wilhelm von Occam, die beiderseitigen Lehrer in der Studienzeit, auch Plato und Aristoteles der Kunst gegenüber" (*Zwingli and Luther*, II, 1953, p. 137). This will be illustrated later, on the point of ubiquity.

In his lectures on Hebrews (1517) Luther had already made it clear that the Sacrament alone does not justify, but rather faith nourished by the Sacrament (*non sacramentum, sed fides sacramenti justificat*). He stressed the necessity of being offered nothing less than the real body and blood of Christ given on the cross, if man in his temptation and fight is to be helped. He also distinguished the two kinds of confidence with which men approach the Sacrament, so that the result was the doctrine of *manducatio indignorum*. Regin Prenter says: "The two key words of Luther's Eucharistic doctrine, 'real presence' and *manducatio impiorum*, are intelligible only in the context of his theology of the Cross" (*More About Luther*, ML Lectures II, 1958, p. 120). Luther's religious assurance derived from his idea of Christ's bodily presence in the Supper. But Zwingli shared the intense desire for religious assurance—except that his derived from his idea of the Spirit's uniting of the believer with the Christ who is beyond all earthly elements. Their philosophical-grammatical division obscured from them—but it should not from us—their essential unity of purpose. Zwingli took Luther's "bodily presence" in the opposite sense, as did Luther in regard to Zwingli's "spiritual work."

The controversy of this early stage showed decisively that the problematic issue was the *Wie-Frage,* as Bonhoeffer called it, the question as to "how" Christ is present in the Sacrament. The emergence of this question illustrates the kind of question it is, namely a christological one, framed against the background of the Two Natures theory, and tempted to appeal to what Pelikan has called an incarnational "alchemy" to solve all our problem. Zwingli was convinced that grammar and logic could provide an adequate answer. A body is that which by (Aristotle's) definition occupies a place. The locale of Christ's glorified humanity is still governed by the rules worked out by scholastic eschatology: bodies in a glorified state have qualities added, but only such qualities as are appropriate to humanity, that is, which modify the localized nature in harmony with the principle that grace perfects nature without destroying it. This view seemed to Luther a triumph of nature over grace, a real presence in a local heaven and a corresponding real absence here on earth . . . a "stork in a nest in the treetop." Against it he brought the Occamist distinctions among modes of presence, claiming that the simple definition of Aristotle was insufficient to deal with *this* sort of presence: it is *sui generis* and therefore one must follow the signs, the declared Word of God testifying to the whereabouts and modes of Christ's work. Therefore in the Eucharist the only "figure" to be allowed had nothing to do with Zwingli's symbolism of the elements, but actually stemmed from the opposite side—the communication of properties means that Zwingli's *alloeosis* is out of order (since both natures share equally in humility and in glory) and instead it is a case of part representing the whole, *synecdoche*. In the famous passage where he calls alloeosis "the devil's mask" (*Confession Concerning Christ's Supper* 1528 pp. 209ff. in Vol. 37 of Works, 1961), Luther speaks of "the old witch, Lady Reason, alloeosis' grandmother." Then he refutes those who accuse him of confusing the two natures of Christ: "Rather, we merge the two distinct natures into one single person, and say: God is man and man is God. We in turn raise a hue and cry against them for separating the person of Christ as though there were two persons."

On this last point, Luther saw the issue properly, and wished to go all the way in behalf of the unity of Christ's person. That is modern enough, but whether his conclusion can stand today is our question: is it enough to say "God is man and man is God?" . . . unless you happen to be Kierkegaard! Even before Marburg, therefore, the battleline was drawn up in the position outlined at Chalcedon. The campaign was to be conducted as between Nestorians and Eutycheans. The real tragedy was that these terms of reference were accepted for all future Lutheran-Reformed engagement, as already noted. From Luther and Zwingli through Westphal and Calvin, Brenz and Peter Martyr, to Andreas and Beza, the posture of debate remains essentially the same. After that there was little real encounter, only long range sniping over a no man's land. I should submit, however, that to the shame of the Reformed side, history seems to have proved the Lutheran caricature to be more substantial than it was originally, because it is the "Zwinglian" sort of spirituality that has become normal for much of the Reformed world. This last point is in direct contradiction to Wilhelm Niesel's, that we may omit Zwingli's view "since this plays no part in the Reformed Churches today" (*Reformed Symbolics*, 1962, p. 271). I should maintain at least that the English-speaking Reformed Churches do not subscribe to genuine Calvinism at this point as presumably the Continentals do (cf. H. Hageman, *Pulpit and Table*, p. 34 in re "Zwingli as their liturgical master").

43

The Role of John Calvin

The figure of Calvin first appeared as a hopeful sign in an already confused and bitter controversy. Melanchthon dubbed him "the Theologian"; Calvin subscribed to the *Augustana Variata* of 1540, expecting that document to contribute to the cause of unity. In the same year he wrote his 'Little Treatise on the Holy Supper of our Lord,' published in French in 1541 and Latin in 1545. After stating his positives in spare and balanced language within thirty-two sections, he deals with Romish errors in the next twenty sections, and then turns to Luther and Zwingli in the concluding eight. He sketches their controversy, reproaches their failure "in not having the patience to listen to each other in order to follow the truth without passion, when it would have been found," and expresses hope for a "final settlement." He concludes with a paragraph stating the essential agreement as follows: "We all then confess with one mouth, that on receiving the Sacrament in faith, according to the ordinance of the Lord, we are truly made partakers of the proper substance of the body and blood of Jesus Christ. How that is done some may deduce better, and explain more clearly than others. Be this as it may, on the one hand, in order to exclude all carnal fancies, we must raise our hearts upwards to heaven, not thinking that our Lord Jesus is so debased as to be enclosed under some corruptible elements; and, on the other hand, not to impair the efficacy of this holy ordinance, we must hold that it is made effectual by the secret and miraculous power of God, and that the Spirit of God is the bond of participation, this being the reason why it is called spiritual."

When Luther read the Latin translation he commented, "I might have entrusted the whole affair of this controversy to him from the beginning. If my opponents had done the like, we should soon have been reconciled." Was this, too, hyperbole? Or was Luther sincere in thinking that Calvin had understood not only what Luther's real intent was but also that Zwingli's real intent was as evangelical as he had now put it? Luther's followers did not so regard Calvin, as the bitter debates with Westphal and Heshus indicate. Luther's words are also an indirect compliment to Martin Bucer. For Calvin wrote his treatise while at Strassburg, where no doubt he was much influenced by Bucer's irenic spirit, and emphasis upon the believer's participation in Christ's new humanity as the essential positive among all parties. It is in this sense that Calvin stands with Bucer and Melanchthon in the ranks of the mediators of the Reformation.

44

But Calvin was already anxious to win the Swiss to a better view, and so courted Zwingli's successor Bullinger. The consummation was achieved with the *Consensus Tigurinus* of 1549, the "Mutual Consent of the churches of Zürich and Geneva as to the Sacraments." Calvin hoped it would serve as a stepping stone across the Lutheran-Reformed deadlock. But instead it hardened the old Marburg lines, for it seemed to come down on the side of the spiritual-symbolic view. The words of institution are figurative, it is impossible to "inclose" Christ under "elements of this world," and—a fact set forth carefully in section 25—the expression "Christ is to be sought in heaven" intimates "distance of place." This was to remain the key to the distinctive Reformed position, appealed to by Beza for instance at the colloquies of Poissy (against the Romans) and Montbeliard (against Andreas), but here it is stated explicitly by Calvin's document: "For though philosophically speaking there is no place above the skies, yet as the body of Christ, bearing the nature and mode of a human body, is finite and is contained in heaven as its place, it is necessarily as distant from us in point of space as heaven is from earth."

This was the point which made the Consent especially distasteful to Bucer. He feared this tendency to "make a new article of faith concerning the certain place of heaven in which the body of Christ is contained." He declared: "I have dealt again and again with so many Lutherans" and have found that they wish "Christ to be truly given and received in the Supper" (CR XLI, p. 350). Bucer's objection continued to be his contribution to the debate, for he never tired of insisting that one must avoid the question of mode (as Luther himself insisted most of the time), and must rest content with negative expressions: "not of this world, not of sense, not of reason." His agreement with the truth of Christ's humanity does not lead him to agree with the conclusion that Aristotle's concept of bodily locale applies here (cf. his *Exomologesis, Scripta Ang.* 538ff.). Bucer therefore tried to stand astride the debate, siding with the Calvinists against the *manducatio indignorum,* and with the Lutherans against localizing Christ's body in heaven. He once likened himself to Sisyphus, worn down with the frustrating activity of this uphill struggle with the stone of contention. Melanchthon also, of course, shared much of this middle ground, and suffered with him the mistrust and misunderstanding to which all peacemakers are heir.

The Humanity of our Lord

It may seem trite today to observe that it is the nature of the Lord which determines the nature of the Lord's Supper. But in the sixteenth century it was something new to say: "Since the Sacraments are appendages of the Gospel, he only can discourse aptly and usefully of their nature, virtue, office, and benefit, who begins with Christ" (Calvin). Such christological orientation was surely the heart of the Reformation. Perhaps it is significant for our study that the Reformed tended to view christology in terms of a dogmatic architectonic, whereas the Lutheran emphasis followed Luther's own correlation of "the forgiveness of sins" with the Christ *pro nobis* (cf. J. Pelikan, ch. 8 of 'Luther the Expositor,' 1959). The medieval way of theologizing derived from the *quaestiones disputatae,* the serial treatment of disparate themes arranged according to philosophical taste. There existed alongside this a mystical piety and theology, in which meditation on the person and work of Christ provided form and content. The Reformers replaced the former by the latter, insofar as they accepted the credal data and constructed a sort of evangelical science, a meditation upon the Gospel facts according to the proportion of faith. The Mediator determines the media; he is the unique Sign whose divine-humanity provides the possibility for other (secondary-derivative) signs to operate in revelation. The Lutheran-Reformed debate showed clearly that only a sustained examination of the *unio hypostatica* is worthy of a eucharistic subject. Both sides, moreover, understood the subtle point within christology that the humanity is interposed toward us, as if the one person of the Mediator—the theandric totality—is itself mediated through the humanity. Even in the glorified state, therefore, Christ is available, "for us," only as the true humanity continues. It is the irony of the debate that both sides wished to make this same point, but each thought to safeguard it from a different point in the christological circumference. Thus the terms substance, reality, body, flesh and truth all relate to it. For example, in expounding the Zürich Consensus, Calvin noted that when he said "spiritual," the Lutherans "roar out as if by this term we were making it not to be what they commonly call real. If they will use *real* for true, and oppose it to *fallacious* or *imaginary,* we will rather speak barbarously than afford material for strife."

46   Here is a basic problem to which the grammar is but introductory. Luther had understood substance or essence (*Wesen*) in the scholastic sense as that which makes an entity what it is—hence, there is even a divine substance. But Zwingli regarded *wesentlich* as *dinglich*—"real in the legal sense of real property, as we speak of a 'man of substance'." (R. H. Fischer, in *Dialog,* Winter '63, p. 53; cf H. Gollwitzer, *Coena Domini,* pp. 97ff., 117 ff.). The meaning of substance for Calvin still requires systematic clarification. He consistently speaks of the substance or matter of the Sacrament as being Christ himself (*res* or *materia sacramenti*). But once the point is made that Sacrament's referent is the divine-human person—even Zwingli knew this *subiectus agens*—then one has split open the scholastic terminology and introduced a dynamic orientation. For instance, Calvin relates all his theology (except predestination?) to this fact of the believer's participation in the new humanity of the living Christ. To prevent a forensic or rationalist misunderstanding of justification by faith, he deliberately reverses his field and treats sanctification first, because only the union effected by the Holy Spirit, in which the 'substance' of our justification and righteousness lies in Christ's flesh, preserves us from error (*Inst.* 3.11.7ff). Moreover, it is of the utmost significance to see the "enemy" through Calvin's eyes—he at once mentions Osiander, whose "essential righteousness" involves a "gross mixture" of Christ's flesh with ours. Osiander appealed to the carnal eating of Christ in the Supper as a sign of his truth—and branded Calvin's view as "Zwinglian." How complex the battlefield becomes! It is a scene full of "confused alarms of struggle and flight," with a variety of protagonists fighting on a number of sides at once, so that no simple plan of the campaign is possible which overlooks this complexity.

When Calvin came to treat of the Supper in his *Institutes,* he began as usual from the "mystery of Christ's secret union with the devout . . . by nature incomprehensible" (4.17.1). Then follows the typical exposition of Christ as the true bread and wine, of whose nourishing body and blood the elements are signs and symbols. Because Christ sets before us these proper elements, therefore "by the showing of the symbol the thing itself is also shown . . . if it is true that a visible sign is given us to seal the gift of a thing invisible, when we have received the symbol of the body, let us no less surely trust that the body itself is also given to us" (4.17.10). Indeed he can state that "the flesh and blood of Christ are no less truly given to the unworthy then to God's elect believers" (4.17.33). Here however, with Westphal in mind, he appeals to one of his favorite Augustinian dicta to say that unbelievers are offered the *res* but can take away only what they can carry in the vessel of faith. Thus there is a "sacramental eating" which is to be distinguished from eating *realiter*. In his *Second Defence* against Westphal, Calvin had made the same point: "Should anyone raise a dispute as to the word substance, we assert that Christ, from the substance of his flesh, breathes life into our souls; nay, infuses his own life into us, provided always that no transfusion of substance be imagined" (*Tracts,* II, p. 248).

47

It is in this context that the distinctive Reformed doctrine of the Holy Spirit is to be understood. The Spirit fulfils his office by bringing us into contact with Christ's substance, which Calvin interprets in terms of a *virtus,* a power judged by its effects in the human realm. Just as much as Luther he wished to preserve objectivity in the Sacrament, the objective presence of the personal Lord. But whereas the Reformed understood the lordship of Christ as a communication of properties of the new humanity by the Spirit, the Lutherans understood it in terms of renewing the promised gift of the Savior: an ordinance of grace guaranteed by the dominical institution. In the latter, the office of the Spirit becomes problematic, except as providing a right intention on the part of the believers: "all that our body does outwardly and physically, if God's Word is added to it and it is done through faith, is in reality and in name done spiritually . . . the heart grasps the words in faith and eats spiritually precisely the same body as the mouth eats physically, for the heart sees very well what the uncomprehending mouth eats physically . . . Thus without doubt he who in faith physically eats Christ's body in the Supper eats spiritually and lives and walks spiritually precisely in the physical eating." (Luther, 'This is My Body,' 1527, pp. 92ff. in LW, 37).

Surely one can see in both sides the same motive, but also the same falling into that very preoccupation with the quiddity of the Lord's body which—in its Romish form—they were out to subvert!

Ubiquity: the Dimension of Transcendence

Probably the central issue in any modern critique of the debate is that of the nature of Christ's continuing divine-human existence, and the kind of religious language appropriate to express it. At once we must reckon with the critique of language which obsesses philosophers these days—even those who disguise themselves as existential theologians in search of a hermeneutic! The language of transcendence is under the gravest suspicion today, and this is a healthy discipline for theology. But theology must never allow that this is a peculiarly modern question, raised first by a Bultmann or a Wittgenstein. It can take heart at Origen's bold analysis of language long ago, Augustine's summary of the "language game" of theological communication, or Athanasius' grappling with the oddness of statements about divinity. It is therefore not surprising that our sixteenth century forefathers recovered something of this critique along with their patristic knowledge. Calvin was never tired of noting the "impropriety" of theological language; Luther called for a "new theological grammar" to express the mysteries better.

The Gospel concerns a divine condescension, a self-abasement in grace which occasions and demands a corresponding accommodation of life and language in faith. It was the grandeur of Greek philosophical theology—according to Werner Jaeger—to have recognized that language about the divine must discriminate as to what is "appropriate" to God; and reason supplies the model. It was surely the grandeur of the Reformers to recall Christian theology from a similar rationalism to face its proper data, the actuality-model of God in Christ. Here the language game being played is very odd indeed; but not without its rules, its interior logic. It was this they were all after. And it seems to me that perhaps the contemporary scene today vindicates Zwingli more than a little, on this question of language. For it was Zwingli who went at linguistic analysis like a modern Oxford don, and came up with answers which anticipate a good deal. (For instance, one category that appeals to many who seek light about religious language, Austen's "performative utterances"?) Luther could not find patience with Zwingli's method: "Let Zwingli regard the words in the Supper as he will, be they command-words or permission-words, action-words or written-words; it doesn't matter to me. But I ask this one question: Are these same action-words of Christ false or true words?. . ." (1528 *Confession Concerning Christ's Supper,* pp. 180f). He at once returns to the question of the object given in the original Supper, the body of Christ. He therefore missed Zwingli's point entirely, that the *meaning* of a word is to be gathered not from etymology or syntax, but from *use.* This point was shared by the Reformed, if in a more positive way, when they insisted on action rather than presence in the Supper; and Melanchthon's formulae are similar, for his "functional doctrine" as Peter Fraenkel calls it, prefers to talk of processes (*ritus, usus*) rather than things (*corpus, panis*), of effects rather than being.

Luther could not be so brief as he desired. To Zwingli he declared clearly, "We must not ask how it happens that Christ's body is in the Supper but simply believe God's Word." But then he found himself spending a ridiculous amount of time and verbiage describing just how this *est* is to be taken, in view of the nature of Christ's glorified body, the quality of faithful reception, and so on. One positive point in his favor should be remarked, that he did not rest in a logically simple doctrine of ubiquity (as others like Westphal and Brenz seemed to) but preferred the idea of multivolent presence ("present where he will"). In famous words he qualified what might have become a pantheistic concept of omnipresence: "It makes a difference whether you say that God is present or whether you say that he is present for you. But he is there for you, when he adds his word and binds himself,

49

saying: Here you shall find me. When you have the word, you can grasp him and have him and say: Now I have thee, as thou sayest. So it is with the right hand of God; it is everywhere, as no one can deny; but it is also nowhere; therefore you cannot apprehend it anywhere unless it binds and confines itself for your benefit to one place. This happens when it moves and dwells in the humanity of Christ. There you will most certainly find it. Otherwise you must run through all creation from end to end, groping and fumbling about, here and there, without finding it. Although it is really there—it is not there for you" (*This is My Body,* 1527). Again, his reliance upon the threefold distinction attributed to Occam and Biel (localiter/circumscriptive, diffinitive and repletive) is posterior to his christological decision: "since Christ is one person with God, you must place this nature of Christ as far outside the creatures as God is outside them, and again as deep and near in all creatures as God is in them" (quoted by Niesel, *op. cit.* 279).

The Calvinists were not convinced that the Lutherans had not divinised the glorified humanity. For them it was the ascension and descent of the Spirit that provided the proper 'moment' in christological-eucharistic discussion. They took them as two sides of the one event; ascension means that the living Christ is not essentially discontinuous with the divine-human One whose presence was circumscribed; Pentecost means that the dynamic of Christ's presence is not a question in the abilities of his new body but in the peculiar power of the Spirit. The question here is whether the Calvinistic doctrine of the Holy Spirit is merely functional? The use of words like *vis, virtus, potentia* and *effectus,* sometimes suggest only instrumentality; yet it is because of their regard for the distinctive office of the Spirit that the Reformed were willing to qualify the being of Christ in a way which the Lutherans were not. The question could be applied to both, and indeed must be, especially if the functional view seems appealing to modern man.

50   In the christology itself, the old lines of Nestorian and Eutychean already mentioned seemed appropriate enough. For the Lutheran conjunction of the natures tended to become identity, while the Reformed distinction of the natures tended to become a separation. Here the quarrel gathered around the concept known as *extra Calvinisticum.* For example: "since the Godhead is incomprehensible and everywhere present, it must follow that it is indeed beyond the bounds of the manhood which it has assumed, and yet is none the less within it as well, and remains personally united to it" (Heidelberg Catechism, Q. 48). It was that "beyond the bounds" which constituted the unacceptable "extra" for the Lutherans. Ursinus' own comment on this question states that if the two natures were equal, they would be united in the inseparable manner of Lutheran theology. "The major proposition is true if it be understood of two natures which are equal, that is, which are equally finite, or infinite; but it is false if it has reference to two natures which are not equal, if one, for instance, be finite, and the other infinite."

At this point we do well to note Karl Barth's analysis of the debates, at various points of his Dogmatics (esp. I.2, section 15.2). He points out that the real issue was one which post-Chalcedon christology had articulated in the twin and complementary concepts of *anhypostasia* and *enhypostasia,* enunciated as dogmata at II Const. 553. The Lutherans stressed the enhypostatic reality of the humanity, but so closely that Lutheran orthodoxy would talk of the "reversal" of the natures—no manhood without the Word, nor Word apart from the humanity. On the other hand, Reformed theology stressed the anhypostatic reality of the Word apart from the humanity, the freedom of the divine even in regard to incarnation. On Barth's ground, therefore, the Reformation debate was not thorough enough in recovering its patristic christology—it was content with Chalcedon without advancing beyond. Indeed, Barth's point is that the *extra* was a traditional theologoumenon, which the Calvinists were forced to recover to meet the Lutheran "innovation"! Today, when Logos christology must necessarily be reviewed in the light of larger questions such as the significance of non-Christian religions and the possibility of life on other planets, this point is more than just historical.

Here the case seemed to rest. The Lutherans retired to their entrenched position in which the *manducatio impiorum* provided the negative test for a real presence, while the Reformed insisted that the circumscription of Christ's body and blood in heaven functioned similarly to guard the work of the Spirit and faith. Both sides had been trapped by the fatal *Wie-Frage.* Now in theology it is usually the rational that constitutes the absurd, if reason fails to follow its data and proudly searches its own recesses for material. So here, where they ought to have acknowledged the limit, the power of negative thinking (as Bucer and Melanchthon tried to do, the one because it would avoid contention and the other because that was the patristic method), they forced each other to transgress the bounds of theo-logic. Is it not significant that subsequent theology on both sides (e.g. Quenstedt, Polanus) went back into the concept of *analogy* to make more careful expression of

51

the mystery? Terms like *proportio, collatio, ratio, tropus* and *signum* indicate analogical predication, and remind us that Luther and Zwingli had looked to each other like those erroneous extremes described by Aristotle, univocity and equivocity.

Mystery and Gift

Both sides, to be sure, understood Jesus Christ as the Analogue, the Sign. And in Luther's idea of *larvae dei,* and Calvin's of the renewed face of the Church we see the move toward positive working out of the "active presence" or "real action" of Christ, as we would phrase it today, with Aulen and Pelikan. The immediate question is that of sign and symbol. Our modern use of these words is unfortunately shaping up as the exact opposite of the classical and traditional usage. In biblical and historical theology, sign (*semeion, signum*) is the stronger word, with symbol the weaker. Thus in the Reformation debates, Luther regarded sign (*Zeichen*) as essentially related to its object, and Calvin used *signum* to mean effective or "activating" signs, usually saying *efficax* to make his point. Both men used *symbolum* to mean an ineffectual or merely symbolic image. Today however, Paul Tillich (who has done much to hasten the reversal of meaning) has observed, "One thing I warn my students is, never to say 'merely a symbol' . . ." The distinction underlines our historical problem: was Zwingli "merely symbolic" in our modern sense? why did Calvin think that the Lutheran insistence on the bodily presence was superfluous, since the sign was sufficient? or why did Luther think that the presence of signs in the Calvinist view meant the absence of the reality?

One thing we must insist on today is that there is only one proper Sacrament and that is Jesus Christ. If "mystery" is used as the normative term, how much better our theology would be! Then we might see what, after all, both sides desired in their debates, the exaltation of Christ himself as the mystery, God in the flesh, Gospel. We might also see that their terms of reference were too narrow. For instance, what have the Anglicans to offer us, with their perception that one must consider the significance of *epiclesis* if one takes seriously a real presence? or the Greek Orthodox with their tradition of mysteries really present? or the still new *Mysterientheologie* of Odo Casel and his disciples in the Church of Rome, with its deep understanding of the *transitus* of Christ and the Christian? These suggest other dimensions which may be necessary before the debate in question can be raised to a better level for solution. This is not the Hegelian cud-chewing process but an attempt to bring history before the ecumenical bar. Otherwise we will languish in mere conservationism.

In order to benefit from our critique, we must take up the chief points in the debates, and perhaps most urgently the question of exegesis. It is to the credit of the framers of the Arnoldshain Theses that they boldly seek to benefit by modern scholarly exegesis of the church catholic. So in interpreting the history we must be prepared to examine their biblical bases. Zwingli's party relied upon John 6:63 ("the spirit quickens; the flesh profits nothing")—Oecolampad called it "my iron wall." Luther stressed not only the Institution but "Lo I am with you always," whereas Calvin's stress was more on the passages denoting Ascension and the *sursum corda*. J. Pelikan has reminded us that historical theology could be written as a history of exegesis, and probably should be written in that style (*Luther the Expositor,* ch. 1). But then we should have to approach the debates not just in terms of how certain texts were used in the heat of battle, but how they functioned in the more positive exposition of whole books, or better, what other texts were prominent in other cognate or parallel doctrines. What about Luther's doctrine of the Spirit, therefore, and Calvin's teaching on the means by which men are damned? or Luther's understanding of the cosmic dimension of the Word, and Calvin's of the finality of the incarnation? This would match the "recent exegetical studies on the New Testament" of Arnoldshain, and would suggest the points at issue between then and now.

It is strange that Luther's position should have become so identified with the *genus majestaticum*—he who was so great a servant of a *theologia crucis*. Would not the note of humility do him more justice here, the Cross as the form in which the glorified Christ still comes in his active presence? If so, then such a *genus tapeinoticon* (suggested by Aulen) would meet the Reformed concern for "the servant form" as that which informs all three offices of prophet, priest and king. This might also allow a better way through the thorny question of the *manducatio impiorum*. It is in such a context, for instance, that T. F. Torrance has written: "Jesus Christ does not withhold himself from anyone in the Holy Supper, any more than he withheld himself from anyone in his incarnation and death, but only through faith do we derive *blessing* from the Body and Blood of Christ, while through unbelief we bring judgment upon ourselves—but there would be no judgment in the Supper if the Body and Blood were not extended to or partaken of by the unbelieving recipient" (S.J.T., March 62, p. 11). It is this same idea that Gollwitzer has in mind when he observes that the *manducatio physica* is the *Realgrund* of the *manducatio spiritualis* (*Coena Dom.* p. 220). Thus, to let the active presence of Christ define

53

the analogical action in the sacrament is to operate with categories better suited to this mystery than those drawn up in the sixteenth century debate.

Finally, perhaps Barth's choice of words suggests the way ahead. In an early essay (1923) on Luther's doctrine of the Eucharist (reprinted in *Theology and Church,* 1962) he claims that Luther was saying *Yes* and Zwingli, *But.* Because Zwingli tried to do without the Yes he seemed to be saying No. And Luther thought he could say Yes without the But. Therefore, "The name of Calvin, the man who later knew and spoke both *Yes* and *But,* points the tragedy of this historical *cul-de-sac*—perhaps also the *way out* and *hope.*" In this paper we have suggested that Calvin himself tended to allow the Swiss *But* too much weight, and therefore does not stand over against the others as Barth maintains. Rather, we must advance from the insights of both men in choosing more helpful categories. What about "dimension" as the mode of presence, as Karl Heim tried to work it out in a modern idiom, for instance? And especially—the critique of language insists that we analyze our meaning (in terms of our use!) and that we respect our limits. When the Arnoldshain Theses said that Christ himself (*Er selbst*) was given in the Supper, German Lutheran critics soon replied (*Informationsblatt,* 2 Nov. 1959) that this does not state explicitly that his body and blood are given: "there is in the Lord's Supper a *materia coelestis,* or it is not a proper Supper." What meaning does modern man give to *materia coelestis?* Is *materia* now more "substantial" than Christ himself? In the land of Kant has the *Ding an sich* become so empirically perceptible that it provides a test of Christ's real presence? These are the questions which need to be asked today, especially when it appears that in some quarters the debate has changed very little, even the terms appearing identical. But unless we can find new forms we are not continuing the Reformation, but only indulging in rhetoric about battles long ago. We still need to revise our language, for Calvin warned that it is bound to be improper, so that theologians must ceaselessly search for the less improper over against the more; while Luther called us all to continue work on the new theological grammar to which he contributed only the preface.

Chapter Four

CHRISTOLOGY AND LORD'S SUPPER IN THE PERSPECTIVE OF HISTORY

by Theodore G. Tappert

I T MAY be helpful at the outset to mention several conscious limitations in this paper:

1. Obviously no claim can be made to completeness in any case, but the treatment here has intentionally been limited to the sixteenth and seventeenth centuries and especially to the continent of Europe. More should not be expected than a fair presentation of the ground covered.

2. Although the labels "Lutheran" and "Reformed" originated as terms of reproach, they are of course employed here without such overtones, and attention is not especially called in what follows to the deplorable slander and recrimination which was characteristic of theological discussion in the sixteenth and seventeenth centuries.

3. Only occasional and oblique reference could be made to "nontheological factors" which played a part in the formation of theological positions. Because of its brevity the treatment which follows runs the risk of placing theology in a sort of timeless vacuum rather than in the context of life situations.

4. This risk might be accentuated if the discussion were confined to commentary on official confessions of faith, and accordingly it seemed desirable to suggest in broader outline what the major views and convictions were which lay behind and alongside of as well as in these confessions.

5. Since the purpose of this paper is not merely to set forth the private opinions of the writer but especially to report the consensus reached by historians in our time, most of the references in the footnotes are to secondary literature.

Martin Luther did not always express himself in the same way concerning the Lord's Supper.[1] This can be accounted for by the fact

55

[1]See especially Hans Grass, *Die Abendmahlslehre bei Luther und Calvin*, 2nd edition (Guetersloh, 1954); Helmut Gollwitzer, *Coena Domiai* (Munich, 1937); Erich Roth,

that he never wrote a comprehensive and systematic treatment of the Sacrament but addressed himself at various times to concrete situations and particular opponents. It can also be accounted for by the fact that there were changes in Luther's understanding.

Three stages may be distinguished in Luther's development. Before 1520 he had little occasion to reflect on the Lord's Supper in the light of his new understanding of the Gospel, and his view of it consequently remained essentially scholastic and medieval. After 1520, when his *Babylonian Captivity* was published, he began to attack the sacrifice of the Mass. He now understood the Sacrament in the light of God's dealing with man through His Word. He attached central importance to the testament of Christ, to the promise of God in the words of institution. After 1524, as a result of his controversies with Ulrich Zwingli and the Anabaptists, Luther shifted his emphasis to the objective presence in the Sacrament of the body and blood of Christ. It was now that he laid weight on a literal interpretation of the "is" in the Greek and Latin (not Aramaic) of "This is my body." From this position he never afterwards departed, although he did not cease to speak of the words of institution as the sum of the Gospel and to regard the Sacrament as a form of the proclamation of the Gospel.

Luther reacted sharply against two views of the Lord's Supper. On the one hand, he rejected the medieval sacrifice of the Mass because he believed that it perverted an act of God by making of it an act of man, that it changed God's gracious gift to man in Christ into man's appeasement of God's wrath. This basic criticism of the Roman Mass was accompanied by a rejection of some things connected with it. Not only transubstantiation, but any kind of mutation of substances, was denied. Accordingly reservation of the host and the adoration of bread and wine were discontinued. The withholding of the cup from the laity was attacked along with the practice of Masses for special intention and the use of a language which was not understood by communicants.

56 On the other hand, Luther was not less critical of Zwingli.[1] The Swiss Reformer had, like Luther, undergone changes in his understanding of the Lord's Supper. Before 1524 Zwingli seems to have held views similar to those of Luther in the same period. But then he became acquainted with a suggestion of Cornelius Hoen which had also attracted

Sakrament nach Luther (Berlin, 1952); Heinrich Bornkamm, *Luther's World of Thought* (St. Louis, 1958); Chap. V; Albrecht Peters, *Realpraesenz: Luthers Zeugnis von Christi Gegenwart im Abendmahl* (Berlin, 1960).

[1]Walther E. Koehler, *Das Marburger Religionsgespraech 1529* (Leipzig, 1929); Walther E. Koehler, *Zwingli und Luther*, 2 vols. (Leipzig, 1924-53); Hermann Sasse, *This Is My Body* (Minneapolis, 1959).

Luther momentarily. Zwingli adopted Hoen's interpretation of the words of institution according to which the words "This is my body" mean "This signifies my body." Such an interpretation was supported by Zwingli's citation of John 6:63, "It is the spirit that gives life, the flesh is of no avail." Zwingli concluded that Christ is not present in the Sacrament in any real way, especially since his body has been in heaven ever since his ascension. Christ, he said, is present only "by the contemplation of faith." Zwingli accordingly denied that the Sacrament is a means of grace, and he emphasized that by participation in it Christians give a public testimony to God's grace and to their own faith.

In the ensuing controversy between Luther and Zwingli the christological question became an issue. Both asserted that in the unity of his person there have been two natures in Christ ever since the incarnation. In his divine nature Christ is omnipresent, Zwingli conceded, but in his human nature he is bound by time and space. It was according to his human nature that Christ was born of Mary, grew in wisdom and stature, suffered and died, and ascended into heaven. There he is seated in his human nature at the right hand of God, and there he will remain until he comes again at the last day. Only according to his divine nature, said Zwingli, could Christ make the blind see and the lame walk, and only so could he say, "Lo, I am with you always."

To this Luther responded by charging that Zwingli so separated the two natures as to lose sight of their unity in one person.[1] Christ, recalled Luther, was born not only of Mary but also of the Spirit. It was not according to his divine nature alone that he passed through closed doors. To be sure, there were times when Christ voluntarily held his divine powers in abeyance. But he was always the God-man, and in support of this Luther appealed to the ancient church's rather mechanical formulation of an exchange of properties (*communicatio idiomatum.*)[2] As elaborated by Luther, (1) the properties of one nature are ascribed to the whole person of the God-man, (2) the person of Christ acts through both natures, each contributing what is peculiar to itself, and (3) the properties of the divine nature are communicated to the human. This construction enabled Luther to deny Zwingli's assertion that it was only in His human nature that Christ died on the cross and to declare that His divine nature participated in the event. Zwingli conceded that the Scriptures did not always distinguish sharply between the two natures but maintained that when they failed to do so this was merely a loose and figurative manner of speaking (*alloeosis*).

57

[1]Paul-Wilhelm Gennrich, *Die Christologie Luthers im Abendmahlsstreit* (Goettingen, 1929).
[2]Cf. Formula of Concord, S.D., VIII, 31-48.

As far as the ascension into heaven is concerned, Luther contended that heaven is non-spatial and that the session at the right hand of God refers not to a particular place but to participation in God's majesty and power everywhere.

When pressed to show that Christ, in his human as well as divine nature, could be in more than one place at a time, Luther advanced an argument concerning the ubiquity of Christ which he adapted from late medieval scholasticism.[3] There are, he suggested, different modes in which the body of Christ can be present in a given place: for example, (1) a comprehensible, corporeal mode, as when Christ walked bodily on earth and occupied space, and (2) an incomprehensible, spiritual mode, as when Christ passed through locked doors without occupying space. It was in the second of these modes that the possibility of Christ's presence in the Sacrament could be imagined. Luther himself did not press this argument after his controversy with Zwingli. In his later years he refused to employ it, preferring to confine himself to the testimony of the Scriptures.

The controversy between Luther and Zwingli was bitter, and in the course of it Luther sometimes made extreme statements (for example, suggesting the mastication of Christ's flesh with one's teeth) which were quoted against him by opponents. The controversy reached its culmination in the Marburg Colloquy in 1529. The extent of the agreement which was reached (especially in opposition to Rome) is notable, but the remaining disagreement was also exposed. The fifteenth of the Marburg Articles, drafted by Luther and signed by him and Zwingli as well as by others, reads: "We all believe and hold concerning the Supper of our dear Lord Jesus Christ that both forms should be used according to the institution; also that the Mass is not a work whereby one obtains grace for another, dead or living; also that the Sacrament of the Altar is a sacrament of the true body and blood of Jesus Christ and that the spiritual partaking of this body and blood is especially necessary to every true Christian. In like manner, as to the use of the Sacrament we believe and hold that, like the Word of almighty God, it has been given and ordained in order that weak consciences may be excited by the Holy Spirit to faith and love. Although we are not at this time agreed as to whether the true body and blood of Christ are bodily present in the bread and wine, nevertheless one party should show the other Christian love, in so far as conscience permits,

---

[3]For a summary see Julius Koestlin, *The Theology of Luther* (Philadelphia, 1897), II, 137-145; cf. Formula of Concord, S.D., VIII, 93-103.

and both should fervently pray almighty God that by his Spirit he may confirm us in the true understanding."

After Zwingli's early death Martin Bucer,[1] who had also participated in the Marburg Colloquy, continued efforts to unite the two parties. After years of preparation by correspondence and consultation, Bucer succeeded in arranging a conference with Luther, and this was held in Wittenberg in 1536. There an agreement, drafted by Philip Melanchthon and known as the Wittenberg Concord, was signed by about a dozen representatives of each of the two parties. The agreement declared that "with the bread and wine the body and blood of Christ are truly and substantially present, offered, and received." Both transubstantiation and "a local inclusion in the bread" were denied, and therefore reservation, "as occurs among the papists," was condemned in words later quoted in the Lutheran Formula of Concord (1577).[2] It was also agreed that in the Sacrament the body and blood of the Lord are offered and received by the unworthy unto judgment. Luther did not insist on the use of the term "unbelievers" in addition to "unworthy," and he remained somewhat conciliatory on this point when he wrote the Smalcald Articles (1537).[3] In fact, Luther entertained high hopes that the Wittenberg Concord might be accepted in Switzerland as well as in southern Germany and prepare the way for unity. In this he was disappointed.

At this time John Calvin,[4] a generation younger than Luther and Zwingli, appeared on the scene. Unlike Luther, he faced the threat of the formidable Counter-Reformation, and it was probably on this account that he was more consciously anti-Roman. Be this as it may, he often expressed indebtedness to Luther and, as Friedrich Loofs has expressed it, "was a 'Lutheran' in a sense in which Zwingli never was."[5] Luther reciprocated by expressing his esteem for Calvin as "a learned and godly man," but the two never met in person or corresponded directly. Calvin sometimes appealed to the Augsburg Confession and subscribed Melanchthon's variata edition "as the author himself in-

59

[1]Hastings Eells, *Martin Bucer* (New Haven, 1931); Ernst Bizer, "Martin Butzer und der Abendmahlsstreit," in *Archiv fuer Reformationsgeschichte*, XXXV (1938), XXXVI (1939).
[2]Formula of Concord, S.D., VII, 12-16.
[3]Otto Ritschl, *Dogmengeschichte des Protestantismus*, 4 vols. (Leipzig & Goettingen, 1908-27), IV, 1-230; cf. Smalcald Articles, III vi, 1.
[4]A. Mitchell Hunter, *The Teaching of Calvin* (London, 1950); Wilhelm Niesel, *The Theology of Calvin* (Philadelphia, 1956); Ronald S. Wallace, *Calvin's Doctrine of the Word and Sacrament* (Grand Rapids, 1957); Wilhelm Niesel, *Calvins Lehre vom Abendmahl* (Munich, 1930).
[5]Friedrich Loofs, *Leitfaden zum Studium der Dogmengeschichte*, 4th edition (Halle, 1906), 881; cf. Ernst Walter Zeeden, "Das Bild Martin Luthers in den Briefen Calvins," in *Archiv fuer Reformationsgeschichte*, XLIX (1958), 177-195; John T. McNeill, "Calvin as an Ecumenical Churchman", in *Church History*, XXXII (1963), 384.

terpreted it." On the other hand, Calvin was critical of Zwingli and dissociated himself from significant features of the latter's teaching concerning the Lord's Supper. However, the agreement reached in Zurich (*Consensus Tigurinus,* 1549) between Calvin and Henry Bullinger, Zwingli's successor, suggested to Lutherans after Luther's death that Calvin's views of the Sacrament were identical with Zwingli's. That this is not the case will appear from a review of Calvin's teaching.

In agreement with Luther, Calvin asserted that the Lord's Supper is a means of grace. From God's side it is a testimony of God's grace even when from the human side it is a testimony of man's faith. It is the Word that makes it a sacrament, and the gift of the Sacrament is the same as that of the Word: redemption, eternal life, and Christ himself as the giver of these. What is promised in the Sacrament is actually conveyed to all who receive it in faith, for the promise that the body of Christ is "given for you" and His blood is "shed for you" can be received only in faith. Involved in the Sacrament is not only a remembrance of past giving, therefore, but an event of present giving: Christ is really present and active.

There were differences from Luther as well as agreements with him. Unlike Luther (and unlike Zwingli), Calvin appealed to John 6 for witness to Christ's presence in the Sacrament. Calvin asserted that the Sacrament remains an empty sign for unbelievers, that Christ is present only to the elect, while Luther had insisted that for unbelievers, too, Christ is present, but active in judgment rather than grace (*manducatio infidelium*). Calvin also gave more prominence to the operation of the Holy Spirit, although this is implied in Luther's repeated assertion that it is the Holy Spirit who calls men through the Gospel and that the Spirit works where and when it pleases God.

During the Reformation a great deal of attention centered on the bread and wine that were used in the Lord's Supper, and as a consequence it was often overlooked that the Lord's Supper is a meal. This can be accounted for, at least in part, by the preoccupation with the elements which had been characteristic of the Middle Ages. Over against the Roman view, both Luther and Calvin emphasized that the bread remains bread and the wine remains wine. Both also insisted that the elements have sacramental significance only when they are eaten and drunk in remembrance of Christ's sacrifice and in association with a recitation of the words of institution. The medieval term "consecration" was conservatively retained but it was made clear that the words of institution are not addressed to the bread and wine but to the assembled people and therefore do not transmute the elements in any way. Despite contemporary misunderstanding and overstatement, Luther and Calvin agreed that the expression "the body and blood of Christ" does not mean things or substances but means Christ himself.[1] Hence neither identified the wine with blood or the bread with body. Neither taught transubstantiation, consubstantiation, impanation, invination, or a local "envelopment" of the body and blood of Christ in the elements of bread and wine. Although Luther underscored the "is" in "This is my body," it is very significant that he usually expounded these words as meaning that Christ's body and blood (that is, the incarnate Christ himself) are "under" or "in and under" the bread and wine as these are eaten and drunk in the sacred meal. By this he asserted not identity but simultaneity.[2]

The common affirmation of Christ's presence and activity in the Lord's Supper involved christology, and Luther and Calvin accounted for Christ's presence and activity differently. Both employed formulations of the ancient church to assert that Christ became incarnate and remains both divine and human. Calvin was more conservative than Zwingli in adhering to the statements of the ancient church concerning an exchange of properties (*communicatio idiomatum*) between the divine and human natures, but he charged that Luther and his followers so extended these statements as virtually to deny the reality of Christ's humanity. Both Luther and Calvin tried to keep the divine and human natures separate and unconfused in the unity of Christ's person. Like Zwingli, Calvin believed that ever since the ascension Christ's body has been in heaven, but that Christ continues to be present and active on earth in his divine nature. Accordingly he sometimes explained Christ's presence in the Sacrament as a spiritual presence of Christ according to his divinity alone. At other times he suggested that communicants are lifted up by the Spirit to heaven, where they are united with the divine-human Saviour. Luther, on the other hand, held that it is more in keeping with the Gospel, as well as with the words of institution, to emphasize that the whole Christ, human and divine, comes to man where he is. To be sure, he added, the body of Christ is no longer like that which men knew when He was on earth, for it is a glorified body, a spiritual body. In this sense it can be said that both Luther and Calvin taught that Christ is spiritually present in the Sacrament. It was Philip Schaff, I believe, who quipped that the

61

---

[1] Cf. Gennrich, *op. cit.*, 64-75; Erich Seeberg, *Luthers Theologie in ihren Grundzuegen* (Stuttgart, 1960), 152, 158; Apology of the Augsburg Confession, X, 4.
[2] Cf. Werner Elert, *The Structure of Lutheranism*, I (St. Louis, 1962), 305; Reinhold Seeberg, *Lehrbuch der Dogmengeschichte*, 3rd edition, IV (Leipzig, 1917), 387.

difference between them was that Luther contended for the real presence of a spiritual Christ and Calvin for the spiritual presence of a real Christ.

Something needs to be said about Luther's colleague, Philip Melanchthon, a contemporary of Calvin and an occasional correspondent of his. When, after Luther's death, some of his followers, like Nicholas Amsdorf and Joachim Westphal, advocated positions which were extreme extensions of Luther's most extravagant anti-Zwinglian statements, Melanchthon was charged with a betrayal of Lutheranism.[1] The charge was mutual, for Melanchthon assailed Amsdorf and Westphal for adhering to the medieval superstition of artolatry. It is true that Melanchthon was sometimes conciliatory to the point of surrender in his dealings with opponents on the right and on the left, but he consistently defended the "substantial presence" of Christ in the Lord's Supper. By "substantial" he meant "personal," that is, that the divine-human Christ is personally there.[2] Melanchthon did not share Luther's speculations about the ubiquity of Christ's body, but Luther did not hold this against Melanchthon, who also explained Christ's presence differently. Distinguishing between body and soul in the Greek fashion, Melanchthon once suggested that although Christ's glorified body is in heaven, his human soul can be on earth. He also cited (as did Calvin) the words of Augustine, *ubique totus est, sed non totum,* according to which the whole Christ can be present in the Sacrament although not everything pertaining to Christ (like a material body) is there.[3] Instead of Luther's "in and under," Melanchthon preferred to say that Christ is present and active "with" the bread and wine when these are received and consumed in the the Lord's Supper. In the Formula of Concord (1577) later Lutherans combined the prepositions so as to read "in, with, and under" while continuing to deny a "local" presence.

It is not without significance that during the sixteenth century there were differences, and even controversies, among Lutherans on the one hand and among Reformed on the other. Interpretations of the Lord's Supper and of christology offered by Luther, Melanchthon, Amsdorf, Westphal, and others on the Lutheran side were not in every respect the same. Nor were interpretations given on the Reformed side by Zwingli and Bullinger or by Calvin, Peter Martyr Vermigli, and

62

[1]O. H. Nebe, *Reine Lehre: Zur Theologie des Niklas Amsdorff* (Goettingen), (1935); Karl Moenckeberg, *Joachim Westphal und Johannes Calvin* (Hamburg, 1865).
[2]Ritschl, *op. cit.,* IV, 25, 26; Friedrich Brunstaed, *Theologie der lutherischen Bekenntnisschriften* (Guetersloh, 1951), p. 154.
[3]Ritschl, *op. cit.,* IV, 4-9, 18-32.

Zachary Ursinus.[1] Party lines between Lutherans and Reformed nevertheless remained. Reduced to simplest terms, with respect to the postascension activity of the Saviour on earth, and therefore in the Sacrament, the Reformed emphasized the distinction between the two naturs of Christ without denying their unity and the Lutherans emphasized the unity of the two natures without denying their distinction. Both appealed to the Scriptures in support of their interpretations and both encountered problems in the testimony of the Scriptures.

Diverse historical circumstances and personal temperaments caused Lutherans to react with special vehemence against left-wing (Anabaptist and Zwinglian) interpretations of the Sacrament and caused the Reformed to react with similar vehemence against right-wing (Roman) interpretations. This is reflected in sacramental practice as well as in theological formulation. Both Lutherans and Reformed agreed in principle that the way in which the Lord's Supper is celebrated, and the kinds of bread and wine employed, belong to the sphere of adiaphora, provided the manner of observance does not express or imply wrong teaching. Both discontinued many practices which were obviously associated with the Roman teaching of the sacrifice of the Mass. However, although uniformity was by no means achieved, or even desired, by either party, Lutherans were more conservative than the Reformed.[2] Different attitudes were taken, for example, toward altars, vestments, art, music, the form of bread, and the posture of communicants. Melanchthon was especially ready to make concessions to Rome for the sake of peace (Leipzig Interim, 1548) and had to be reminded by his fellow-Lutheran Matthias Flacius that the relation between doctrine and ceremony could not be ignored.

Melanchthon also had a large hand in the reintroduction of scholasticism, which became characteristic of both Lutheran and Reformed theology in the seventeenth century. After 1580 the differences between Lutherans and Reformed became hardened. Despite a few attempts at reconciliation by individuals like John Durie, the hallmark of the scholastic theology of the seventeenth century was polemics. Political considerations intensified the polemics, and Lutheran and Reformed theologians aimed less at convincing and persuading their opponents than at defending and protecting their own positions. With astonishing acumen and diligence they marshalled arguments. Supported by a common theory of inspiration, they brought texts of the Bible to bear on

63

[1]*Ibid.*, III, 243-458. See especially Joseph C. Mc Lelland *The Visible Word of God: an Exposition of the Sacramental Theology of Peter Martyr Vermigli* (Edinburgh, 1957).
[2]Cf. H. G. Hageman, *Pulpit and Table. Some Chapters in the History of Worship in the Reformed Churches* (Richmond, 1962).

the issues which divided the churches. For our purpose the competing theologies of the seventeenth century can conveniently be compared in two anthologies prepared in the middle of the nineteenth century: for the Lutheran side by Heinrich Schmid, *The Doctrinal Theology of the Evangelical Lutheran Church*, and for the Reformed side by Heinrich Heppe, *Reformed Dogmatics*.

Turning first to christology, the agreement between Lutherans and Reformed was summarized in these words by J. F. Cotta, the editor of John Gerhard's *Loci* (1610-21) : "They agree (1) that in Christ there is only one person but two natures, namely, a divine and a human; (2) that these two natures have been joined in the closest and most intimate union, which is generally called personal; (3) that by this union, a more intimate one than which cannot be conceived, the natures are neither mingled, as has been condemned in the Eutychians, nor the person divided, as has been condemned in the Nestorians; but (4) that this union must be regarded as without change, mixture, division, and interruption; and therefore (5) that by this union neither the difference of natures nor the peculiar conditions of either have been removed, for the human nature of Christ is always human, nor has it ever, by its own natural act, ceased to be finite, extended, circumscribed, capable of suffering, but the divine nature is and always remains infinite, immeasurable, incapable of suffering. Nevertheless, (6) that by the power of the personal union the properties of both natures have become common to the person of Christ, so that the person of Christ, the God-man, possesses divine properties, uses them, and is named by them. But in addition to this (7) that by means of the hypostatic union there have been imparted to the human nature of Christ the very highest gifts of acquired condition—for example, the greatest power, the highest wisdom, although finite—but (8) that to the mediatorial acts of Christ each nature contributed its own part and that the divine nature conferred upon the human nature infinite power to redeem and save the human race. In a word, (9) that the intimate union of God and man in Christ is so wonderful and sublime that it surpasses in the highest degree the comprehension of our mind."[1]

This was substantial agreement. The disagreement between Lutherans and Reformed centered in the question of the ubiquity or omnipresence (or, rather, omnivolipresence) of the humanity of Christ. J. H. Heidegger (1700) summarized the Reformed view by declar-

---

[1]Quoted in Heinrich Schmid, *The Doctrinal Theology of the Evangelical Lutheran Church*, translated by C. A. Hay and H. E. Jacobs (Philadelphia, 1876), 352.

ing:[1] "The Gospel story teaches very clearly that Christ's human nature was conceived in the womb of the blessed Virgin, formed in it, born of it, and so came into a light in which it was not, and that the man Christ moved from place to place both before and after the resurrection and ascended from earth to heaven. . . . The presence of a visible, local body is nothing but a visible, local, circumscribed one, and the opposite presence to that is the invisible, definitive, and non-local presence of spirits." The Lutheran answer of David Hollaz (1707) was:[2] "(1) The doctrine concerning the reality of the flesh of Christ is not neutralized thereby [by the ascription of omnipresence to it], for it is not omnipresent by a physical and extensive but by a hyperphysical, divine, and illocal presence, which belongs to it not formally and *per se* but by way of participation and by virtue of the personal union. (2) The doctrine concerning the death of Christ is not overturned by it, for the natural union of body and soul was indeed dissolved by death, but without disturbing the permanent hypostatic union of the divine and human natures. (3) The doctrine of the ascension of Christ is not disproved by it, for before the ascension the flesh of Christ was present in heaven by an uninterrupted presence as a personal act, but he ascended visibly to heaven in a glorified body according to the divine economy so that he might fill all things with the omnipresence of his dominion. For Christ, by virtue of his divine omnipotence, can make himself present in various ways." Less important was the difference between Lutherans and Reformed on the states of Christ's humiliation and exaltation.

With respect to the Lord's Supper a large area of agreement between Lutherans and Reformed can again be established. Both asserted that the gift conferred in the Sacrament is the same as that conferred in oral proclamation of the Gospel. Both considered the Sacrament a means of grace in which Christ gives himself and the benefits, secured by Christ on the cross, to the believing communicant. In its essential character, therefore, the Lord's Supper is not a sacrifice made by man to God. The movement is from God to man, effected by the working of the Spirit and taking place in a public assembly of Christians rather than in a private action performed by a priest.

Disagreement between Lutherans and Reformed continued to center in two areas. The first is that the Reformed thought of the body of Christ as being in heaven and accordingly maintained that Christ

[1]Quoted in Heinrich Heppe *Reformed Dogmatics*, revised by Ernst Bizer and translated by G. T. Thomson (London, 1950), 447.
[2]Schmid, *op. cit.*, 355.

is present in the Sacrament "spiritually," while the Lutherans contended that he is present "bodily" and reintroduced Luther's early formulation of ubiquity to show the possibility of a corporeal presence. In fact, Lutherans went so far now as to speak of a "celestial matter" (*materia coelestis*) in the sacrament and in effect to substitute this for the personal presence of Christ. This appears to have intensified the Reformed rejection of the Lutheran locution that the body and blood of Christ are "in, with, and under" the elements of bread and wine.[1] Moreover, the Reformed were more careful than the Lutherans in emphasizing that Christ is present in the whole action of the Lord's Supper and not merely in connection with the elements, although Lutherans also made this observation in the Formula of Concord[2] and in subsequent theological works.

The second area of continuing disagreement revolved around the Lutheran insistence that unbelieving as well as believing participants in the Sacrament receive the body and blood of Christ, while the Reformed held that the unbelieving receive only bread and wine. The Reformed did not mean by this that faith effects the presence of Christ and his benefits but rather that faith alone can accept and receive what is objectively offered. The Lutherans also held that faith is necessary to receive the gifts of the Sacrament but declared that unbelievers receive unto judgment what is objectively offered. The difference was more sharply expressed when the Lutherans asserted that "the wicked receive the same body and the same blood of Christ with their mouth" (*manducatio impiorum*),[3] while the Reformed asserted that "bread and wine are taken with the bodily mouth, the body and blood with the soul's mouth, i.e. by true faith."[4] Predestination was prominently introduced by the Reformed in this connection. Meanwhile, both Lutherans and Reformed tended, under the influence of scholastic intellectualism, to replace faith in God's promise with assent to a theory about the Sacrament.

Difference in the understanding of the Lord's Supper was aggravated by difference in practice. In fact, there was sometimes conscious cultivation of difference in practice. The Reformed allowed only lawfully called ministers to administer the Sacrament. Generally this was also the case among Lutherans, although allowance was made (at least in theory) for lay administration in emergency. Lutherans

---

[1]Cf. Westminster Confession, XXIX 7, in John H. Leith ed., Creeds of the Churches (Garden City, N.Y., 1963), 226.
[2]Cf. Formula of Concord, S.D., VII, 83, 84.
[3]Schmid, *op. cit.*, 592.
[4]Heppe, *op. cit.*, 650.

conservatively continued to use unleavened wafers, which they inherited from the Middle Ages, but the Reformed replaced them with leavened bread because of the association of wafers with Roman teaching. The fraction of the bread was deemed a necessary (although not absolutely necessary) ceremony by the Reformed, and partly because the Reformed approved of fraction the Lutheran disapproved of it. Altars were usually retained by Lutherans, but the Reformed supplanted them with tables in order to make clear that the Lord's Supper is not a sacrifice in the medieval sense. In many (although by no means all) places bread and wine were placed directly into the mouths of Lutheran communicants by their ministers, but this medieval practice was uniformly given up by the Reformed as tending to superstition.

Most of the differences in doctrine and practice which were so sharply defined in the seventeenth century were retained either as conventions or as convictions during succeeding centuries. To be sure, some softening of accent occurred, and the polemical spirit subsided or disappeared. The following are a few of the questions which we today need to raise as we review the record of the sixteenth and seventeenth centuries.

1. To what extent did misunderstanding between Lutherans and Reformed make their differences appear to be greater than they actually were?
2. To what extent did Lutherans obscure their teaching by conservatively adhering to practices which suggested or expressed what they denied? On the other hand, to what extent did the Reformed foreshorten their teaching by a more radical rejection of traditional forms and of a creative use of art?
3. To what extent have modern studies in the Reformation, notably in Luther and Calvin, clarified the historical differences between Lutherans and Reformed? In addition, to what extent have modern biblical studies, with texts and tools not formerly available, helped to settle questions which used to be in dispute?

67

MAJOR LUTHERAN-REFORMED
CONVERSATIONS

This check-list is intended to show that conversations between Lutherans and Reformed did not end in Marburg four centuries ago and to illustrate the changing circumstances in which conversations continued to be held. Political considerations played a part from Marburg to the Prussian Union. Relative theological indifference contributed to some agreements in the eighteenth and nineteenth centuries.

Increased mobility of people and easier communication provided occasion for more recent conversations.

1529. *Marburg Colloquy.* Martin Luther, Philip Melanchthon, et al. met with Ulrich Zwingli, John Oecolampadius, et al. in Marburg. They failed to agree on the Lord's Supper, the major topic of discussion, although there appeared to be agreement on other topics.

1536. *Wittenberg Concord.* Martin Bucer, Wolfgang Capito, et al. met with Martin Luther, Philip Melanchthon, et al in Wittenberg. Agreement on the Lord's Supper helped to unite the North and South Germans but did not include the Swiss.

1564. *Maulbronn Colloquy.* James Andreae, John Brenz, et al. met with Zachary Ursinus, Caspar Olevian, et al. in Maulbronn, a village near Stuttgart. They discussed the Lord's Supper and especially the ubiquity of Christ but without achieving agreement.

1570. *Consensus of Sendomir.* A group of Lutherans, Reformed, and Bohemian Brethren met in Sendomir, near Warsaw, in the interest of Protestant unity over against the Roman Catholic majority in Poland. The proposal to draft a new Polish confession of faith was not realized.

1586. *Montbeliard Colloquy.* Theodore Beza, P. Huebner, et al. met with Lucas Osiander, James Andreae, et al. in Montbeliard, France. They discussed the Lord's Supper, christology, and predestination. The question whether Huguenot refugees might receive the Lord's Supper in Lutheran churches was answered in the negative by the Reformed on the ground that participation in the Sacrament is a mark of profession.

1645. *Conference of Thorn.* Among others, Abraham Calovius and John Huelsemann (Lutherans), Amos Comenius and John Bythner (Reformed), and Gregory Schoenhof (Roman Catholic) met in Thorn, Poland. The conference was called by the king in the hope of ending religious controversy in his land. It did not succeed.

1661. *Colloquy of Cassel.* Meetings were arranged by the landgrave of Hesse in the hope of uniting Reformed and Lutherans in his land. The topics discussed included the Lord's Supper, christology, predestination, baptism. Tentative agreements were later repudiated, but the two churches recognized each other as true churches.

1788. *Unio Ecclesiastica of the German Protestant Churches.* An administrative union of a handful of German-speaking Lutheran and Reformed congregations in South Carolina which survived only to 1794. There was no attempt at a theological consensus.

1817. *Prussian Union.* An administrative union of Lutheran and Reformed churches in Prussia, imposed by the king and imitated in several other German states. Theological differences were ignored for the most part.

1841. *Church Society of the West.* This "Kirchenverein" was organized by German immigrants, of Lutheran and Reformed origin, in the American Middle West, became the Evangelical Synod of North America, and later merged into the Evangelical and Reformed Church, now part of the United Church of Christ. Both Luther's Small Catechism and the Heidelberg Catechism were recognized without defining wherein they agreed or differed.

1891. *Evangelical Church of the Augsburg and Helvetic Confessions.* The minority Lutheran and Reformed churches in Austria formed an administrative union to represent them in dealings with the Roman Catholic state.

1956. *Consensus on the Holy Communion.* A common statement was adopted by the Netherlands Reformed Church and the Lutheran Church in the Netherlands by which intercommunion was established. Differences as well as agreements are acknowledged in the statement.

1957. *Arnoldshain Theses.* A statement by a commission of Lutheran, Reformed, and Union theologians in Germany, setting forth the extent of existing agreement on the Lord's Supper and offering a basis for further discussion and possible official action by the several churches.

1958-61. Intercommunion was authorized (?) between the Church of Scotland on the one hand and the Church of Denmark and the Church of Sweden on the other. An agreement on ordination was reached by the Reformed and Lutheran churches in France.

69

THE NATURE AND MANNER OF THE IMPARTATION OF JESUS CHRIST IN THE SACRAMENT OF THE LORD'S SUPPER

by William O. Fennell

I understand my task to be the attempt to make a constructive statement on the Lord's Supper and christology that takes into account the conflicting views on these subjects that have from Reformation times to the present separated Lutheran and Reformed churches. In undertaking this task it has seemed wise not to make direct reference to the historical definitions of the problems or to attempt a resolution of the problems in the theological language commonly used in the two traditions. For such a procedure would inevitably lead into the *cul de sac* of unresolved disagreement into which the traditional debates led. It would seem better to venture a series of constructive statements formulated with the ancient controversies in mind and then invite the theologians of each tradition to say whether or not their doctrinal concerns have been adequately represented or met. Of course, I suffer no illusion that this essay will meet the test of adequacy. Indeed, in its preparation I have become more consciously aware of the gaps in my historical knowledge and of the riches of understanding of the sacramental mystery that are to be found in approaching Scripture by way of a dialogue with the whole of church history. But despite its inadequacies, I hope that the members of the conference will find in this essay sufficient common ground for our present purpose of seeking greater mutual understanding and indeterminate measures of concord.

The title represents my understanding of the central issue with regard to the Lord's Supper. It may very well be that the concentration on the question of the nature and mode of the real presence of Jesus Christ in the Sacrament resulted in a certain lack of wholeness in the sacramental teaching of the reformation churches. But there can be no doubt that the controversy centered on a fundamental issue of Christian thought and life. Although our long-range task must be that of seeking through ecumenical conversations the achievement of a greater whole-

70

ness in our theology of the sacraments, our present task is the more limited one of attempting some kind of resolution of historic disagreements and misunderstandings. Therefore it seemed best to concentrate on the questions implied in the title.

The most fruitful starting point for our discussion would seem to be one that thinks of the Lord's Supper as *visible word*. Whether everything that one wishes to say about the nature and the function of the sacrament can be exhaustively said from this point of view remains to be seen. But initially we would no doubt all agree that to think of the sacraments as visible words is historically authoritative and contemporaneously meaningful.

The Gospel of God's saving presence and deed in Jesus Christ is made available to men in the Spirit-enabled proclamation and reception of the Word through preaching and sacrament. Valid preaching intends that through the human words of the sermon, based upon the written record of the prophetic and apostolic witness, Jesus Christ will be present calling forth and confirming faith. "He who hears you hears me, and he who rejects you rejects me." (Luke 10:16). The commandment to preach is accompanied by the promise of presence. (Matthew 28:20). Through the apostolic continuity of proclamation in the lively word of witness which is preaching, the living Word of God incarnate in the life, death and resurrection of Jesus Christ is made present through the Spirit. All true preaching is sacramental. It is an action whereby God makes his presence real, objectively through the Word of the Gospel that is the content of the words of the sermon, and subjectively through his presence in his Spirit. Both modes of presence serve to call forth and strengthen the faith that makes the Word a gracious saving presence; or contrariwise, where faith is wanting, they serve to effect a judging, heart-hardening and therefore damning presence.

Now the Gospel is proclaimed not through the spoken word alone. It is also proclaimed through the visible, enacted word of the sacrament. The commandment of our Lord to preach the Gospel, accompanied by the promise of Presence[1], has a counterpart in the commandment to enact the Lord's Supper, accompanied by the promise of "eating and drinking" the "body and blood" of Jesus Christ.[2] The same Gospel of God's saving presence and deed in Jesus Christ that is administered through Spirit-accompanied preaching is also administered through Spirit-accompanied visible and enacted word, the Sacrament. If it is asked

71

---

[1]Matthew 28: 19-20.
[2]I Corinthians 11: 23-26.

why the Gospel should be made available by two kinds of proclamation, the verbal, auditory, spoken word of witness and the visual, material, enacted word of witness, the first answer must be: Because the Lord commanded it. But if one seeks further for understanding of the grace imbedded in the command, there are meaningful ways of answering the question: Why sacraments? From the point of view of both objective proclamation and subjective response there is a more total involvement of the person in "observing" and "receiving" the enacted word than is the case with the spoken word alone. There is an accommodation by God to our humanity in the administration of the Gospel, just as there was in his reconciling presence and work that is the Gospel to be administered. It is as spirit-body beings that we have been reconciled and made new; and it is as spirit-body beings that we are addressed with the Gospel of our salvation. There is an adequacy of presentation when the Gospel is proclaimed by both the spoken and the enacted word in the total event which is the sacramental celebration of the Lord's Supper. The Gospel which is for the whole person is administered to the whole person. The object of faith for the Christian is not spiritual ideas or ideals, or moral principles. It is God in his personal, embodied presence in Jesus Christ who accomplishes our salvation by participation in our creaturely and fallen humanity. So it becomes apparent that the act of worship that is a means of grace whereby God makes himself available to men is most adequate when spoken and visible words together are used to administer his grace.

It is from this perspective that we might go on to ask about the relation between the real presence of Jesus Christ and the instrument through which it is administered. Can we not find considerable help toward a resolution of traditional difficulties concerning the mode of the presence in relation to the elements of the Lord's Supper by comparing the preached word with the enacted word? All valid preaching, we have maintained, is sacramental. Through it there is realized the promise "He that heareth you heareth Me." Jesus Christ ordains the continuance of his personal self-testimony, firstly in the apostolic testimony to him, and then in the continuance of that testimony in the ministry of the Church. The Word of God—God's presence in the Gospel word of witness to him—is given in and with the human words of men. The human words are used as instruments of the Divine Word. There is a correlation but no identity between the two. God takes the faithful and obedient witness of man to the given received revelation and through his Holy Spirit makes it to become an occasion for his contemporaneous self-speaking to man. Is there therefore a sense in which it would be right to say that Jesus Christ is given to us in, with and under the human words of proclamation? If so, is it not precisely in the same sense appropriate to speak of him as given in, with and under the visible word of the bread and wine? In neither case is there an identity between the sign and the thing signified. But in neither case is the thing signified given apart from the sign.

At this point it may be asked whether this way of viewing the Sacrament as a visible word does full justice to the reality of the sacramental presence of the Christ. Does it confine us too narrowly to an "I-Thou-encounter" conception of the Christian man's or believing community's relation to Him? Is there not a sacramental participation in the reality of the Christ which is ontic and not simply noetic? And is it not precisely in the effecting of this ontic union between Jesus Christ and us that the Sacrament of the Lord's Supper differs from that mode of the presence of the Christ that is given through preaching? Is it not in the sacramental eating and drinking of the body and blood of Jesus Christ that we are enabled to become bone of his bone and flesh of his flesh, even as in the incarnation he became bone of our bone and flesh of our flesh? Does not the analogy of preaching and sacramental action break down here and the concept of sacrament as visible word show its inadequacy?

It is my conviction that the answers we give to these questions ought to confirm rather than call into question the analogical identity between spoken and seen word as instruments for the self-impartation of Jesus Christ. As Edmund Schlink has said: "It is the same life which the believer receives when he hears the Gospel and when he receives the Sacrament."[1] No radical distinction can be made between the kind of presence that is conveyed in each or in the effects that each is intended to convey. It would be a failure rightly to understand the creative power of the Word of God if we thought to make in relation to it a fundamental distinction between noetic and ontic modes of impartation or reception. Moreover, is it not a calling into question the once-for-all, finished work of our redemption to think in terms of an ontic union between the believer and Christ as being in some way granted as the grace of sacramental eating and drinking? Does the ontic union between God and man accomplished for us in the incarnation, when the Son of God became bone of our bone and flesh of our flesh, need to be completed by a *new work,* accomplished for us in the Sacrament, when we through faithful eating and drinking become bone of his bone and flesh of his flesh? Are we to think that just as in

73

---

[1] Theology of the Lutheran Confessions, p. 183.

the incarnation there was an ontic oneness accomplished between God
and man by God's assumption in Jesus Christ of our humanity, so there
must now be, again by God's prior, self-initiated work, an ontic *oneness*
accomplished from *our side* by our spiritual eating and drinking of the
body and blood of Jesus Christ? Although some historical statements
about the matter seem to lead to these conclusions, surely we must find
that they are unwarranted. However much we are constrained to assert
the real, contemporaneous presence of the Christ in the Sacrament, we
cannot think of him as coming to complete an incomplete work, but
rather as making available to us the benefits of a saving work already
complete in itself. It is for this reason that we may affirm that the same
life—our new life—is mediated to us both through a believing hearing
of the Gospel that is preached and through a believing receiving of the
Gospel that is enacted in the seen-word of the Sacrament. In either
case, our becoming one plant with Jesus Christ is achieved by our
believing reception of Him who comes in sermon and Sacrament to
announce his reconciling oneness with us in the events of His incarnation, atoning death and resurrection. And in either case, it is the Holy
Spirit that enables the believing reception of the Word.

It would seem appropriate just here to raise a question that has
occupied a central place in the historical disputes about the Lord's
Supper, viz. that concerning the *manducatio impiorum*. Before taking
up the question, I should like to note in passing that the *locus classicus*
for the expression would seem to have had other things in mind than
some theologians have thought. Commenting on the passage I Corinthians 11:17f., Robert Nelson has written:

> The purpose of the Lord's Supper, according to Paul, is twofold:
> attention is centered upon the sacrificial suffering and death of Jesus,
> but also on the fellowship of the faithful brethren who are united in
> Christ. When the Corinthians turned the supper into an occasion
> for gluttony and revelry, the wealthy ignoring the hunger of the poorer,
> they saw neither the sacrificed body of the Lord nor the loving fellow-
> ship of the *ecclesia*. As Paul demanded of them in verse 22: "Do you
> despise the Church of God?"[1]

74

As I have indicated elsewhere,[2] I substantially agree with this interpretation of the passage. The unworthy eating that brings judgment here
is the profanation of the Sacrament through a failure to love. I believe
that one particular form such unworthy eating takes today is the
failure to discern the body of Christ whenever we fail to act upon

---

[1] *The Realm of Redemption*, p, 74.
[2] In an article entitled: *The Essential Oneness of Christ's Body*, CJT, Vol. IV:1.

the truth that all who believe in and love the Lord Jesus Christ are essentially one in him by admitting to fellowship at his table fellow-members of the *ecclesia* of God.

Whether or not we are agreed on this exegesis of the passage, and its significance for the question of intercommunion, we may still ask the question of the nature and effect of Christ's presence in the Lord's Supper for the unworthy. Assuming for the moment that the unworthy are the unbelieving, is the presence of our Lord in the Sacrament so objectively real that he is present to unbelievers as well as believers? Our answer is yes. It is not our faith that effects his presence; so our unbelief cannot cause his absence. He is present *to* all, if not *for* all, in the Sacrament. But here again, in seeking to understand the meaning of that presence for the unbelieving, do we not find a parallel in preaching? "He who hears you hears me, and he who rejects you rejects me." Those who reject the message concerning the Christ reject the Christ who identifies himself with the proclamation. The consequence of that rejection is surely that they are judged by the Word of the Gospel and are hardened in their unbelief. Is it not a dangerous thing to hear the Gospel truly preached and not accord him who comes thereby the grateful, accepting response of faith? If because of that one should ask what makes for worthy listening that need not fear judgment, surely the answer is a readiness on the part of the hearer to allow himself to be judged and forgiven and made new by Him who comes as the content of the Gospel word of judgment, forgiveness and renewal. So also is it with the Sacrament. The Christ comes in the judging, forgiving word of the Gospel made visible and enacted in the Lord's Supper. To see and eat and drink in faith is to enter into union and communion with Him who is made "our wisdom, righteousness and sanctification and redemption." (I Cor. 1:30). To see and eat and drink faithlessly is to be judged by the Christ present in the word of the enacted Gospel and to become hardened in unbelief. But it remains a sobering thought that unseeing lovelessness as well as unseeing unbelief can be a cause and occasion for unworthy eating and drinking at the Lord's Table. Worthy eating and drinking must also consist of allowing him to be the Lord of his own table and to feed with his Word all whom he has made his own.

We should now say something further about the relation between Jesus Christ and Holy Spirit in realizing the real presence of the Christ in the sacrament of the Lord's Supper. We have already made passing remarks on the subject. But since historically much was made of the differences in theological understanding of it, and since the matter

75

is still of contemporary concern, we should seek further clarification of the issues involved.

Again I believe we find a key to the solution of our theological difficulty here by thinking of the Sacrament as visible Word. But in order to understand more clearly the relation between Jesus Christ and Holy Spirit in the proclamation of the Word in the Sacrament we will have to say something more generally about the biblical understanding of the way in which God makes himself known to man in his redeeming action in history. In the Old Covenant the order of redemption, which at the same time is the order of God's self-manifestation, is: a) God's presence and action in history; b) the prophetic witness to that presence and action which is a second mode of presence and action. That is, God is present both in history and in the word of witness to that presence. Through the second mode of presence participation in the first mode is made possible. But, c) there is a third mode of presence which is the uniting link between the first and the second. It is God's presence in the Holy Spirit, inspiring the prophetic witness and enabling the believing reception of it. In the New Covenant, the same order of redemption is preserved: a) God is present and active in history, but now in a mode of presence and action wondrously unique named Jesus Christ; b) God is present and active in a second mode that is the apostolic witness to Jesus Christ; c) it is the Holy Spirit that enables both the believing witness to Jesus Christ through the believing acceptance of him (Mtt. 16:17; 2 Cor. 4:6; I Cor. 12:3) and the believing receiving of the apostolic witness to him through which participation in the first mode of his incarnate presence is made possible.

Now when we realize that the apostolic testimony to Jesus Christ that enables participation in his historical presence, begins with, and is an extension of, the self-testimony of Jesus, we see how the Lord's Supper, considered as visible Word, fits into the foregoing discussion of modes of God's presence. The Last Supper of our Lord with his **76** disciples was a visible word of self-testimony, accompanied by the auditory word of self-witness, whereby he bore witness to his historical person and action on the cross as saving gift to man. Now, in the continued celebration of the Lord's Supper, this apostolic self-testimony of Jesus (which is God's presence in the word of witness) enables our participation in the salvatory action of the Cross (which is God's presence in the incarnate history of Jesus). And it is God's presence in the Holy Spirit in the Church that effects the union of his presence in the witness and his presence in the history of Jesus Christ.

From the foregoing theological perspective it becomes impossible to separate the presence of Jesus Christ from the presence of the Holy Spirit; or to separate the presence of Jesus Christ—either here with us on earth or there in heaven—from his presence in the spoken and enacted word of proclamation; or to make the kind of radical distinction implied in the question whether in the Sacrament Jesus Christ comes into our time or we are taken from our time and brought into his. From this point of view, also, we must affirm that it is the whole Christ who is present through the instrumentality of the sacramental word of witness to him. This secondary mode of presence in the word of witness brings us, through the presence and action of the Holy Spirit, to participate in the primary mode of presence which is the historical Godmanhood of Jesus Christ, in His salvatory life, death, resurrection and ascension. Thus we are brought into union and communion with the total Christ who comes in Word and Spirit to present unto us the totality of his saving gifts in the wholeness of his saving presence. The Holy Spirit is no substitute for an absent Christ. He is rather the subjective presence and agency of God through whom the objective presence of the Christ, mediated through the enacted Word of the Sacrament, is made available to faith.

From this way of viewing the real presence of Jesus Christ in the Sacrament we are not led into the christological questions that historically proved to be so divisive in the Protestant community. We are not forced to formulate either a doctrine of the *communcatio idiomatum* to "explain" how Christ in his human nature can be present in the Sacrament, or a doctrine of a localized Christ in heaven with whom we come into communion only through the Holy Spirit lifting up our hearts on high. We take up the christological question now, not in order to answer the question *how* the total Christ might be conceived to be present, but in order to answer the question of *who* the total Christ is who comes in the Sacrament to commune with and impart himself to the worshipping community. Here the question of the adequacy of the Chalcedonian formulation is bound to arise. Although we agree with those who think that the conceptual tools of Chalcedon were inadequate for their task (what conceptual tools are not?), and although today we would wish to speak in dynamic terms rather than in the static, substantive terms of Chalcedon, nevertheless we remain committed to the fundamental truth concerning the person of Jesus Christ which Chalcedon sought to preserve and affirm. In the person of Jesus Christ God entered into a full participation in our humanity, himself becoming man that as true man he might work the work of our forgiveness and recreate out of our old sinful humanity the one new man. Therefore we must confess him very God and very man; not once God and now man; nor once God and then man and now God again. But once and for all, because of incarnation, both very God and very man, at once God's forgiveness of us sinners and our new humanity in him. No longer in need of a doctrine of *communicatio idiomatum* to answer the problem how the total Christ may be conceived to be truly present in the Sacrament, which has seemed to many an explanation of presence at the cost of Christ's genuine humanity, our christology can be developed in terms of the *communicatio gratiae* from God to man in the Godmanhood of Jesus Christ. Donald Baillie in his book *God Was In Christ* has invited us to seek a clue for the mystery of Christ's *being* in the experienced mystery of grace. (Gal. 2:20; Phil. 2:12). I have never been happy with the Adoptionist and Nestorian tendencies in the development of this suggestion in Baillie's book. Nonetheless, there may be great merit in thinking christologically in terms of the mystery of grace. The supreme difference between Jesus Christ and ourselves viewed from the point of view of that mystery is that, whereas the grace that flows toward and in us, enabling us to be the men of faith we are, is a grace that we are not, in Jesus Christ the grace that flowed toward and in him, enabling him to be the man he was, is a grace that he also was. That is, the "paradox of grace" in us is a "paradox of being" in him, though the paradox of being can also be understood in terms of the communication of grace. It is not our intention to pursue these themes further here, nor equally important christological themes such as *anhypostasia* and *enhypostasia*. Our brief excursion into the christological field will enable us to take up these and kindred subjects in our discussion. We have thought it necessary to touch upon the christological subject here because traditionally the doctrine of the real presence of Christ in the Sacrament has led directly into the christological discussion. Our understanding of the doctrine has not as such led in this direction.

78

   We mentioned at the beginning of our paper that we were going to narrow our subject to a discussion of the nature and the manner of the impartation of Jesus Christ in the Sacrament of the Lord's Supper. This subject has been further narrowed by our dealing almost exclusively with the question of the real presence understood from the point of view of thinking of the Sacrament as visible Word. Before concluding, I think it important to broaden our discussion somewhat by speaking briefly of two other themes related to the question of the impartation of Jesus Christ in the Sacrament, viz the themes of *eucharistic sacrifice* and *eschatology*.

There is no way of thinking about the self-impartation of Jesus Christ in the Sacrament that would validate our speaking about the Church offering Christ to God the Father as her eucharistic sacrifice. There is nothing wrong with an attempt to relate the Church's celebration of the Sacrament with the perpetual intercession of the Christ in heaven as spoken of in the epistle to the Hebrews. But it is a false understanding to believe that as Christ our mediating High-Priest in heaven presents himself to the Father as our atoning sacrifice, so the Church on earth, by virtue of his real presence in the Sacrament, and the priestly function of the ministry, offers Christ to the Father as atoning sacrifice. Nevertheless, there may indeed be a valid way of thinking of the Sacrament in terms of sacrifice.

According to the account of the Last Supper in the Gospels, and the tradition concerning it received by Paul, the atoning sacrifice of Christ is central to its meaning. The broken bread and poured out wine, by virtue of the spoken words by which our Lord identifies himself with them, witness to his atoning sacrifice upon the cross. Priesthood and sacrifice are always conjoined. There on the altar of the Cross, Jesus Christ, God as man, offers himself to the Father as our atoning sacrifice. His sacrifice is self-sacrifice; His oblation is self-oblation. He is both offerer and that which is offered—the Lamb slain from the foundation of the world.

By this sacrifice and oblation of Christ on the cross we are made kings and priests unto God. As priests we are called to make a sacrifice and oblation of our own. Our sacrifice, like his, must be self-sacrifice, and our offering must be self-offering. We offer ourselves a living sacrifice of prayer and praise and service. But we do so only by the mercies of God that are ours in Christ Jesus our Lord. That is, our sacrifice and offering are made both possible and acceptable by the fact that Christ in his incarnation and atoning death has so identified himself with us that we are included in his self-sacrifice and self-oblation. Thus, drawing the power for our self-offering from his self-offering, and counting on the grace of forgiving acceptance that derives from his pure and acceptable sacrifice, we make the offering of ourselves to God. It is in this way that we think of our action in the so-called eucharistic sacrifice as conjoined with the perpetual intercession of the Christ in heaven. Our lives are hid in Christ with God. He who has made himself one with us takes us with him into the presence of God, offering us with him in his self-offering to the Father. Thus, finding

79

ourselves in him, and finding ourselves acceptable to God through him, we come bearing the gift we have in our keeping to offer, namely ourselves. So as we come with our grace-enabled offering we plead his eternal sacrifice as the sole ground for the possibility and acceptability of the offering of ourselves to God and to the neighbour whom God has given us to love. The theme of sacrifice, then, also belongs to the doctrine of the self-impartation of Jesus Christ in the Sacrament of the Lord's Supper.

Finally, we add a word on Sacrament and Eschatology. "For as often as you eat this bread and drink this cup, you proclaim the Lord's death until he come." (I Cor. 11:26) It is significant that the risen, ascended, glorified and living Lord comes to impart his presence to men under the sign of the cross. It will not always be. For there is a presence that will not be mediated through spoken and visible words which signify broken body and shed blood. The proclaiming of the Lord under the signs of his death is only "until He comes". This word of hope and promise concerning the eschatalogical end gives to the Lord's Supper here and now a significance that has the future in it. The Lord's Supper becomes for the Church that celebrates it not only an occasion for Holy Communion with Him who comes as a personal presence to offer himself and his benefits to the faith that will receive him, the *eucharistia* is also informed with hope for the promised fulfilment. As part of the gracious benefit derived from the Christ who is present, she is enabled to pray *maranatha* in hope and expectation of the Lord who will come in the future. Thereby the Lord's Supper becomes an anticipation of the heavenly banquet eaten in the presence of the Lord in the fulfilled Kingdom of God.

Chapter Six

CHRISTOLOGY, THE LORD'S SUPPER AND ITS OBSERVANCE IN THE CHURCH

by Martin J. Heinecken

An attempt at a constructive, contemporary evaluation of the theological issues with respect to christology and the Lord's Supper, especially as this concerns the conversation between the Reformed and the Lutheran Churches.

I. The Christological Basis of the Lord's Supper

THE history of the controversy between the Lutherans and the Reformed shows that the chief point at issue was whether or not the risen and ascended Christ could be present in the Lord's Supper in his human as well as in his divine nature. It is a question, therefore, of the implications of the Chalcedonian christology.

Luther and the Chalcedonian Formula

Luther's understanding of the Chalcedonian formula led him to assert the ubiquity of Christ. That is to say, the risen and ascended Christ, in whom the human and the divine natures are "unconfusedly and unchangeably", as well as "indivisibly and inseparably" united, shares in the omnipresence of the Father, in as much as the right hand of God is everywhere. This presence is not *localiter* (occupying a space as when Jesus walked the earth), nor is it that of the *esse definitive* (the non-spatial mode in which Christ rose from the dead 'clauso sepulchro' in which he remained prior to the ascension). It is rather the presence of the *esse repletive* in which the risen and ascended Christ shares in the omnipresence of God. This was further bolstered by the doctrine of the *communicatio idiomatum* according to which the properties of the divine nature (e.g. omnipresence) were believed to be conferred upon the human nature.

In the Lord's Supper, then, the Christ who shares God's omnipresence, is present in accordance with his promise imparting his body and blood for the forgiveness of sins. It is only in the Gospel that the everywhere present God, whom the natural man knows only as the

81

God of wrath, becomes the *gracious God-for-man*. The same thing happens in the Sacrament, since "the Sacrament is the Gospel." The gift of the Sacrament is the same as that of the preached word of forgiveness *but the mode is different*. In preaching, absolution, the mutual consolation of the brethren, and baptism, the body and blood of Christ are not given because it is not in accord with Christ's promise. Nor do you receive the body and blood of Christ in the daily meal or when drinking wine in the tavern. The body and blood of Christ are given for the remission of sins, life and salvation only when connected with Christ's own words of promise.

As the historical study has shown this whole argumentation was for Luther an accommodation to the reasoning of his opponents. His own christology was of a much more dynamic nature so that you cannot really speak of his christology but only of his Christ. His concern was soteriological and fidelity to the Gospel and he was not bound by the time-conditioned forms of expressions as the later orthodoxists came to be.

Furthermore, it should be quite clear that Luther did not derive his doctrine of the "real presence" in the Lord's Supper from the Chalcedonian christology, of which he may be said to have taken a dim view, as far as its form of expression is concerned. He derived it rather from the witness of the Scriptures and his manner of interpreting Scriptures without allegorizing or correction by the reason. He derived it from what he regarded as the simple, direct meaning of the words of institution and from his whole organic understanding of the Gospel.

What shall be said then about this use of the Chalcedonian christology? Since it is agreed that every theological formulation is addressed to a specific historical situation in the terms of that situation and is to a certain extent, therefore, time-bound, it is a question of whether the intention of Chalcedon and of the Nicene Creed underlying it can be preserved in a contemporary reformulation or whether it is to be given up as no longer tenable. The question is: Is it enough today simply to repeat the old formula, or must things be said differently today in order to say the same thing? Or else is Chalcedon simply to be repudiated in view of a more enlightened understanding of the issues today? We take our stand with the second of these three options.

The Soteriological Concern and a Functional Christology

The concern that motivated the doctrinal struggles that ended in Nicea and Chalcedon was unquestionably soteriological. The insistence is that it takes no less than "very God of very God", "of the *same* substance with the Father" and not only of *like* substance, not only fully to reveal God but fully to effect man's redemption. At the same time, the soteriological concern demands that Jesus be fully man. There is to be no Gnostic depreciation of the material, neither so as to require a being less than God for this contaminating contact, nor so as to imply a docetic Christ, not fully human but man in appearance only. Hence it is the second person (*hypostasis*) of the Trinity who becomes incarnate uniting a fully divine nature with a fully human nature in one person (*enhypostasia*). Nothing less than a full and complete man is the bearer of God's own revelatory and redemptive presence upon the earth. The same God who created the world also redeems it, sanctifies it and will bring it to completion. This God entered fully into the life of man, humbling himself to equality with the lowliest (Phil. 2:6ff.) and sharing all the conditions of human existence. Only so could he be the mediator, the revealer, the redeemer of man. The Redeemer-God who is Lord of the Church and who will come again to judge the quick and the dead is the one who has united Himself with human flesh and blood *forever*.

By thus putting the emphasis upon a *functional* christology there is no intention of setting up a false disjunction between act (*Akt*) and being (*Sein*) (See Dietrich Bonhoeffer, *Akt u. Sein*). Nor are we setting up a false disjunction between "act" and "word". These two are inseparable. God does not act in self-revelation apart from the interpretative, disclosing word and the word is always itself an act. It is to recognize, however, that apart from God's acts in his relation to us we know nothing about God as he is in and for himself. Of course, what God *does* is rooted in what he *is* quite apart from his relation to us. That still does not alter the fact that when we make assertions about God as he is in and for himself, this is based entirely upon his revelatory acts. We say we know God's essence, i.e. what he truly is. Yet this does not put God into our control as when we possess other "essences" fully in our thought, as when, e.g. we grasp the essence of a chair, which is our 'baby', the creation of our own mind. It is not in this way that we grasp God's essence when we affirm that "God is love". Love is an act, an act of relationship. Thus the heart of God in his relation to us is revealed in his acts of love toward us. And from this it is concluded that this is *what God is,* an inexhaustible fountain of love. He *is* what he *does,* and he *does* what he *is.* His love (*agape*) is, therefore, the true expression of his unchanging heart and will. And *everything we say about him is a statement about his love,* even when we speak of his wrath, for this is what he does in a certain relationship to man. All God's so-called attributes are never just qualities which

83

may be abstracted from his essence and laid off like a garment as is presupposed by the doctrines of the *communicatio idiomatum* and the *kenosis,* as sometimes interpreted.

So it is un-biblical to assert *an abstract omnipotence* of God as one of the qualities inhering in his essence. This is a static definition of a god under man's control and is not the living God of the Bible. Psalm 139, e.g., speaks differently. There it is a matter of being unable to escape from God's love: "If I ascend up into heaven thou art there; if I make my bed in hell, thou art there. If I take the wings of the morning and dwell in the uttermost parts of the sea, even there thy hand shall lead me and thy right hand shall hold me" (vv. 8-10). And the same goes for the inability of the sinner to escape from God's wrath, from which only God's love can save. How different from this are the distinctions between local, definitive and repletive presence! What matters is that God is inescapable in both judgment and grace and this has the most profound implications for his presence in preaching, in the Sacrament, and in fact, his presence everywhere.

So if it is not a matter of being able to define God (via essence and attributes), but of faithfully describing him in his creative, redemptive, sanctifying activity, and being confident that these actions are the expression of his true heart and will, by the same token the christology is not a matter of abstract speculations about the union of two "natures" in one "person" and just how this was accomplished (*unitio, unio personalis, perichoresis, communicatio idiomatum, exinanitio*). Granted that each of these tried to do justice to the biblical witness in an historical situation, it does not follow that these formulations in terms of a Platonic or Aristotelian metaphysics are to be fixated for all times. They were addressed to a situation and the same issues must be dealt with in terms of the situation today.

Then the issue seems to be quite clear. It is today, as it was then, soteriological. It is not only a matter of finding in Jesus, the Christ, the full revelation of God. It is rather a matter of finding in Christ the work of man's redemption fully accomplished in the act of victory over the powers that held man in thrall because of his sin. Thus a real distinction can be made between creation, redemption, and sanctification. It is necessary to speak of creation, before one speaks of the fall, and then of redemption and of sanctification and the final recapitulation of the original creation (Eph. 1). This will have the most profound implications not only for preaching (law and Gospel) but also for what is believed to take place in the Lord's Supper, where forgiveness of sins, life and salvation, are imparted on the basis of a once and for all (*ephapax*) act of atonement, reconciliation, victory.

Nor is it then just a matter of self-understanding and the realization of authentic existence (cp. R. Bultman and especially his left-wing followers). Granted that "knowledge of God" and "knowledge of self" are inseparable and that every way of conceiving God involves a certain way of understanding oneself. (Luther: As you believe, so you have him). Yet what happened in Jesus, the Christ, is not only that here a man surrendered himself fully in obedience-in-trust to God, thus becoming a clear channel for God's love to flow through him to the neighbor. (Or Paul Tillich—He who was subjected like all men to all the conditions of existence, without succumbing, in every moment surrendering himself as Jesus to himself as the Christ—both of which statements may be readily affirmed). But here was the actual condescension of God himself into human flesh, without the implication that this is the reflection of a pagan mythology no longer tenable today. This involves both a *kenosis* (John 17:5; Phil. 2:6-7; II Cor. 8:9) and an incarnation (John 1:17; Col. 2:19). It is not just that the so-called Christ event (cross and resurrection) becomes the occasion for a different self-understanding and for the birth of a new being (authentic existence), but there is in the whole life, suffering, death, and resurrection of Jesus, a once and for all atonement made for the sins of the world and a decisive victory won over the powers to which man had been given over because of his sin (II Cor. 6:19; Rom. 5:10); I John 5:4). See especially Luther's explanation of the second article of the creed: I believe that Jesus Christ, true God . . . and true man . . . is my Lord, who has redeemed me . . . in order that I might be His own . . .) Granted that all this is in anthropomorphic language, this is the only way we can speak about the God who has come down to man.

New Testament Christology

So New Testament studies (see especially Oscar Cullman: The Christology of the New Testament) show that the christological affirmations were not just the creation of the later church, but are based upon Jesus' own sayings and actions. Granted that the New Testament (as well as the Old Testament) is testimony literature (Cf. Martin Kähler: *Die Urkunde der kirchengründenden Predigt*) and that all the witness to the person and work of Christ is post-Pentecost, yet this witness is based upon what Jesus said and did in history in fulfillment of prophecy. Hence all the titles ascribed to Jesus (the

Christ, Son of Man, kyrios, soter, high-priest) take individually a current conception and fill it with new meaning, which both corrects and fulfills the current usage. So, e.g., Jesus is the promised Christ, but in a manner not expected by any who were looking for the consolation in Israel. So also Jesus corrects and fulfills the current expectations of the apocalyptic "Son of Man," etc. There are marked differences in witness in the New Testament and it took time, in conflict with heresies, to work out the implications of the unique thing that had happened, and thus to safeguard both the fullness of revelation and the once and for all, complete redemption. And to safeguard this in ever changing situations of conflict is the theological task.

The Mystery and Miracle of the Incarnation

The New Testament witness as well as the subsequent historical development thus show the absoluteness of the miracle and the mystery of the incarnation and the work of redemption. Even if the peculiar Kierkegaardian language of paradox is not to be forced upon all or canonized by enthusiastic "followers", yet what he said can be helpful. The paradoxical runs counter to appearance, counter to the general opinion, and counter to the reason (in a sense still to be specified). What is true of all affirmations of faith (viz. their paradoxicalness) is *a fortiore* true of the affirmations about the man, Jesus, faith in whom is decisive for man's eternal happiness.

Here then is the absolute paradox, which, first of all runs counter to appearance. God never appears directly for all to see. This is paganism. God is, therefore, effectively *hidden* in the man Jesus and Jesus did not somehow *fully and directly* betray his divinity to his contemporaries, either by his looks or his deeds. Just as God is *hidden* effectively in the masks of creation and in the proclaimed Word, so he is hidden also in the "mediated immediacy" (John Baillie's phrase) of the incarnation.

Here is the absolute paradox, for secondly, it runs counter to the general opinion. Neither the general public of Jesus' day nor the natural man of any day discerns the fullness of the Godhead revealed in the man Jesus. For this the enlightenment of the Holy Spirit is necessary (I Cor. 12:3; Matt. 16:7).

Here is the absolute paradox, for thirdly, it is an offense to the reason of man, in the sense that he cannot fathom the mystery (I Tim. 3:16), but he can understand only that he cannot understand it. To be sure, the primary offense is not to man's intellect but to his pride of virtue and of power, which makes his absolute dependence upon

God's grace a *skandalon*. But there accompanies this also a pride of intellect, which will not admit, "How unsearchable are God's judgments and His ways past finding out" (Rom. 11:33). The incarnation is a mystery, which seals man's lips (*muein*) and makes it impossible for him to describe fully in human language what has taken place. All human language is, therefore, only a pointing to an incredible fact. The "knowledge" of God conveyed in and through Jesus, the Christ, is, therefore the "knowledge" of the most intimate personal relationship in the biblical sense rather than a mere intellectual apprehension of an historic fact or of a truth of the reason. It is the self-impartation of God himself and this is not accomplished except through the transformation in his existence of the one so apprehended (John 3:5). The alternatives when confronted by the claim which Jesus, the Christ, puts upon man are not belief or doubt, but "faith" or "offense", and neither "faith" nor "offense" are possible except where the absoluteness of the paradox in the sense defined is recognized. The way is blocked then to a mere intellectual acceptance or doubt and man is forced either to acknowledge or to resist the unconditional claim put upon him. (*Hoc est Christum cognoscere, eius beneficia cognoscere:* Melanchthon).

A Kenosis

So there is here involved a *kenosis,* or self-emptying of God himself into the servant form (Phil. 2:5 ff.). Luther never wearied of saying that man is not to climb into heaven but stay upon the earth and see God there where He has chosen to reveal himself in the manger and the swaddling clothes, the flesh, the suffering, the shame of the cross. This is a *theologia crucis* and not *gloriae.* There is to be no climbing up to God to the beatific vision nor any flight on the wings of faith up to God, because in Jesus, the Christ, God has fully come down to man and released him from his ignorance, his fears, his imprisonment in his ego-centricity, the just judgment of condemnation upon him, and set him free for service to the neighbor, to be a man, as Jesus was a man and to live *in* and *for* the world as the man God created him to be.

It is not then the fact only that by Jesus certain truths are revealed but that in Jesus, the Christ, God is fully present upon the earth, Immanuel, God-with-us (Matt. 1:23) in the fullness of his judgment and his grace, so that he is a savor of death to some and of life to others (II Cor. 2:16).

The Soteriological Concern and the *finitum est capax infiniti*

It is in the interest of soteriology, therefore, that there must be this

87

full indwelling of God and by no means just a coming down out of the sky of a being among other beings, which, now that we know a little bit more about the heavens, becomes impossible. This has nothing to do with possible scientific cosmologies. But the question is whether or not the finite, space and time, flesh and blood, will really at a time and place contain the fullness of the Godhead without bursting (Col. 2:9) or whether God really remains remote, aloof, uncontaminated with the earthly.

It is not enough then to say that although Jesus was fully human God acted decisively in him. If this is all that is said it would be impossible, in fact, it would be blasphemy to worship Christ, to see him sharing God's prerogatives, ever living and making intercession for men, being present to his own (Matt. 18:20; 28:20), and bound to come again in glory to judge the quick and the dead (Matt. 24:30) and to establish "a new heaven and a new earth" (Rev. 21). If all that is said is that God acted decisively in the man Jesus, then to speak of the "real presence" of this Jesus in the Sacrament would make no sense. The God who acted in Jesus could be so present, but not the man Jesus, who, if raised from the dead, could, like any other human being, be present only at one place and would thus be confined to a place at God's right hand. This is only a variant of saying that the divine nature could be present but not the human nature. It is nothing other than the denial of the finite's capacity to contain the infinite.

This then is the issue in the twentieth century as it was in the sixteenth. To be sure, the Chalcedonian formulation was accepted on both sides, particularly by Calvin. But it seems not to have been taken seriously in its full implications. If the Chalcedonian formula with its famous four adverbs says something that is vital, then there can be no separation of the human and the divine—*ever*. Though the natures are not to be confused in any way or somehow changed into each other, they cannot ever be divided or separated from each other either. If this is really so, then, if Christ is present in the Sacrament at all, it *can* only be in accordance with both natures. If he gives himself to his own in the Sacrament in a peculiar mode, then *it will have to be the body given on Calvary and the blood shed for the sins of the world,* without implying substances or particles of flesh and blood, because it is with the personal presence and self-giving of the risen Christ we are dealing. Otherwise the joyful feasts of the early Christian community at which they believed the same Christ (with whom they had once shared bread and who would one day share it with them again in the perfected kingdom) to be present at table with them, would indeed have to be written off as a sad and tragic delusion, if the human nature did not share in the properties of the divine (to use this quaint language). This is why the adjective may indeed have proved to be the enemy of the noun, when "real" was added to "presence". What can the word "real" add to a presence, which, if present at all, can be present only as what it is, i.e., the presence of Him, who in the mystery of the incarnation, lived, died, rose again, and was raised to glory?

Unless, then, there is fidelity to the intention of Chalcedon and one or the other of the heresies refuted throughout the bitter struggles is not to be repeated, there is no choice but to recognize what was intended by the "real" presence in th sacrament. At least, since we are still dealing with the christology and not yet with the presence in the sacrament, the soteriological concern that motivated the Fathers can be preserved only by taking seriously the full mystery of the incarnation and the fact that God not only acted in Jesus, the Christ, once, at a turning point in history, but that he united himself with the man Jesus in a unique, incomparable way. The church that is nurtured by Word and sacrament makes sense in no other way. All the heaped up expressions for the church, the body of Christ, the bride of Christ, the branches on the true vine, the sheep of the one shepherd, the building of which He is the cornerstone, would have to be abandoned, if there is no Christ present everywhere in the church.

The Church as the Extension of the Incarnation

This christology would also repudiate a regarding of the church as the extension of the incarnation, if this means that the church is simply the continuation in time of what happened when the Word became flesh. The biblical witness implies a difference between Christ and his church, however intimate the relation. Christ is the Head, while the church is the body; He is the bridegroom, while the church is the bride; He is the vine, the church is the branches; He is the cornerstone and the apostles are laid into the foundation on which the church is built. What happened, therefore, in the life, death, resurrection, and ascension of the Lord is unique, once-for-all, unrepeatable. The act of atonement for the world's sins and the victory won are unique, once-for-all, unrepeatable.

89

It is true then that while in the priesthood of believers the reconciling work of Christ continues, this priesthood is not the extension of the incarnation, but it is the congregation, the gathering of the believers by and about a living Lord, gathered, sustained, nurtured by him through his Word in the power of the Holy Spirit.

The Personal Encounter

This christology also preserves the personal nature of the encounter between God and man whether in preaching or absolution, or the sacraments, or the mutual consolation of the brethren. It is not by an impersonal infusion of graces that the Christian life is nurtured but by the presence of the gracious God in Christ.

The Finite Is Capable of the Infinite

The central issue then is that the finite is capable of the infinite. To turn this around and to say, as Gustav Aulen does, that the *infinitum est capax finiti* does not solve or avoid the problem. The fact that the infinite God encompasses the finite presents no problem. The question is whether or not the earthly flesh can really contain and have present in it the unlimited fullness of God. It is the question concerning the salvatory events in history, the so-called *Heilsgeschichte.* Do these events take place only outside of history, in eternity, outside of space and time, or do they actually take place in history, at a time and place, in flesh and blood, although in a hidden way, discernible only to "faith" or "offense"? The crucial point is then—to use the familiar Lutheran formula—that God acts "in, with, and under" the medium of the earthly, not alongside of it, or in any way separated from it either in space or time, so that the earthly is only a sign or an illustration or an acted out parable, merely pointing to but not participating in that which happens apart from the earthly.

Luther's View of the Relation Between the Word and the Earthly Elements

Luther's view is determined, if I understand him correctly, by his conception of the presence of God in the masks of creation. God's omnipresence is not an abstract assertion, but it means God being present to men and acting upon them in judgment and in grace, never directly, never as the *deus nudus,* but always in the mask of the earthly. This is by no means pantheism, because creator and creature are clearly distinguished and the great idolatry of confusing creator and creature recognized. (Rom. 1) But it means that God does cloak himself in sun, wind, rain, father, mother, magistrate, farmer, etc. and so works in and through these media in the "mediated immediacy" of which we have spoken. In and through these media God actually encounters men and calls them to worship, obedience, and joyful, thankful acceptance of his gifts. But since all men confuse creator and creature, boast and glory in themselves, giving the glory to the creature rather than the creator, thus manifesting their enmity against God, they encounter the

90

wrathful God (Rom. 1). It is actually the God of love who confronts them and manifests his goodness to them (Acts 14), but his love is hidden in his wrath, because of man's idolatry.

But in the proclamation of the Gospel it is different. In it God meets man in Christ explicitly revealed as the gracious one, but once more in a hidden way, in the mask of the earthly, in the human word, in the servant form. In all worship (*Gottesdienst:* a subjective genitive,) God serves man. Wherever the Gospel is rightly proclaimed and the sacraments administered in accordance with it, there the everywhere present God who is experienced only as the wrathful God outside of this proclamation, speaks and acts and gives himself as the gracious God-for-man. If *Anfechtung* threatens to destroy confidence and cheerful obedience, then the only refuge is in God's own word of promise, which once more opens God's gracious heart and prompts man to put his trust not in his own faith but in the ever faithful God.

On this background it is easy to see how Luther conceived of God acting *in and through the earthly medium in the sacraments.* The water of baptism is not an empty sign which merely accompanies God's word, but God is present and active in and through the water itself, so that it may be called a "gracious water of life" (The Small Catechism). Without the Word the water is nothing but a barber's bath, but with the Word it is a "gracious water of life and washing of regeneration in the Holy Ghost" (Titus 3:5). There is no question about the water becoming holy by means of an act of priestly consecration. The water which God created is itself a fit vehicle for the presence of the holy God, whenever he so chooses. At times he chooses through it to quench man's thirst or float his ships; at other times he uses it to wash man clean of sin, and to drown the old Adam in him.

In the Lord's Supper then the bread and the wine remain what they are, yet become the vehicles, in and through which Jesus, the Christ, imparts himself, his body and his blood. The humble, earthly vessels are the vehicles of the gracious presence.

II. An Orientation Toward the Lord's Supper on the Basis of the Stated Christology

IN this section summary statements will be given on such matters as there is believed to be agreement, giving more detailed explications where the differences seem to be. *Vis a vis* the Reformed the difficulty is at the point of the so-called "real" presence, but we are hopeful that the stated christology will provide an orientation (*Frage-*

stellung) by means of which the difficulties may be overcome. The second crucial issue concerns the eucharistic sacrifice, not only as held by Roman Catholics but increasingly by many Protestant churches. Finally there is the question of open and closed communion and the shaping of practice in general.

A. First then the points on which there is believed to be agreement:

1. *The Sacrament is the Gospel*

   a. The gift of the Sacrament is the same as that of the preached Word in which the fullness of God's gift to men in Jesus, the Christ, viz, forgiveness of sins and with it life and salvation are imparted.

   b. The Sacrament is altogether gift in which the direction is from God to man and it is not a propitiatory sacrifice offered from man's side to God. ". . . you should hold fast to the word that says: 'Take and eat, this is my body.' This word is the whole Gospel. You will observe and understand that it says nothing about a sacrifice or a good work but about a present and a gift, which Christ offers and gives to us, and which we should receive and with faith appropriate and hold fast. He tells you to take and keep and would you make an offering of it and give it away? How can you say to God, 'I give you your Word?' Neither can you say to another person, 'I am offering God this Word on your behalf?' On the contrary you should say: 'Dear Lord, since you say that you freely give it to me, I receive it with gratitude and joy.' Just as you cannot make out of the Gospel a sacrifice or work, so you cannot make a sacrifice or work out of this Sacrament; for this Sacrament is the Gospel." (Word and Sacrament II, Luther's Works, II, vol. 36, Phila., Muhlenberg, 1957, pp. 288-9. See also G. Aulen, Eucharist and Sacrifice, Phila., Muhlenberg, 1957, p. 199: "A formula such as this, we offer Christ, turns the biblical kerygma upside-down".)

   c. It is appropriately designated as "the Sacrament of suffering and victorious love", in as much as the suffering love which gave itself on Calvary and won the victory over all the powers that held men enslaved, now gives itself in the Sacrament.

d. "The grace in the Sacrament is that of God himself in his gracious resolution to restore man to life with himself (the God-for-man), and its gift is not an impersonal infusion of grace. The grace is the sustaining and empowering presence of Christ himself. It is from the Spirit-engendered faith relation to him that the powers of the new life emerge" (ULCA Statement, Basic Affirmations #21).

e. The Sacrament is properly also designated as the *"verbum visibile"* or *"actuale"*, since the power of the Sacrament lies in the Word alone without which there is no Sacrament. (*Accedit Verbum ad elementum et fit sacramentum.*) It is this dynamic Word of God which has within it the power to effect what it says. (Luther: "All the people that have written against us write as if we spoke of the Sacrament without the Word. As to the power of the words and their alleged mere significative character: A human word is a mere sound. Emperor Maximilian is dead. ((Consequently his words are no longer powerful)). When, however, something is said by 'the high majesty', by God himself, such a word does not only 'signify' but it effects and brings about that which it signifies, not through our power, but through God's. Then the words are not only the sound of a speaking man, but of God, and thus sound conveys something to him who eats the bread. When God says, Take, do that, speak these words, then it comes to pass. He speaks, and already it is done". Quoted by H. Sasse from the Marburg Colloquy, in "This is my Body", Augsburg, 1959, p. 246).

This designation as the *verbum actuale* is, however, not to imply that the Word in preaching is not equally active, objective and powerful. There is nothing more objective and potent than God's Word for it is God himself in his self-manifestation.

2. In the Sacrament the personal relationship is to be maintained and a sub-personal, *ex opere operato* infusion of grace as well as "capernaitic" notions of partaking of inert substances of flesh and blood repudiated. Corresponding

93

to the personal nature of the encounter there is the personal response of either faith or offense.

3. The Sacrament is a memorial of the event of Calvary which occurred in history at a specific time and place. Without this backward reference to a once and for all act of atonement and of decisive victory which marks the turning point (crisis) of history and the beginning of the new age (*kairos*) in the fullness of time (Gal. 4:4), there could be no Sacrament. Such memorial is, however, other than a mere recalling of a past event; it is contemporaneity with that event in faith, which is the only way in which there can be contemporaneity with the salvatory event. Every celebration of the Sacrament is therefore a proclamation of the Lord's death in its salvatory significance (I Cor. 11:26).

4. The Sacrament is at the same time expectation and a joyful looking forward to the Lord's return, the new heaven and the new earth and the fulfillment of the whole creation. This mood of joy was certainly the dominant aspect of the earliest celebrations of the Sacrament. They who had eaten and drunk with their Lord rejoiced both in the presence of the Lord with them at the Supper, while at the same time they looked confidently forward to the consummation at the banquet table in the Father's kingdom (Cp. Jesus' own eschatological reference in all the synoptic accounts—Also the "maranatha"). The Sacrament, like the passover, is the *viaticum* that accompanies the pilgrims from their exodus (baptism) to their entrance into the promised land (resurrection).

5. The Sacrament is "mystery" in the sense in which the Gospel itself is mystery (I Tim. 3:16). It defies understanding and therefore seals the lips and prevents adequate description. It is significant that the Latin *sacramentum* is in the Vulgate the translation of the Greek *mysterion* to designate the revelation of that which remains hidden even in the revelation. This is indication enough that the Sacrament defies understanding, but it is always to be remembered that it is the whole miracle of the incarnation and the self-impartation of the gracious God in Jesus, the Christ which is the mystery and not some mysterious change in the elements.

6. The Sacrament is the pledge of the promise of God, i.e. of forgiveness of sins, life and salvation. (Cp. the original meaning of *sacramentum* as the pledge which the litigants in a law suit deposited that they would speak the truth and as the oath of allegiance which the soldier took to his emperor). Much has been made in the past of this external, visible, tangible pledge as an accommodation of God to the weakness of man, who is in need of such assurance. It is true that the external action of the Sacrament and the visible, tangible earthly element provide a sort of guaranty to the senses, but the psychological assurance which this may give is not to be overplayed. If the Sacrament is taken seriously as the presence of Christ, the earthly element may be equally an occasion for offense as of faith. The very thing that is to give assurance becomes the occasion for stumbling, just as the lowly servant form caused many to turn from Him while he walked the earth.

7. The Sacrament is the communion of the believers not only with their Lord (see below on the "real" presence), but also with each other. The individualization of the Gospel and the personal assurance of the "given and shed for thee" are not to obscure the corporate nature of the Sacrament, which is not for individual soul-nurture but for the strengthening of believers together as the church, the body of Christ. The vertical and the horizontal relations belong indissolubly together. In the Sacrament the participants are not joined directly to each other by natural ties of blood or social status or common interests but as forgiven sinners they are joined to each other only in their union with their common Lord. This makes them into a true fellowship (*koinonia*) and erases all the divisive distinctions (Gal. 3:28), although the God-given inegalities which make men dependent upon each other in community always remain. "Participation in the Sacrament serves to counteract both false individualism and false collectivism, and the needs of the moment will decide where the emphasis may fall and the necessary corrective applied. When the individual is lost in the crowd he will find himself addressed and acted upon by name; where he is wrapped up in his selfish concerns he will be summoned out of himself to be a member in the whole body" (ULCA

95

Statement #30).

8. A certain appropriateness of the elements (water in baptism; bread and wine in the Supper) is to be recognized. These elements have no powers within themselves, but they do serve as appropriate, universally intelligible symbols (the water that cleanses from sin and in which the old Adam is drowned; the bread and wine as the common elements of daily sustenance and the joys of the table fellowship. That, in another culture, other elements would be representative of the same thing is taken for granted). They are symbols and not simply signs which only point to that which they signify. "They share in that which they symbolize by virtue of the natural order; but they are what they symbolize by virtue of the Word of God" (ULCA Statement #22).

9. As the divinely appointed vehicles the elements are capable of being the bearers of the divine presence. The finite is thus capable of the infinite. The suggestion that the earthly substance must give place to the divine substance (transubstantiation) is an offense both against the goodness of the creation and the "mediated immediacy" of God's presence at all times. The *"how"* of the presence of Christ "in, with and under" the earthly elements remains a mystery in the same sense in which the Gospel of the incarnation itself remains a mystery. Rationalistic speculations upon the exact nature of this "how" are, therefore, out of place (theories of consubstantiation, impanation).

B. Controversial Issues:

1. *The "real" presence*

Lutherans have in the past affirmed the "real" presence as opposed to a merely "spiritual" presence. As has been stated, this was based upon a christology which refused to separate the two natures in Christ and, therefore, affirmed the presence of the human nature in the sacrament as well as the divine in virtue of the *communicatio idiomatum.* This was in denial of the notion that the body of Christ had to be localized at one place in heaven and could not be present upon the earth in many places at the same time. If, however, the glorified body of Christ is regarded as no longer limited to time and place but as sharing in the omnipresence of God, and if the right hand of God is taken not as a place but as the exercise of a function, the right hand of God being everywhere, then the distinction between a "real" and a merely "spiritual" presence drops away. It is the total Christ who is present on the earth and there is no need to rise into heaven on the wings of faith. Likewise all notions of a capernaitic eating of inert particles of flesh and blood are repudiated by the insistence that it is the risen living Lord who is present and imparts his body and blood. Thus the "real" presence is "spiritual", in the sense of not being particles of flesh and blood, and the "spiritual" presence is "real", in the sense of the total glorified Christ, including his body and blood, being immediately present in the earthly medium. *The full mystery of the impartation of the body that was broken and the blood that was shed on Calvary is thus preserved without any speculations about the "how".* The gift of the Sacrament is the same as that of the Word but the mode of the giving is different. Heathen notions of the eating of flesh and drinking of blood in a crude literal sense are avoided. As stated above, the Sacrament is a personal encounter. (The prepositions "in" and "with", as Martin Heidegger and other existentialists point out, have quite a different meaning on the personal level than on the level of inanimate objects. A match is "in" a box but man lives "in" a community in quite a different set of relationships. The chair is "with" the table in the same room but two people are "with" each other in quite a differ- ent sense of personal communion).

The crux of the matter then lies in the recognition of the finite, earthly element being able to be the bearer of the fullness of the infinite. Thus the three affirmations which have played such a significant role in past controversy could become the occasion for mutual understanding and acceptance.

97

a. The *sacramental union* of the "body and blood of Christ" with the elements. This expression replaces no- tions of transubstantiation, consubstantiation, impana- tion. It says that the union is *sui generis,* taking place only in the Sacrament during the actual celebration (*extra usum non est sacramentum*), without specifying the exact beginning or ending of the presence. It is in virtue of Christ's promise in the words of institution that he is present without making these words into a formula of consecration.

(Luther: "That bread and wine should be the body and blood of Jesus is not due to our doing, speaking, or acting, let alone to our consecration as priests, but to Christ's order, command and institution . . . We do no more than administer the bread and wine with his words according to his command and institution". WA 38, 240, 248. See also #40 of the Basic Affirmations, ULCA Statement on the Sacrament of the Altar).

b. The *manducatio oralis*. Although susceptible of grave misunderstandings this expression aims at the preservation of something vital. It is intended to refute a false "spiritualization" of the God-man relation and particularly of the Sacrament. It should not allow crude notions of "capernaitic" eating to be reintroduced. On the other hand, without destroying the personal nature of the Sacrament, it stresses both the presence of the "body and blood of Christ", in the sense defined above, and the fact that the total man is affected. It is not an immortal soul only that survives the corruption of the body, but it is *the total man* who is to be resurrected (1 Cor. 15). The Word always affects *the total man* (Luther: *der ganze Kerl*) and so does the *verbum visibile* of the Sacrament. This is not to assert some kind of a *materia coelestis* by means of which the resurrection body is quantitatively nurtured. The notion that the Word feeds the soul while the Sacrament nourishes the body, gives it health, longevity, etc., is ruled out. The *manducatio oralis* thus preserves both the *totality of the gift* as well as the *totality of the recipient of the gift*. What is at stake once more is the goodness of the material and its inclusion in the redemption (*finitum est capax infiniti*).

c. The *communio impiorum*. In spite of the misunderstandings and the false fears of unworthy participation, here, too, there is something vital at stake, if the objectivity of the presence of Christ is to be preserved. *Negatively,* this expression does not mean that in some mechanical, sub-personal, *ex opere operato* way the Sacrament affects those who receive it, some to salvation, some to damnation. The Sacrament is not like a live wire charged with death-dealing or life-giving current, but a personal encounter in either faith or offense. *Positively,* the powerful presence of Christ is there regardless of whether it is believed to be there. It is not produced by faith, but simply acknowledged in faith. Nor is it destroyed by unfaith; it simply remains unacknowledged by unfaith or else becomes a stumbling block. It is, therefore, a redeeming presence for faith, while it is a judgment upon unfaith.

Furthermore, the "unworthiness" is not the failure to hold the correctly formulated doctrine of the real presence, just as saving faith is never simply a matter of holding right doctrine. Nor is it a matter of the lack of proper outward preparation or of degree of sorrow or even of the degree of faith. Luther says simply, "He is truly worthy and well-prepared who has faith in these words, 'Given and shed for you for the remission of sins'" (Small Catechism). Since man is, however, *simul justus et peccator* such faith is always accompanied by unfaith. Therefore, faith in one's faith is not to replace faith in Him who alone can give and strengthen faith. ("Lord, I believe; help thou my unbelief").

On the basis of I Cor. 11 unworthiness consists in the failure to discern the body of Christ. In the context this seems to have a double reference. First to the body of Christ in union with the earthly element (I Cor. 10, 16-17). Secondly, it seems definitely also to refer to those who joined in the Sacrament as the body of Christ on the earth. The loveless party spirit in the Corinthian congregation, their despising of the poor, their drunkenness were the indication of their unworthiness in that they did not recognize the presence of the Lord in their midst and his self-giving to them in the Sacrament, and did not recognize properly, either, their koinonia with one another in their common Lord. Such failure to discern the body of Christ, in the double sense, therefore, had to be a judgment upon them. It

99

could not leave them unaffected because it was not an innocuous presence, but the presence of Him who is the savor of death to some and of life to others (II Cor. 2:16). The context makes clear Paul's reasoning. Participation in idol feasts was not an innocuous matter but an objective, demonic pollution (I Cor. 10: 19-22). The presence in the Sacrament could not be less objective and called for proper self-examination, proper behavior, proper discernment of the reality with which they had to do, lest that which should be a blessing become judgment (I Cor. 11:27-29).

This recognition then became the occasion for safeguarding the table of the Lord. Participation in the Sacrament requires proper self-examination (confession of sins and confession of faith), together with the discernment of the body of Christ.

2. *The eucharistic sacrifice*

For all evangelical churches of the reformation tradition the view of the Mass as the unbloody repetition of the sacrifice of Christ, as traditionally held by the Roman Catholic and Anglo-Catholic churches, is out of the question and need not be further dwelt on. There is, however, a two-fold sense in which the notion of sacrifice is necessarily associated with the celebration of the Sacrament. First, there is the becoming contemporary with the atoning sacrifice of Christ, which was offered once and for all for the sins of the world. This was, however, not a sacrifice offered from man's side to God but was the self-giving of God in Christ reconciling the world to himself, covering the sins of the world and winning the victory over the enslaving powers. This sacrifice abrogates and fulfills all the Old Testament sacrifices. It is the sacrifice which God himself provides in his Son to put an end to all man's propitiatory sacrifices and efforts at atonement and reconciliation. It means also that Christ lives as our eternal high-priest ever making intercession for us. (See ULCA Statement, #31).

Secondly, there are connected with the celebration of the Sacrament in which the gifts of forgiveness, life and salvation are imparted, "sacrifices" of thanksgiving and praise and the "sacrifice" of the total man (Romans 12:1), which

100

are offered from man's side to God. These are, however, in no sense propitiatory or meritorious. They are offered in thanksgiving for and in response to what God has done and are, therefore, best designated as "eucharist", since in all thanksgiving the direction is from man to God. *The term "eucharist" should then not be used to designate the central action of the Sacrament in which God gives his supreme gift to man but rather "to designate the entire gift-engendered and responsive involvement of the people to whom the gift is given"* (ULCA Statement, #33; see also #39).

If gifts of bread and wine are offered then this is also in grateful response to God's prior self-giving and has no meritorious or propitiatory significance. The elements are put at God's disposal to become the vehicles of his gracious presence.

All this would seem to be in harmony with what Donald Baillie says: "Now if we gather together all that we have been thinking about the real presence of Christ in the Sacrament, about the offering that we make to God in the Sacrament, and about the eternal sacrifice of Christ whose high-priestly work continues forever at the heavenly altar, may we not say something like this: that in the Sacrament, Christ himself being truly present, he unites us by faith with his eternal sacrifice, that we may plead and receive its benefits and offer ourselves in prayer and praise to God. If we can say this, then surely we Protestants, we Presbyterians, have our doctrine of eucharistic sacrifice". (The Theology of the Sacraments, N.Y. Scribners, 1957, p. 118).

3. *The question of open and closed communion*
   There is no "Communion" which is open to all comers. The Communion is for those who share consciously and deliberately in the church's confession of faith, who have the ability to examine themselves, and who, therefore, come in penitence and faith, aware of the presence of Christ in the Sacrament and of the gift he imparts in it, as well as of the judgment which it brings upon the willfully impenitent and unbelieving.
   There is no full agreement among Lutherans, however, as to whether the Communion should be open only to mem-

101

bers of the same "confession" or also to the members of other Christian churches on a selective basis.

The overwhelming majority of Lutherans take for granted that there is "open Communion" between all churches which subscribe to the Augsburg Confession without any express declaration of such fellowship. A limited number, however, hold that such fellowship is to be declared only after there is assurance that the confessions are interpreted in the same way and that there is no open discrepancy between confession and practice.

Similarly most Lutherans hold that in the present state of divided Christendom a policy of selective fellowship with respect to the members of other communions should be followed, depending on the immediate situation and on whether or not the church's confession is thereby compromised. A so-called "general invitation" is, however, not given because of the obvious difficulties in framing such an invitation and the danger of making it either too narrow or too broad.

For the most part, also, it is held that it is not possible to give outward expression to the actual, existing oneness of the church by an "open Communion". The oneness of the church exists and cuts across the lines of all denominations even where they do not commune at the same table. Moreover, it is wrong to pretend to an outward unity at the Lord's Supper when this unity does not in fact exist. The Lord's Supper is not to be used as a device to create unity but to give expression to an existing unity. Therefore, as long as separate confessions are held to be justified, there is no greater scandal involved in a separate Communion than in a separate denomination. All Christians are joined to each other only through their common Lord and they will know and feel their oneness even when separated as much as they will be pained by the scandal of their separation.

Therefore, if the members of various denominations who do not share the same confession may nevertheless freely have intercommunion, what happens to the urgency of ending the scandal of disunity and coming to a common confession? So the overwhelming opinion is for having each denomination safeguard its own Communion even while engaging in honest ecumenical dialogue and allowing for a selective fellowship where the particular circumstances warrant it.

4. *The shaping of practice*

It is not thought necessary at this stage to go into the details of practice. The position of the Augsburg Confession (Article VII) is clear that there need be no uniformity with respect to rites and ceremonies instituted by men as long as there is agreement on the Gospel. Yet rites and ceremonies are by no means a matter of indifference and they may at any time enter into "statu confessionis" if they compromise the Gospel. They must, therefore, not only not be in open contradiction to what is believed but they must be in harmony with and give positive expression to the confession of faith. They must be transparent to the Gospel. (See the section on "The Shaping of Practice" in the ULCA Statement on the Sacrament of the Altar).

* * *

SUMMARY STATEMENT

*Christology, The Lord's Supper and
Its Observance In The Church*

1. In the present situation, in which windows are opening between Protestants and Roman Catholics as well as between Protestant and Eastern Orthodox, it is especially important that Lutheran and Reformed churches appreciate and bear witness to their common evangelical heritage in the Reformation.

2. We acknowledge the abiding significance of the recovery of the gospel granted to our churches in the Reformation. We confess that this gospel imposes on us the necessity of constant re-examination of our theological-formulations in the light of the word of God.

3. During the Reformation both Reformed and Lutheran churches exhibited an evangelical intention when they understood the Lord's Supper in the light of the saving act of God in Christ. Despite this common intention, different terms and concepts were employed which not only shared in the inadequacy of all human thought and language but also led to mutual misunderstanding and misrepresenta-

tion. Properly interpreted, the differing terms and concepts were often complementary rather than contradictory.

4. In the last four centuries both Lutheran and Reformed churches tended to be one-sided in their teaching and practice. Unfortunately, they did not support or correct one another as they might have done if they had mutually recognized how much they had in common.

5. Ever since the sixteenth century Reformed and Lutheran churches have held the conviction that the same gift is offered in the preached word and in the administered sacrament. Each of these is both word and deed, for in preaching word is action and in the Lord's Supper action is word.

6. When by word is meant the proclamation of the gospel, the sacrament is a form of visible, enacted word through which Christ and his saving benefits are effectively offered to men. Accordingly, the sacrament is a means of grace.

The assurance of his presence is given in the self-witness of Christ in the instituting rite: This is my body, this is my blood. The realization of his presence in the sacrament is effected by the Holy Spirit through the word.

We are agreed that the sacrament does not simply serve to confirm a faith that is awakened by preaching: it also arouses faith through its presentation of the gospel.

7. An adequate doctrine of the Lord's Supper requires some reference to sacrifice. The perfect self-offering of the Son of God is the atoning sacrifice whereby our self-offering to God in worship and in loving gift to the neighbor is made possible and acceptable.

8. We are agreed that the presence of Christ in the sacrament is not effected by faith but acknowledged by faith. The worthy participant is the one who receives in faith and repentance the Christ who offers himself in the sacrament. The unworthy participant is the one who fails to acknowledge the Lordship of Christ, his presence **104** in the sacrament, and the fellowship of the brethren in the common Lord. Such unworthy participation brings judgment.

9. The significance of christology for the Lord's Supper is that it provides assurance that it is the total Christ, the divine-human person, who is present in the sacrament, but it does not explain how he is present.

10. Our churches are not in full agreement on the practice of inter-communion because they hold different views of the relation of doctrine to the unity of the Church.

Chapter Seven

JUSTIFICATION AND SANCTIFICATION: LITURGY AND ETHICS
by *Henry Stob*

Introduction

W HEN St. Augustine considered what it was that he ought to know, he concluded that it was two things only: God and the soul, and nothing more. It is true that this conclusion and the consequent dual concern was not peculiar to him. It grew out of the turning that Socrates had made in the history of philosophy, and it was shared by most hellenistic thinkers, notably by the Neo-Platonists. But the concern was in accord with the Christian scriptures, and it both dominated medieval thought and gave shape to Reformation doctrine. Calvin, at any rate, allowed it to control his systematic exposition of Christian truth. The very opening statements of the *Institutes* are these: "Nearly all the wisdom we possess, that is to say, true and sound wisdom, consists of two parts: the knowledge of God and of ourselves. But, while joined by many bonds, which one precedes and brings forth the other is not easy to discern. . . . Yet, however the knowledge of God and of ourselves may be mutually connected, the order of right teaching requires that we discuss the former first, then proceed afterward to treat the latter."[1] This essay is organized in accordance with this scheme.

God

It is sometimes charged that in his doctrine of God Calvin was more speculative than Luther. The charge sometimes takes the form of the assertion that Calvin, unlike Luther, recognizes a God prior to and beyond the Christ, a God other than the one active in the drama of man's salvation, a God resplendent in his self-contained holiness and concerned with nothing so much as his exclusive glory, a God who exists not *pro nobis* but in and for himself. This charge is sometimes summarized by saying that, whereas Luther's theology is Christocentric, Calvin's is theocentric. What must be said to this?

I hazard no opinion about Lutheran theology, but as respects the theology of Calvin, the charge, I suggest, is both true and false. Calvin's theology is neither merely theocentric nor merely Christocentric,

105

[1]*Institutes* I, 1, 1-3.

but both of these at once, though in differing perspectives. These perspectives are formed by making a distinction between God in his being and God in his act, between the God who inhabits eternity and the God who has entered into a covenant with man in time, between the God who in his aseity is wholly independent of the world and the God who, having created a world, in ineluctably involved with it and ceaselessly concerned about it. This distinction is perhaps not dissimilar to that which the philosopher makes between the static structures and the dynamic operations of Deity.

When Calvin contemplates God in his dynamic operations *ad extra,* particularly in redemption, he knows no other name than Jesus; he is then as Christocentric as is Luther—perhaps more so. He finds that, though scripture is the word of and about God, it speaks of no one but the Christ, and, what is equally important, that, though scripture comes in many parts, no part fails to articulate the Savior. Calvin, accordingly, finds Christ no less in the book of James than in the book of Romans, no less in the Old Testament than in the New, no less in the law than in the gospel. Christ is what the Bible is about from first to last. What to some may appear, therefore, to be Calvin's undue orientation to Old Testament motifs or his sub-Christian legalism, is in fact his Christocentrism, his conviction that it is the whole of Scripture and the entire fabric of revelation *was Christum treibet.*

But Calvin does know, I suggest, a God "beyond" and "prior" to Jesus Christ, a God who is "more" than the Revelation he has given, a God who in the infinite fulness of his trinitarian being cannot be contained in anything finite, a God mysterious, incomprehensible, highly exalted, and "wholly other." This God is the *Deus absconditus,* the hidden God, whose ways are past finding out. He is the sovereign God whose providential rule is over all, the absolute God of the fixed and eternal decrees whose inexorable sway none can withstand. This is the God who is man's destiny. It is, I suspect, in so far as Calvin has confessed this God that his theology has come to be called theocentric, rather than Christocentric.

1) God In and For Himself

(*Theocentrism*)—There is nothing in Calvin or in Calvinism which suggests that there is that in God which is at variance with the Christ who stoops to save. Yet there is the recognition of a God who is wholly self-sufficient and self-contained, who needs no world at all to be himself and therein perfectly blessed, and who even when he acts, as in creation and redemption, is his own final end. Also, there is in Calvin and Calvinism a sense of God's greatness, independence, power, and transcendence, which has imparted to the tradition its undeniable "theocentrism," its characteristic "God-consciousness," and its own consequent "style." The lofty God of Calvinism is not a God into whose presence one enters boldly or with whom one associates on easy and intimate terms; mysticism can hardly grow on Calvinist soil. Nor is the God of Calvinism a God whose worship can be framed and fashioned in accordance with man's sense of fitness and propriety; God is the sole determiner of how he is to be acknowledged, praised, and served; church order and church liturgy are therefore fitted closely to the scriptural pattern. Nor is the God of Calvinism a God whose commands can be taken lightly; he is the imperious law-giver whose will must be unconditionally obeyed; he is not a God before whom it is possible to "sin boldly." Nor is the God of Calvinism a God before whom one vaunts himself; he is a God who veritably abases men.

But this abasement had a curious effect upon the Calvinist; it stood him erect among his fellows. Having become a slave of God he lost the capacity to act slavishly toward any creature. Having bowed at one point he could do so at no other. Having given his allegiance to the King of kings, he could count no man his master. The Calvinist in history became therefore two men: one all self-abasement, the other "proud, calm, inflexible"; one all meek and worshipful, the other set like flint against all tyranny. The Puritan, in Macaulay's view, was of this sort: "He prostrated himself in the dust before his Maker; but he set his foot on the neck of his king."[1]

2) God In And For Man

(*Christocentrism*)—Although the Scriptures do not allow us to ignore the existence of the *mysterium tremendum,* and although all their representations of God are made against the background of his distant and awe-ful holiness, yet the God they announce is centrally not one who exists in splendid isolation in and for himself, but one who moves outward in creating, preserving, and redeeming love. This Calvin knew well.

a) *Creation*—Although the central function of the Christian doctrine of *creatio ex nihilo* is to cut off any thought of the continuity between God and man, i.e., to assert God's absolute transcendence and man's radical contingence, the doctrine also serves to express God's gratuitous benevolence. God, we learn from the apostle John, is *agape,* self-giving love, and while this love is centrally displayed in God's redeeming work through Christ, it is by no means absent from creation.

107

---

[1]T. B. Macaulay, *Essay on Milton,* Margaret A. Eaton, editor (Boston: Educational Publishing Company, 1899), p. 97.

In a sense, indeed, it is there exhibited in its purest form. If to love is to impart, and to impart without regard to any foundation in the beloved, then the giving of existence (and essence) to a creature who before "was not" at all, is the most basic sort of giving or loving that there possibly can be.

Ever since Augustine the Church has accordingly ascribed creation to God's love, and has discerned in God's creative work the gracious divine determination to share with others his inexhaustible perfections. God, who is all glorious and cannot be enriched by anything outside himself, was not in creation seeking himself, but only man, and man's beatitude. Calvin is not slow to acknowledge this; when he considers the end God had in view in creating the world, he declares that this end lies in man: "God has ordained all things to our profit and salvation . . . and that he created all things for man this he has shown by the order that he has kept."[1] If, as Calvin acknowledges, "God's glory" is also an end, this can only mean that the God of love is glorified precisely herein that a community of men should possess, enjoy, and mirror forth the excellencies he freely confers.

The basic continuity between creation and redemption is thereby indicated. The God who created a world designed to share in his goodness is the same God who is active in redeeming a world that has turned aside from its true beatitude. And the name of Christ appears in both contexts of operation: the personal Word through whom God saves the world is also He through whom God made the world.

b) *Providence*—There is no call to enter here into all the knotty problems that inhere in the Christian doctrine of divine providence. It is enough to say that the Reformers did not surrender the created world to the ultimate direction of the creature, but kept the governance of it in the hands of the loving creator, whose concern for the establishment of a "kingdom of life" never suffers abatement, and whose determination to effect it cannot be thwarted. Calvin, as is well known, everywhere stresses God's ceaseless activity in the world. God is active directly in "the order of nature," where no so-called "natural laws" exist to obstruct the free exercise of his power. He is directly active in "the order of history," where, through general and special providences, he sets up and puts down men and nations in his determination to secure the ends of love and justice. And he governs "the hearts and lives of his children" through the power of the Holy Spirit, living and reigning within them to the end that, being justified and sanctified, they may eventually be glorified.

---

[1] *Institutes* 1, 14, 22.

Indeed, all God's providential ministrations are directed centrally to this end. This is why Christ stands, in Calvin's view, in the center of providence as well as in the center of creation and redemption. The movements of the stars and planets, and the rise and fall of nations subserve Christ's kingdom. Understanding this, Jonathan Edwards could say of the members of this kingdom, the saints: "The wheels of the chariot of the universe move for them; and the progress that God makes therein on his throne above the firmament, the pavement of his chariot, is for them; and every event in the universe is in subserviency to their help and benefit."[1] In his essay on Milton, Thomas Babington Macaulay recognizes the same mind in the English Puritans:

> Not content with acknowledging, in general terms, an overruling Providence, they habitually ascribed every event to the will of the Great Being, for whose power nothing was too vast, for whose inspection nothing was too minute. . . . If their steps were not accompanied by a splendid train of menials, legions of ministering angels had charge over them. . . . The very meanest of them was a being to whose fate a mysterious and terrible importance belonged, on whose slightest action the spirits of light and darkness looked with anxious interest. . . . Events which shortsighted politicians ascribed to earthly causes had been ordained on his account. For his sake empires had risen, and flourished, and decayed. . . . It was for him that the sun had been darkened, that the rocks had been rent, that the dead had risen, that all nature had shuddered at the suffering of her expiring God.[2]

c) *Redemption*—Clearly, the culminating act of God in behalf of a race of men estranged from him—in behalf of men in flight from him or in rebellion against him—took place in Palestine, A.D. 1-30. In the incarnation, crucifixion, resurrection, and ascension of Jesus Christ redemption was once-for-all accomplished: God was in Christ reconciling the world unto himself.

It is, of course, not the purpose of this essay to exposit the Calvinist Christology and soteriology, nor to expound in depth the nature and meaning of those key events by which salvation was obtained for men. It is enough here to declare that in the view of the Reformers all that God means or can mean for men who are lost and undone is contained in Christ: he and he alone is our salvation; there is no other name given under heaven by which we can be saved.

109

It may be said, however, that in Calvin's view it was not what Christ *was*—God and man—so much as what Christ the God-Man *did*

---

[1]Henry Rogers and Edward Hickman, eds., *The Works of Jonathan Edwards* (2 vols.; London: Ball, Arnold and Company, 1840), I, 100.
[2]Macaulay, *op. cit.*, pp. 94-96.

that matters. The incarnation was the precondition for the work of redemption, but it did not in and by itself redeem. The incarnation did not humanize God, nor did it deify man, as some in the history of Christian thought have tended to suppose. Even the unique conjunction of two natures in one person, as in Christ, could not be considered by Calvin as forming an exception to the absolute transcendence of divinity or the ineluctable finitude of man. It is at this point, it will be remembered, that a difference arose with Luther about the *communicatio idiomata.*

Although Calvin regarded the Biblical language used concerning what Christ *did* as not altogether "appropriate," he does not hesitate to say, in accommodation to such language, that Christ's task in offering atonement was to "interpose between us and God's anger and [to] satisfy his righteous judgment." He represents Christ as "beaten and struck by the hand of God," thereby appeasing the wrath of God and giving God satisfaction. What this comes down to is that Christ was and is our substitute, the propitiation for our sins. What Christ *did*—in dying, rising, and ascending—was to pay the debt of sin man owed to God, thus laying the foundation for that forgiveness which God grants to his elect; and what he did was to bring that life and immortality to light which was to make new creatures of all who believed in his name. In short, through what he did Christ became man's justification and sanctification; he became the remedy both for man's guilt and for his depravity. In and through his substitutionary atonement Christ made available to men the righteousness and life of God.

He who takes Christ's name upon his lips says many things, but among the things he says—and this is central—is that the way of salvation leads from God to man, and not vice versa. There being no way from man to God, every form of autosoterism must be cut off at the root. There is no word or work or attitude of man that can move him one step toward heaven. Neither obedience nor aspiration, neither *nomos* nor *eros,* neither circumcision nor uncircumcision—nothing human at all —can extricate man from his predicament. It is only Christ who is the lost world's hope.

110

Man

1) Man In And For Himself:

(*The Creature*)—Since man does not and cannot exist in and for himself, the heading of this section is basically inappropriate. If it is nevertheless set down, this is to draw a parallel between it and the corresponding section under God, and to strike a contrast between it and the section yet to follow. Having made these concessions to formality and artificiality, it is now to be observed that man, in the biblical view, most certainly does not exist in and for himself. This may be expressed by saying that man, unlike the self-contained and uncreating God, does not so much exist as *co-exist*. He is always *in relation,* and this essentially; he is by definition relative. What defines him is his relation to the world in which he is caught up, especially the social world of men, and, most basically, his relation to his Maker.

a) *Man and Society*—Unlike the angels who presumably exist discretely, man exists as a member of a race. He is born in relation to a mother, is normally fixed and nurtured in a family, is united by ties of law and consanguinity to many others with whom he forms a clan or tribe, and is enclosed by other ever-widening circles of human association. He is by nature a "political animal," as Aristotle already knew, and he is by creation set "in company," as Moses teaches: "male and female created he them." This is mentioned here, not for its own sake, but in order that it may serve as a point of reference when we consider that unique community, the Church, a type of association and organization which, though effected by grace, is founded on nature, i.e., on the necessity men are under to *co*-exist.

b) *Man and God*—If man is a social being, he is even more definitively a *religious* being; if he is tied in with men and things, he is even more securely tied in with *God*. The one all-determinative fact of human existence is that God cannot be escaped. There is no way that can circumvent him; there is no maneuver that can evade him. Man cannot flee God, for as Augustine already pointed out, to flee him is but to go *from* him pleased *to* him displeased. All men both know God and are haunted by him. Perhaps no one stressed this more than Calvin. There is in all men, he insisted, a *sensus divinitatus,* a sense of God that never can be lost. All men are therefore "religious." Without exception they make response to Him whom they cannot but perceive. The religions of the world are just such responses, but even when a man disdains the cultic and throws himself into what are called "secular" pursuits, he is articulating an unavoidable, even though mistaken, "ultimate concern." Man cannot but have a "god," either the true God or a spurious one. It is man's fate to be "religious," to commit himself to something, and to have that commitment govern at the bottom all of life's expressions.

2) Man In And For God:

(*The Christian*)—Grace does not destroy nature, but perfects it. Redemption does not negate the creation, but restores it. Christ does not make a literally new man of us; he inwardly renews the old man that we were. This means that the Christian Church is made up of people who were social before they entered the fellowship, were religious before they were confronted by the Christ, and were liturgically and morally expressive before they were made right with God. This is not said, however, to minimize the change that does take place when a man becomes a Christian. The change that takes place is radical. From being enemies of God we are made his friends; from being afar off we are brought near; from being under judgment we are made at peace. The outer darkness that awaited us at the end of our flight from God, and the consuming fire that awaited us at the end of our hostile ascent up the holy mountain of the Lord—this has been averted. The God of grace arrested us in our flight, and the God of peace halted us in our assault, and he set us before his face. What is involved here can, I think, be put down under three heads; incorporation, involvement, and articulation.

a) *Incorporation: Faith*

Christ. Christ is the repository of all grace. In him are contained all the blessings and benefits that can possibly accrue to man. He is the true "blessed possessor." In him resides righteousness and truth and life, and every other perfection which God is willing, and even concerned, to share with men. Christ is in particular the justified one, and the sanctified one, the very foundation of salvation.

Union. The question now is, as Calvin poses it: "How do we receive those benefits which the Father bestowed on his only begotten Son —not for Christ's own private use, but that he might enrich poor and needy men?"[1] The answer to that question is simple and direct: we must be joined to Christ, a spiritual union between himself and us must be effected, for "we must understand that as long as Christ remains outside of us, and we are separated from him, all that he has suffered and done for the salvation of the human race remains useless and of no value for us."[2]

112   The union that is necessary, and which is never merely external or adventitious but always inward and spiritual, can be described in either of two ways: Christ dwelling in us, or we dwelling in Christ. In either case what is required is a vital connection, by which the merits of Christ are transferred to ourselves. An ontological identification between Christ and the sinner there cannot be, but a living union is indispensable. As Calvin conceives of it, this union is not a *unio mystica* in the

[1]*Institutes* III, 1, 1.
[2]*Ibid.,* III, 1, 1.

technical sense, but it is an *insitio in Christum,* a veritable participation in the savior's life.

The Spirit. This union cannot be effected by man; no one can insinuate himself into Christ and thus tap the divine resources resident in him. The author of this union can only be God himself. It is in fact the Holy Spirit: it is "the secret energy of the Spirit by which we come to enjoy Christ and all his benefits."[1]

Faith. But how, it may be asked, does the Holy Spirit effect the union? The answer is: by creating in us a true and living *faith.* This faith is of course something in us (it is we who believe, not God), but it is not a human property, quality, or virtue. It is a bond. It may be likened to an umbilical cord, made and maintained by the Holy Spirit himself. It is never a basis upon which Christ's benefits are conferred; it is ever only an instrument by which the divinely directed transference of Christ's graces is effected. It is therefore not anything valuable in itself; whatever value it has lies in its content, which is Jesus Christ.

Preaching. And how by the power of the Holy Spirit is this faith brought into being? The answer is: through the preaching and the hearing of the word, more particularly of the word of promise, the gospel or good news, for "man's heart is not aroused to faith at every word of God."[2] Accordingly, "we need the promise of grace, which can testify to us that the father is merciful, since . . . upon grace alone the heart of man can rest."[3] Calvin comes then to define faith as "a firm and certain knowledge of God's benevolence toward us, founded upon the truth of the freely given promise in Christ, both revealed to our minds and sealed upon our hearts through the Holy Spirit."[4]

Justification and Sanctification. If we ask what, in Calvin's view, are the benefits that Christ imparts to us when we partake of him through faith, the answer is succinct and unmistakable. What he imparts to us is justification and sanctification. "By partaking of him, we principally receive a double grace: namely, that being reconciled to God through Christ's blamelessness, we may have in heaven instead of a judge a gracious father; and secondly, that sanctified by Christ's spirit we may cultivate blamelessness and purity of life."[5]

What is especially to be noted here is that, though Calvin makes a conceptual distinction between justification and sanctification, he never allows a real separation between them. The two are indeed logically

113

[1] *Ibid.*
[2] *Ibid.,* III, 2, 7.
[3] *Ibid.*
[4] *Ibid.*
[5] *Ibid.,* III, 11, 1.

distinct and mutually independent; sanctification is not the basis of justification, and justification is not the basis of sanctification. But one never appears without the other. If a man is justified, if his sins are forgiven him, if Christ's righteousness is imputed to him, if he is declared innocent, then he is also set upon the way of sanctification; a new life-giving power has entered into him; he has become in principle a new man, and he will do works of repentance. The faith that justifies is also the faith that regenerates. Calvin here is wholly on the side of James, as indeed James is on the side of Paul. Faith without works is dead; it is a faith that does not justify. To be forgiven is to be moved to forgive. There is only one way to be justified, namely, to be incorporated into Christ. But to be incorporated into Christ is to have his regenerating life pulsate through our being; a branch engrafted on the vine *must* bear fruit.

b) *Involvement*—The first fruit that faith bears is social in nature. When through a living faith one is joined to Christ one is at once ushered into a fellowship. To be incorporated into Christ is to be set in the company of others who are similarly incorporated. To be a member of Christ is to be a member of Christ's body. The vertical dimension when pluralized generates the horizontal. It is not possible to be in Christ without being in the Church, for the Church is nothing more nor less than the company of those who are in Christ.

The Church needs an organization; it must become institutionalized, but it is not on its institutional side that its true character is revealed. What the Church truly is, is not an organization but an organism, not an institution but a fellowship, not a cult but a *koinonia*. It is in that fellowship that the word of promise is heard and repeated, that the common faith is confessed, nourished, and exercised, that brotherly affection is developed and displayed, and that the mission to the world is announced and implemented. The Church is not the company of the perfected, but the company of the justified embarked on the way to perfection. Of that company Christ is the head and the Spirit is the life.

Although the Church must be centrally defined as the fellowship of Christians, i.e., as the fellowship of those who by grace exist in and for God, it may also be defined as an *ecclesia,* i.e., as the community of those who have been called out from the world. The Church is inherently separatistic. It exists not to express and body forth the values and ideals of the world or the changing forms of culture, but it exists to lay these under judgment and to witness to a higher reality. But the withdrawal which is of the very essence of the Church is not a withdrawal that has its end in itself. It is a withdrawal and consequent *koinonial* involvement which has as its purpose another and subsequent involvement, an

114

involvement with the world designed to "save" it or at any rate to illumine and preserve it in accordance with our Lord's description: "Ye are the light of the world," "ye are the salt of the earth." Such an involvement may also be regarded as a fulfillment of the apostle Peter's injunction: "supplement *philadelphia* with *agape*" (II Peter 1:7).

c) *Articulation: Love*—The Christian, joined to Christ in faith and joined to his Christian fellows in brotherly affection, must live out his life in obedience to the command: Thou shalt love the Lord thy God with all thy heart and thy neighbor as thyself. There is, it could be said, no other law than this. But the question may be asked: Is this two laws or one? A brief answer to this question will conclude this discussion.

Linear and Rhythmic Love. When one considers that there is ultimately only one who can lay man under obligation, that there is only one who can claim man's unconditional allegiance, one is driven to conclude that man is in the last analysis responsible to no one else but God. When it is asked with what or with whom does the creature have ultimately to do, the answer can only be: with God. This can only mean that however many and diverse his responses may turn out to be, they articulate at bottom but one response: the response to God. But this is just another way of saying that man is ceaselessly religious, that every thought and word and deed of man is religiously qualified and determined. And so, I dare say, it is.

It is one of the glories of the Reformation that it put God back into the common life and into the work-a-day world of man. It was recognized by the Reformers—certainly by Calvin—that religion is not merely one area of existence, but the whole of it; that God is to be met not merely on Sunday or in church, but on every day and in every honorable vocation in which one labors. The reformers knew—and their children know—that a Christian man lives always before the face of God, and that in everything he does and says and thinks he is bound to reckon with his Lord and to pay him homage. It is the glory of true Protestantism to have bridged the gap between the secular and the sacred, and to have left no section of life godless or profane.

Theologians such as Rudolph Otto, Paul Tillich, Dietrich Bonhoeffer, and John Robinson therefore speak to our condition when they deprecate a periodic "flight" from a supposedly "profane" domain into some "holy" place in which alone God can be met. Whatever Calvinists and Lutherans may think of John Robinson's *Honest to God,* they are natively conditioned to appreciate the author's remark that "this is the essence of religious perversion, when worship becomes a realm into which to withdraw from the ['godless'] world [in order] to 'be with

God.' " The Calvinist certainly knows of no "religious" life discontinuous with that which he lives during every waking hour of every working day. He recognizes nothing as legitimately secular or profane; he allows no moment undedicated to God's praise, no realm unsanctified by God's presence. With Robinson he is ever prepared to find the "beyond" in the midst of life, the "holy" in the common, the "divine" in the mundane. He is prepared to repudiate a Christianity which reserves for God a mere "sphere" of religion, a "last secret place" in the "private" world of the individual's need. If "religion" is to be thought of as a separate and sacred garden plot in the much wider field of the world, then with Bonhoeffer the Calvinist is prepared to advocate a "religionless" Christianity. What he wants is nothing less than to love God with all his heart and soul and mind, everywhere and always, on every road, in every task, and at every hour.

But a perceptive Calvinist who claims all of life for God, and who recognizes religion as embracing every area of existence, does not on this account fail to distinguish, *within religion,* between worship and work, prayer and service, communion and accomplishment. Religion, like all of life, is, he knows, a matter of inhaling and exhaling. He knows that the "quiet hour," the "retreat," the resort to the "inner room" is not to be identified or confused with the "outward thrust" and the "worldly activity" of the dedicated Christian. Religion is indeed all-encompassing, but it has its characteristic rhythm. Religion is an ellipse with two foci. There is in it a certain alternation in which its nature is displayed. Prayer and service, which are *not* the same, are both embraced within it. As the institution of the Sabbath amply indicates, worship and work support and complement each other. It is, however, not only to the "holy day," as contrasted with the other six, that a special kind of sacredness attaches, but also to those special times on every day in which, through prayer and scriptural meditation, we hold communion with our God and find new strength for daily tasks.

Liturgy and Ethics. Although *leitourgia* is an inclusive word which can mean both worship and work, and which can therefore stand for that centered and unified response which I have called "religious." I use it in this section to stand more narrowly for worship, or for that which goes on in church. By the same token, the term ethics is here taken to designate the moral relations that persons or groups of persons sustain to each other. What needs to be considered, I suppose, is the bearing within Christian existence that liturgy and ethics have or should have upon each other.

That the scriptures establish a close relation between the two is evident. Our Lord's summary of the law, already cited, joins our duties towards God most closely with our duties toward our fellow men. It has therefore become a commonplace of Christian teaching that only as we love God can we truly love our fellows, and only as we love our fellows are we fit to enter into God's presence. It is also generally recognized that only as we are spiritually attuned to God will we find and exploit areas of service to men, and only as we are morally sensitive will we discern spiritual truth: "if any man's will is to do his will, he shall know whether the teaching is from God . . ." (John 7:17).

As far as I am able to judge the Reformed churches have always sought to keep worship and service, piety and love, cultus and ethos in a mutually fruitful relationship. Of course, as many ethicists have observed, it is difficult to move at once in a vertical and horizontal direction. It frequently happens therefore that as was the case with the priest and the Levite, one is too much involved with the affairs of the temple to pause at the side of the road to bind a neighbor's wounds. By the same token, one can become so much concerned with programs of social reform as not to lay them or oneself either upon God's altar or under his judgment.

However that may be, there has been in the Reformed tradition— as no doubt in the Lutheran—a steady attempt to fit the liturgy of worship to the demands of everyday existence, and infuse the common relationships of life with the sense of God's presence. In the Reformed churches the Lord's table has usually been strictly guarded; an untoward walk of life has usually earned for the offender banishment from the Supper and in extreme cases other forms of discipline. The preaching has usually been both declarative and didactic; the gospel has been proclaimed, but in imitation of Paul the *kerugma* has usually been attended by the *didache*. The reading of the ten commandments is a feature of every Christian Reformed worship service, though it is not always plain to the worshipper precisely what function it serves; it is meant to serve both as a mirror of sin thus inducing repentance and stimulating prayer for pardon and as a rule for a holy life. The regular offering not only supports the work of the church but also effectually symbolizes for the worshipper the Christian necessity he is under to make his whole life a sacrifice.

117

Whether or not the Reformed churches or any other churches are succeeding in keeping the two together, it would seem right that Christians should combine adoration with resolution, pardon with effort, the mystic with the moral, the passive with the active. It seems indisputable that every *Gabe* is an *Aufgabe,* that justification must be attended by sanctification, and that liturgy should be in alliance with ethics.

Chapter Eight

JUSTIFICATION AND SANCTIFICATION; LITURGY AND ETHICS

by *Conrad Bergendoff*

A CENTURY after the Lutheran doctrine of justification had received its classic formulation in the Formula of Concord it was severely tested by the movement associated with Spener's name, Pietism. One of the criticisms leveled against Pietism by the orthodox Lutherans was that its most prominent feature, the conventicle, was a Reformed innovation. Spener had in fact received early impressions in Geneva of the effectiveness of Calvinist discipline, and he was acquainted with the preaching of Labadie whose spiritual conferences were remarkably similar to Spener's conventicles, though Spener asserted they were not the model for his practice. Kliefoth went so far as to claim that "Spener's concept of the Church and all his views on the life of the Church, its institutions, its means and measures, are alien and opposed to Lutheran views, and are essentially reformed."[1] Of more importance is the question, in what respect was Spener not Lutheran, and Heinrich Schmid, who cites Kliefoth, went on to elaborate this point. Schmid presents Spener's complaint in the latter's own words: "Though many preach of justification by faith almost exclusively they neglect to teach their congregations thoroughly what faith is, namely, not a human, ineffective, imagining of Christ, but a divine, powerful light in the soul, which brings about a new birth in man and makes of him an entirely new person, bringing the Holy Spirit."[2] Schmid concedes that Spener's criticism of orthodox preaching was justified. There was in much of it the kind of emphasis on a doctrine which left in the hearers a sense of false security because of the merits of Christ. But he would not concede that the error lay in a proclamation of justification by faith. For if this were a fault, then Luther was at fault, for assuredly this was almost the sole message of Luther. Rather the error lay in this, that the preachers "did not sufficiently emphasize that the faith which grasps the merit of Christ must be a living faith, a faith that hates sin, and comprehends within itself an urge and impetus towards a holy life!"[3]

---

[1]Quoted by Heinrich Schmid, *Die Geschichte des Pietismus* (Nordlingen: C. H. Beck, 1865), p. 441.
[2]*Ibid.*, p. 448, Cf. Spener, *Beantwortung des Unfugs*, p. 95.
[3]Schmid, *op. cit.*, p. 449.

It would be difficult to charge that the Reformed differed from the Lutheran on this point. Hence the un-Lutheran aspect must be sought elsewhere. Schmid goes on, "Spener awakens the idea that the doctrine of justification is not adequate, and that another teaching must be brought in. And then the doctrine of justification was in danger of losing the central place which it had always held in the Lutheran church —whatever was happening in the congregation, whatever the errors and strayings to which they might be tempted, the doctrine of justification must retain its revered place and its ancient power would always be sufficient to correct the errors and strayings. If the congregations of the day were morally loose, if they prematurely depended on the merits of Christ, it did not mean that it was necessary to preach another doctrine than justification. Rather, it called for the correct preaching of the doctrine of justification. For whoever rightly proclaims the doctrine of justification will not be morally lax and will not prematurely depend on Christ's merit. Spener should not have expressed himself as he did. He did not do well insofar as he separated between justification and faith."[1] His adherents, Schmid claimed, spoke little about justification but much about faith and sanctification. They were less concerned about whether they were justified than if they were converted, or twice-born. The attention had shifted from what Christ has done, or does, to what man does. If we accept the orthodox Schmid's estimate of what is the criterion of Lutheranism, and leave aside the Reformed source of Pietism, we have this result—that nothing can take the place of the article on justification by faith.

John T. McNeill, certainly a competent interpreter of Calvinism, declared that "it is not easy to say with confidence precisely where Calvin's thought has its center or what he would have us regard as its dominant theme. Is the sovereign majesty of God the conception about which his whole message revolves? Or does it center, as is often popularly assumed, in the doctrine of election? Or is he really indifferent to the priority of any one major doctrine over another and primarily concerned to be an interpreter of the divine Book, the Word of God, by which man obtains a knowledge of salvation?—Indeed, so serious is the problem of harmony and primary emphasis in his theology, that we have been invited by H. Bauke to understand it as essentially comprised of inharmonious elements, a *complexio oppositorum,* or conjunction of opposites."[2] And would this suggest something of the difference between Lutheran and Reformed theology? For if one has a central, orienting

119

[1]*Ibid.,* p. 450.
[2]*The History and Character of Calvinism,* (New York: Oxford Press, 1957), pp. 201-2.

point and another does not, it would quite certainly lead to differences in the selection and treatment of the contents of the message and in the practices of each.

It is of importance, then, clearly to delineate what is meant by justification before we go on to see its relationship to sanctification. The Formula of Concord was an attempt to reach agreement on points of controversy arising in the Reformation. One of those points was the nature of righteousness. Was the righteousness of Christ, on which justification depends, as Osiander held, that "Christ himself as the true, natural, essential Son of God, dwells in the elect, impels them to do what is right, and in this way is their righteousness? Or was faith a trust in what Christ had done in his human nature? The Formula repeated what the Apology had said about this article, that it is "the chief article of the entire Christian doctrine" and Luther's words that "where it does not remain pure, it is impossible to repel any error or heretical spirit." Then it makes clear that there can be no distinction here between the human and the divine natures. It is because "as God and man Christ has saved us by his perfect obedience, redeemed us from our sins, justified and saved us." "Faith does not justify us because it is so good a work and so God-pleasing a virtue, but because it lays hold on and accepts the merit of Christ in the promise of the Holy Gospel." "The righteousness which by grace is reckoned to faith or to the believers is the obedience, the passion, and the resurrection of Christ when he satisfied the law for us and paid for our sin. This righteousness is offered to us by the Holy Spirit through the gospel and in the sacraments, and is applied, appropriated, and accepted by faith so that thus believers have reconciliation with God, forgiveness of sins, the grace of God, adoption and the inheritance of eternal life."[1]

From this sense of justification, regeneration is to be distinguished. The Formula admits that "the word 'regeneration' is sometimes used in place of 'justification'." But when we so use "regeneration" we must exclude from it the "subsequent renewal which the Holy Spirit works in those who are justified by faith." "If the article of justification is to remain pure", the Formula warns, "we must give especially diligent heed that we do not mingle or insert that which precedes faith or follows faith into the article of justification." "The only essential and necessary elements of justification are the grace of God, the merit of Christ, and faith which accepts these in the promise of the gospel, whereby the righteousness of Christ is reckoned to us, and by which we obtain the forgiveness of sin, reconciliation with God, adoption, and the inheritance

120

---

[1] *Formula of Concord, Solid Declaration, Art. III.*

of eternal life." "Such a faith," the Formula adds, "exists only in or with true repentance." That additional statement, I think, is very important. It comes as a sort of postscript after the assertion that all the righteousness we are speaking about in justification is in Christ—none of it is in us. But since this righteousness is received by faith, the nature of faith is essential. While justification depends entirely on Christ, something precedes as well as follows, though we do not "mingle or insert that which precedes faith or follows faith." And as "renewal" is subsequent, so "genuine contrition must precede". For justification does not "mean that we may or should follow in the ways of sin, abide and continue therein without repentance, conversion and improvement."[1] We might, it seems to me, put it this way: that inasmuch as justification involves the forgiveness of sins, there can hardly be a forgiveness when the sinner intends to remain in sin.

While the action involved in justification is on God's side, a granting of forgiveness to the believer, it is equally clear that something happens on man's side, something that bears significantly on sanctification. Karl Holl finds that "in Luther faith culminates in a consciousness of a full unity with God" but he does not consider the *unio mystica* of orthodoxy as a true representation of Luther's thought. "This union" in Luther, he says, "has nothing to do with the absorption into the Eternal toward which mysticism strives."[2] Holl claims that while Luther could speak of the believer as *ein Kuchen* with Christ, he never uses this expression concerning the believer's relationship to God. He does say, *fides facit ex te et Christo quasi unam personam*[3] while orthodoxy affirms a union with the Trinity. But this distinction may be less important, since neither Luther nor orthodoxy teaches a union of substance. Both affirm a unity of will.

In still another aspect Luther's "union" differs from that of mysticism; namely, the part played by the "Ego" or "I". The "I" in Holl's interpretation of Luther "is involved in the paradox which inheres in the ambiguity (*Doppelsinn*) of forgiveness. For in Luther forgiveness does not imply that the memory of past sins is completely extinguished. Like Paul, he means on the contrary that true repentance grows out of forgiveness, since man then first understands against what kind of a God, against what a benevolent God, he has transgressed. So the relationship to the "I" that has sinned remains. But forgiveness itself gives man the right to make an inner break with this "I". It creates a new "I" and fills it with a self-consciousness more exalted than, and sharply con-

121

[1]*Ibid.*
[2]*Gesammelte Aufsaetze zur Kirchengeschichte* (Tuebingen: J. C. B. Mohr, 1921), 1, 81.
[3]*Ibid.*, p. 81, quoting WA XL 1:285, 5 ff.

trasted with, the earlier condition which rested on the awareness of natural powers.—Whoever experiences the meaning of this new relationship with God feels within himself spontaneously welling forth a new estimation of values, new emotions and new powers of the will. One cannot know himself at one with God without at the same time affirming his will as alone valid. And one cannot sincerely thank God without experiencing simultaneously the impulse to do freely and joyfully and with inner desire that which accords with the mind of God. It is not, as the scholastics dreamt, a mysterious inspired power which, along with the forgiveness of sins, brings about the renewal of man but forgiveness itself which gives immediately to the will a God-ward direction when it is understood and appreciated as the consciousness of being accepted by God."[1]

Einar Billing, a Swedish Luther scholar, writes in a book on the doctrine of the call, "Whoever knows Luther knows that his various thoughts do not lie alongside each other, like pearls on a string, held together only by common authority or perchance by a line of logical argument, but that they all, as tightly as the petals of a rosebud, adhere to a common center, and radiate out like the rays of the sun from one glowing core, namely the gospel of the forgiveness of sins."[2] Billing undertakes to survey the whole life of the Christian as he fulfills God's will for his life, in the light of this doctrine of forgiveness of sins, or, justification by faith. That it is possible to do so should be evident from what we have found to be the meaning of justification. In it sanctification and ethics are rooted, and no understanding of Lutheran theology or ethics is adequate which fails to start out from this point.

But, before going on to the field of worship and ethics, we need to dwell a moment on Luther's idea of the will and what its place is in conversion and sanctification. It is both easy and fashionable to discuss Luther's ideas as belonging to a pre-scientific age, and to dismiss its "faculty" psychology as outdated. But when one reads what Luther had to say about the "I" one is impressed that Freud has no monopoly on the knowledge of "Ego" and its powers. Conversion is no process wherein the will of man decides, on deliberation, to alter its course. The will is affected, rather, by a deep emotional experience wherein man comes to realize the unspeakable mercy of God in Jesus Christ. In the will of God he finds a greater will than his own and surrenders to it. This is a recognition of the unique significance of the human will. It cannot be broken without causing the disintegration of the human personality. But it is not sovereign, not autonomous. It must be turned toward God, it

122

---

[1]*Ibid.,* pp. 81-3.
[2]Einar Billing, *Our Calling* (Rock Island, Ill.: Augustana Book Concern, 1952), p. 7.

must find its inmost satisfaction in doing the will of God. This it cannot do unless the knowledge of God's will become the star it follows. In this sense, the intellect must become enlightened before the will can know its way. Orthodoxy's concern about the true doctrine arose from the necessity of the believer's knowing what God has done for man. If this knowledge was absent no appeal to man's moral sense would bring the power to do the will of God. Pietism's appeal to man to analyze himself diverted the attention from a constant looking to the grace of God out of which would come the impulse to do what was pleasing in His sight. "Where the intellect goes", Luther once wrote, "there the will follows; where the will goes, love and desire follow. The entire person must become new, and become an entirely new person, who thinks otherwise than before, who otherwise judges, evaluates, imagines, speaks, loves, desires, acts than before."[1] But this description was of the believer after the new light had come into the darkness of his soul. This was after the will had been turned in the direction of God. Before that, in man's "natural" estate, will and reason went their own way, for the will was actuated by selfishness and only when reason and selfishness agreed on a goal would they go together. Even in such a state it was true that reason might rule but not govern, for the will would reveal its subservience to a more powerful force—love of self, and would use reason to forward its aim. Man's will expresses what he most profoundly desires. Conversion does not destroy the will but the grace of God turns it completely around and makes it serve rather than command.

The point at which our questions arise is apt to be here. How can the act of God in which he forgives sins in a moment illuminate all the life of man so that he knows henceforth what is the will of God in each circumstance? The answer must be, I think, that this illumination is a very gradual process. Once I know that God exists as my Creator and Redeemer, and that my life has meaning before him, I am on a road of many windings and pitfalls, but a road that leads to him. The world is suddenly lit up for me as God's world but my way through it will require constant faith, daily forgiveness, love to fellow-man, unquenchable hope. It is a way I cannot walk alone, but in the fellowship of the Church I find guidance, comfort, and strength. It is a world in which I have duties to fulfill, and my attitude towards these duties will be a testimony of my faith in Him whose world it is. We have traditionally considered these aspects of Christian life under the title of sanctification. Two phases of it are included in our title, Liturgy and Ethics. I take it that

123

[1]WA X, 1:1, p. 233, 7 ff. Quoted in Herbert Olsson, Grundproblemet: Luthers Social etik (Lund: Hakan Ohlsson's Boktrycheri, 1934), p. 80.

the intention of the title is to relate them particularly to justification, but also to view their place in sanctification.

In our Lutheran churches the term liturgy has a more familiar ring than in the Reformed, and the Lutheran is often classed with the Roman and the Orthodox churches as liturgical churches. Does this have any bearing on either justification or sanctification in the Lutheran Church?

I have sometimes wondered at the apparent paradox in our Church Augsburg Confession clearly asserts that there need be no uniformity in customs and ceremonies, while on the other hand the Church has proved very conservative in its traditions of worship. The century and a half after the Reformation saw a quite widespread uniformity in all parts of the Church. The Lessons were retained from the medieval system. The sermon, of course, had a prominent place, but in one way or another confession and absolution remained. The Creed, the form of Communion, even Matins and Vespers showed remarkable uniformity. Even Latin and Greek survived in some rubrics—the Kyrie, the Gloria. When in the 18th century Pietism and Rationalism corroded the ancient forms, in the 19th and our own century this was seen as a retrogression or decay and a new interest developed for the older usages. In the U.S.A. Lutherans have cooperated in a new Service Book and there is probably more uniformity today than ever before in this country. Similar revivals could be mentioned in Europe. Is there some unconscious belief here that a liturgical worship is essential to Lutheranism?

My own answer is in the affirmative. And the reason? The objectivity which led orthodoxy to criticize Pietism as subjective finds expression in a form of worship which prefers lessons and prayers and ceremonies that do not depend on the whims of influential ministers but somehow represent a consensus of churches united in faith. A gospel of grace which stresses the work of Christ as over against any meritorious work of man is better expressed in forms that do not essentially vary from place to place or generation to generation. The wealth of hymnody which characterizes Lutheran countries has provided a means of congregational worship, and subjective expression and free prayer has usually found a place at some point of the service. Despite the fixity of the pericopes they have yielded to many various types of sermonic treatment.

In this area of objective proclamation are found the arguments which have been employed by the defenders of Lutheran churches closely allied with the state. We may have our reservations about a state-church, but we must face the fact that in many Lutheran countries this has been the historic form. It is conceivable that a change might have been effective by now had there been a concerted effort by churchmen. But devoted Christian leaders have defended the folk-church—a name they prefer to state-church—by holding that the duty of the Church is to proclaim the gospel to all the inhabitants of the land. They look on the free-church as the orthodox did on the Pietists, as small groups of like-minded who arrogate to themselves the promises of the Word and look on themselves as the people of God. To the argument that their stand is influenced by a state which guarantees their economic existence these men reply that in a free-church which depends on the good-will and generosity of its members there is an economic influence no less than in the state-supported church—the free-church will be cautious in its attack on sins of those who contribute most. I have no intention of entering the debate. I simply point out that there probably is no organization of the Church which does not subtly influence it. We need not go out of our own country to learn how social and racial attitudes of the community decide what is preached, and not preached. Without agreeing at all to a system of churches in which the government plays a decisive role, we must wonder that in spite of it the liturgy and preaching have maintained a relative independence.

From the Reformation period on Lutherans have looked admiringly on the Calvinist laity and the discipline of Presbyterianism. In the United States Lutherans have paid the Reformed the high compliment of imitation, for in this country Lutheran synods in the main adopted the Presbyterian form of church government. If in American Presbyterianism the elder seems to be more deeply involved in the message and government of the Church than any Lutheran counterpart it is because American Lutherans inherited from their homelands something of the hierarchical superiority over the laity. The Church of Sweden may not consider the episcopacy essential but it has never lost a certain succession of priestly predominance in the congregation. Within the universal priesthood of believers, the priesthood of the "ministerium" has, in varying degrees in different parts of the Lutheran church, retained vestiges of a particular estate.

Melanchthon distinguished between the power given the ministry and the Church as a whole—doctrine and sacrament were by *iure divino* entrusted to the ministry, the power of the keys to the Church. But Lutheran orthodoxy gave the keys also to the ministry. The political economy envisioned in early Lutheranism divided Christian society into three estates: the ecclesiastical, "which is called to arouse, maintain, and increase faith in the Church by the preaching of the divine Word and the administration of the Sacrament;" the political, which is "to care for the outward, temporal, well-being of the community;" "both these

125

estates, therefore, minister, each in its own way, to the third, that of the family (the economic estate) for which they are to provide a well-ordered life, and which they are to aid in fulfilling its spiritual calling."[1] This beautifully simple scheme had little relationship to practical political life, but it does throw light on the place the ministry chose for itself. The thinking of the theologians had as its consequence, in the words of a Lutheran student of polity, that "the ministry assumed all churchly initiative, responsibility, and activity. Government got the role mainly of protecting the ministry in its functions, and the members of the economic estate were assigned the place of faithful and attentive listeners."[2] In such a development of the teaching of the universal priesthood of believers the original view of Luther was pretty well eclipsed. It is no wonder that some Lutherans looked jealously at Geneva.

Something of the difference in ethos-and ethics- between the Lutherans and the Reformed is exemplified in the situation in Geneva as compared with Wittenberg. In the latter the Elector was the government. Luther preached, and certainly his sermons affected life in the city. But the theologians did not make laws. Wherever the Reformation prevailed the distinction between minister and jurist was carefully guarded. City councils could and did listen to the clergy, but they did not long let theologians spell out ordinances. Indeed, it was the fate of Lutheran churches to have to be governed by consistories in which the secular predominated. The minister might be ever so stringent in his condemnation of sins in his parish—in the punishment of them, even in the use of the ban, he had to defer to town council or prince. Even in Sweden where the bishops held their ancient office, the proceedings of the chapter were subject to the review of provincial governors.

It may be urged that the situation in Geneva was no different. But the real difference lies in the presence of a man like Calvin, who, at least long enough to set an example, bent the organs of city government to the councils of the ministry. This he did in the name of the Church, and by appeal to scripture. From such a course the Lutheran hesitated. He was held back, not only by the actual political situation, but by a feeling that this was not the task of the Church. A modern Lutheran theologian expresses what has been a common axiom throughout most of Lutheran history, "Christian believers must carefully distinguish between the provinces of the church and of the state, bearing in mind, on the one hand, that the state cannot be governed by God's Word, or 'Christian

126

[1]H. Schmid, *The Doctrinal Theology of the Evangelical Lutheran Church*, Trans. Charles A. Hay and Henry E. Jacobs (3rd edition, revised, reprint; Minneapolis: Augsburg Publishing House, 1961), pp. 604-5.
[2]Ragnar Askmark, *Ambelet I Den Svenska Kyrkan* (Lund, 1949), p. 200.

principles,' but only by reason and common sense (*lex naturalis*), while, on the other, the Church is governed alone by God's Word, and not by and dictates of reason or by the external coercion of laws."[1]

Of course, the Lutheran believed that the officer of state, himself a Christian who had experienced the forgiveness of sins, would, in his vocation, testify to the grace of God, and court preachers did in some cases influence rulers to govern as Christians. But if "reason and common sense" sufficed in affairs of state it was not essential that the rulers be interested in sanctification and it could end by relegating the Church only to private affairs. The Lutheran Church has been accused of just such a retreat from social ethics. But to return to the orthodox defence, we would have to say that the error is not in the proclamation of justification by faith but in an inadequate proclamation. For if only the penitent really understand the nature of sin, then the justified should know better than any one else the failures of love to fellow-men which are revealed in transgressions of the law. In monarchical nations of Europe the Christian might plead that the true Christians were too few to determine the course of government. One may ask if this holds in a democracy where individual citizens have, at least theoretically, a part in government.

It is often asserted that Calvinism succeeded better in cities and republics, while Lutheranism throve in monarchical states, and that Lutherans were less prone to participate in revolutions than the Reformed. Such generalizations are difficult to prove, or disprove. But Calvin's power in Geneva, a city of less than 15,000 population, did create a precedent for ecclesiastical influence in government that Lutheranism cannot parallel. Yet the ultimate effect of the preaching of the gospel in the lands of northern Europe did have something to do with the formation of the character of those lands. The type of piety created there did depend on the preaching of justification by faith, even though it must be conceded that the ethics of these lands owed much to literature and leaders in Reformed or Anglican churches. Despite all the changes through which Lutheranism has passed during four centuries, the unity of Lutheran churches of the world rests on the centrality of justification. At Helsinki the Lutheran World Federation found difficulty in restating the doctrine in modern terms but the Lutheran World Federation has no other common ground than this interpretation of scripture and Christian life.

127

---

[1] J. T. Mueller, *Christian Dogmatics* (St. Louis: Concordia Publishing House, 1954), p. 553.

Chapter Nine

LAW AND GOSPEL

by George W. Forell

THE distinction between law and gospel and the relationship of creation and redemption has become one of the central problems in contemporary theological discussion. It relates to questions ranging from nature and grace to science and religion, reason and revelation and Bonhoeffer's distinction between the penultimate and the ultimate.

In view of the centrality of the problem, it is of interest that some years ago Professor Gustaf Wingren claimed that the major difficulty with the theological system of three of the most prominent theologians of this century was their confusion of law and gospel. He accuses Nygren, Barth and Bultmann of speaking about God apart from concrete revelation in which God has spoken and of which the scriptures are the record. Among his own teachers, the Lundensians and especially Anders Nygren, he says that agape-love was developed as a dominant motif in which all other aspects of revelation are dissolved. "The Christian message of God as forgiving agape is in reality an answer to a pregnant question, viz. the question of guilt. This message is meaningless unless the man who hears it is standing under the claim of God even before he hears the gospel. There is a continual danger that in Nygren's theology the center of the Christian faith, the gospel becomes erroneously interpreted, since the gospel is divorced from the question of guilt and tied to a formal philosophical question."[1] Here the essence of God, namely the "motif," is abstracted from the concrete revelation. But when law and gospel are only apparent contradictions, the biblical theology of the cross has been surrendered in favor of a theology of glory.

In criticizing Karl Barth, Wingren points out that the *knowledge* of God is the central concern of Barth's theological system. "The main question with Luther is the question of righteousness. But with Barth the main question is whether we have knowledge of God, or whether, in ourselves, we lack such knowledge and must receive it from the outside . . . Luther holds that natural law compels us to do works; there is no encroachment on the gospel which deals with an entirely different righteousness . . . Barth cannot bear to hear about a natural law,

---

[1]G. Wingren, *Theology in Conflict* (Philadelphia: Muhlenberg Press, 1958), pp. 16-17.

because in that case the will of God would be known independently of the incarnation, and the revelation in Christ would only complement something natural, i.e. something human.[1]

Because of this epistemological emphasis (rather than the soteriological emphasis of the New Testament) Barth has no use for the law as man's enemy. Here, too, law and gospel are not distinguished. This expresses itself in Barth's famous reversal of law and gospel into gospel and law: *Das Gesetz ist nichts anderes als die notwendige Form des Evangeliums, dessen Inhalt die Gnade ist.*[2] This means, "Law is nothing but the necessary form of the gospel whose content is grace." In Barth the law has lost its terror; it does not bring wrath as St. Paul says (Rom. 4:15). And if the law is only the form of the gospel, what shall we do with St. Paul's words, "Likewise, my brethren, you have died to the law through the body of Christ, so that you may belong to another, to him who has been raised from the dead in order that we may bear fruit for God." (Rom. 7:4).

The confusion of law and gospel in Barth's theology results in a situation described by Wingren as follows: "There is in Barth's theology no active power of sin, no tyrannical, demonic power that subjects man to slavery and which God destroys in His work of redemption. There is no devil in Barth's theology. This is a constant feature in his theological production."[3] Or, as Thielicke puts it, *Durch diese Lehre von Gesetz und Evangelium kommt der abstrakte Monismus in die Theologie und macht sie zu einer Weltanschauung der Gnade.*[4]

In Bultmann Wingren claims that the New Testament message which tells of God's becoming man, living with men, dying for men and rising from the dead is dissolved in an essentially philosophical concern. However, Bultmann does not ignore man's guilt. In fact, this guilt is the basic presupposition of his theology. However, it is a guilt which is significantly different from the guilt of which the Scriptures speak. In the Bible we are guilty before God (Rom. 3:19). In Bultmann guilt is lack of self-realization. Again quoting Wingren, "Human life (*Dasein*) has fallen, but it has fallen exclusively from itself."[5] Bultmann himself says to his critics, "Some have objected that I am borrowing Heidegger's categories and forcing them upon the New Testament. I am afraid that this only shows that they are blinding their eyes to the real problem, which is that the philosophers

129

---

[1]*Ibid.,* p. 26.
[2]K. Barth, *Evangelism und Gesetz;* Theologische Existenz, N. F., 50, p. 13.
[3]Wingren, *op cit.,* p. 25.
[4]H. Thielicke, *Theologische Ethik,* Tübingen, 1951, Volume I, No. 569, p. 193.
[5]Wingren, *op. cit.,* p. 131.

are saying the same thing as the New Testament and saying it quite independently."[1] However, they are saying it without reference to Jesus Christ. Bultmann would like to retain what he calls "the act of God through which man becomes capable of self-commitment, capable of faith and love, of his authentic life."[2] In order to do so, he dispenses with all the concrete statements of the New Testament concerning this Christ, he discards the pre-existent Son of God, the Virgin Birth, miracles, resurrection, etc., and he adds, "We are compelled to ask whether all this mythological language is not simply an attempt to express the meaning of the historical figure of Jesus and the events of his life; in other words, significance of these as a figure and event of salvation. If that be so, we can dispense with the objective form in which they are cast."[3]

What is left when the New Testament is thus demythologized is a philosophy of existence which for some illogical subjective and emotional reason attributes extraordinary significance to a certain Jew who was killed in Palestine a long time ago. Or perhaps the reason is not quite so illogical. Actually, psychologically, this Jesus does help people. Bultmann makes again and again statements like these, *Hilft er mir weil er der Sohn Gottes ist, oder ist er der Sohn Gottes weil er mir hilft.*[4] The saving efficacy of the cross is not derived from the fact that it is the cross of Christ: it is the cross of Christ because it has this saving efficacy.[5]

The key sentence which may give a clue to the peculiar attachment to the demythologized Jesus—though he represents philosophically an acute embarrassment—is, "Does Christ help me because he is the Son of God or is he the Son of God because he helps me?" (see above). For Bultmann he is the Son of God because he helps me. The concern is now *only* what this faith does for the hearer. In this theology there is no room for the distinction between law and gospel; the law has been egocentrically spiritualized and the gospel has been demythologized, the distinction between the two has been abolished.

130   While the scope of Wingren's interpretation has been severely criticized[6] (with special bitterness in Sweden), the significance of the Wingren analysis has not been questioned.

[1]H. W. Bartsch, (ed.), Kerygma and Myth (London, S.P.C.K., 1957), p. 25.
[2]Ibid., p. 33.
[3]Ibid., p. 35.
[4]R. Bultmann, Glauben und Verstehen: Gesammelte Aufsatze (Three Volumes; Tubingen: J. C. B. Mohr, 1933-60), II, 252.
[5]R. Bultmann in Bartsch, op. cit., p. 41.
[6]See e.g. the important correction of the analysis of Barth in Robert W. Jenson, Alpha and Omega, A Study in the Theology of Karl Barth (New York: Thomas Nelson and Sons, 1963), especially p. 138, note II.

It is against the background of this admitted importance of the law-gospel dichotomy that its significance for the ecumenical engagement of the Lutheran Church should be discussed.

The Nature of the Law in Theological Discourse

According to the dictionary, law is "the binding custom or practice of a community; rules of conduct enforced by a controlling authority; also any single rule of conduct so enforced." (*Webster's New Collegiate Dictionary*). Paul Lehmann in the *Handbook of Christian Theology* says, "Law is the principle and operation of order in the world. As principle, law is expressed in the form of prescriptive statements. As operation, law expresses the fact that diverse and changing relations unfold in a dependable and an intelligible pattern."[1] This is law in general, in all its cosmic, social, moral, and religious forms.

In theological discourse, law is a personal demand of God. The controlling authority which makes it binding is God. In the law we are confronted by God who establishes a relationship with us. This God is the almighty maker of heaven and earth. And he confronts *all men* in his law; it is the personal demand of God's almighty authority. Within the context of the Christian proclamation the law is not a propositional code (doctrine) but a personal (existential) demand. It is the claim of God upon us and all men. It confronts us quite independent of our familiarity with one or the other legal code—which may more or less adequately express these demands at a certain time and in a certain place. Man experiences the law even if he has no formal knowledge of it. He may experience it differently at different periods of history, or different individuals may experience it in different ways. Nevertheless all men everywhere and at all times are confronted by the law.[2]

1) Old Testament

In the Old Testament we find the record of this personal confrontation of man by God which expresses itself in law.

131

Covenant and Law—The law in the Old Testament is not independent of the covenant, or contrary to it, but rather its byproduct. The covenant fact is always associated with the covenant law. But

---

[1]Halverson and Cohen, *A Handbook of Christian Theology* (New York: Meridian, 1958), p. 203 f.
[2]Here lies the significance of Tillich's analysis of anxiety in his *Courage To Be* (New Haven: Yale University Press, 1952). Fate and death, guilt and condemnation, emptiness and meaninglessness are different ways in which the reality of law is experienced in different times and by different people.

a covenant is a relationship, and in the Old Testament this relationship, true to the nature of all personal relationships, implies obligation. E.g., Noah is given certain obligations, (Gen. 9), when God establishes his covenant with him. This obligation is central in the Sinaitic Covenant: "Now therefore, if you will obey my voice and keep my covenant, you shall be my own possession among all peoples; for all the earth is mine, and you shall be to me a kingdom of priests and a holy nation." (Ex. 19:5)

Law and Legalism—The perversion of the law which always threatens to reduce it to mere legalism is the reduction of the personal demand into a propositional code. Isaiah 1:11: " 'What to me is the multitude of your sacrifices?' says the Lord; 'I have had enough of burnt offerings of rams and the fat of fed beasts . . . Wash yourselves make yourselves clean; remove the evil of your doings from before my eyes; cease to do evil, learn to do good; seek justice, correct oppression; defend the fatherless, plead for the widow.' " (cf. Ps. 50, Jer. 7). The development of legal skill for the purpose of circumventing the personal demand of God is a deviation characteristic of later Jewish casuistry.[1]

New Covenant—Because man abuses the law in legalism as the prophets complained and reduces the personal demand of God to a propositional code, the prophets see the need for a new covenant which reestablishes the personal relationship: "I will put my law within them, and I will write upon their hearts; and I will be their God and they shall be my people." (Jer. 31:31, Cf. Ex. 34:25, Is. 55). In the Old Testament law is the divine demand expressing a personal relationship between God and His people. Because man breaks this relationship the law condemns and the hope is a new law.

2) New Testament

The New Testament does not abolish God's personal demands. In the New Testament the law as confrontation with God's personal demand is emphasized and focused through Jesus Christ and his law of love (John 13:34: "A new commandment I give to you, that you love one another even as I have loved you, that you also love one another.") Everywhere in the New Testament we are summoned to this

132

---

[1]Cf. A. Heschel, *God in Search of Man* (New York: Meridian, 1959), p. 328: "The outstanding expression of the anti-agadic attitude is contained in a classical rabbinic question with which Rashi opens his famous commentary on the Book of Genesis." Rabbi Isaac said: The Torah (which is the law book of Israel) should have commenced with chapter 12 of Exodus, "since prior to that chapter hardly any laws are set forth." See also p. 329: "In justification of their view, exponents of religious behaviorism cite the passage in which the Rabbis paraphrased the words of Jeremiah (16:11), 'They have forsaken Me and have not kept My Torah in the following way: Would that they had forsaken Me and kept My Torah.' "

love. ("Truly I say to you, as you did it to one of the least of these my brethren, you did it to me." Matt. 25:40). Love is the fulfillment of the law (Rom. 13:10).

The New Testament proclamation of the law is not immune to legalism, the perversion of personal demand into a propositional code results in a highly developed legalistic casuistry and the domination of Christendom for centuries by lawyers.

The New Testament law accuses man, and the efforts to reduce the demands of the New Testament law of love to counsels of perfection for the elect tends to obscure the function of the law as taskmaster, *paidagogos,* driving us to Christ. (Gal. 3:24).

Both in Old and New Testament God addresses us by means of the law. We are confronted by God's holy will and by his willingness to meet us to deal with us. If anything, the demands of God's law are more personal and more total in the New Testament. In both Old and New Testaments man is guilty because he has broken the relationship which God has offered him. He is separated from God through his own fault. And because this relationship to God is in fact broken, the law always accuses.

3) The Lutheran Church

In the Church of the Augsburg Confession the distinction between law and gospel has been methodologically central. As early as 1518 Luther uses it in his *Explanations of the 95 Theses* (LW, 31, p. 230 ff.) commenting on Thesis 62: "The true treasure of the Church is the most holy gospel of the glory and grace of God," as follows, "The gospel is a preaching of the incarnate Son of God, given to us without any merit on our part for salvation and peace. It is a word of salvation, a word of grace, a word of comfort, a word of joy, a voice of the bridegroom and the bride, a good word, a word of peace." And he describes the law as follows (WA 1, p. 616): *Lex vero est verbum perditionis, verbum irae, verbum tristitiae, verbum doloris, vox iudicis et rei, verbum inquietudinis, verbum maledicti.* ("The law is a word of destruction, a word of wrath, a word of sadness, a word of grief, a voice of the judge and the defendant, a word of restlessness, a word of curse.") And he refers to 1 Cor. 15:56, Rom. 4:15 and 7:5 and then continues, *Ex lege enim nihil habemus nisi malam conscientiam, inquietum cor, pavidum pectus a facie peccatorum nostrorum, quae lex ostendit nec tollit nec nos tollere possumus.* ("Through the law we have nothing except an evil conscience, a restless heart, a troubled breast, because of our sins, which the law points out but does not take away. And we ourselves cannot take it away.")

133

This distinction between law and gospel is a consistent feature of Luther's theology throughout his entire life. We find it developed in detail in his commentaries on Galatians and in his sermons. Though he considers the distinction crucial, he is also convinced that it is impossible to accomplish it consistently. The tendency is always either to become what he calls a *glaublose Werkeler* or a *werkloser Gläubling* (WA 45, p. 689). His awareness of the difficulty of making the right distinction is perhaps most clearly expressed in a remark at table in 1531 reported by Johannes Schlaginhaufen:

> "Non est homo qui vivit in terris qui sciat discernere inter legem et evangelium. Wir lassens uns wol gedunken wen wir horen predigen, wir verstehens; aber es felet weit. Solus Spiritus Sanctus hoc scit. Dem man Christus hats auch gefelt, am berge, ita ut Angelus cogebatur eum consolari; der war doch Doctor, vom himel, durch den Engel confirmirt. Ich hett gemeint, ich kundt es, weill ich so lang und vill darvon geschrieben, aber wenn es an das treffen gett, so sich ich wol, das es mir weitt, weitt felet. Also soll und mus allein Gott der heiligist meister sein." (WA T. 2, p. 4, No. 1234)

But while the distinction is difficult, it has to be made, for out of the confusion of law and gospel grow both legalism and antinomianism, thus obscuring and perverting the Christian proclamation. Once the distinction has been made, Luther insists that the law has two purposes (WA 40, I, p. 479 ff.): the civil and the theological uses of the law. This he summarizes in the second disputation against the Antinomians (WA 39, I, p. 441): *Scitis duplicem esse usum legis, primum coercendi delicta, et diende ostendendi delicta.* This mean that all Christians are under the law. As the FC later put it in regard to the believers, "Although they are regenerated and renewed in the spirit of their minds, yet regeneration and renovation are not perfect in all respects in this life, but only begun . . . and on account of the old Adam who yet dwells in the understanding, the will and all the powers of man, it is necessary that the law of God should always shine before us . . ." (FC Epit. VI, p. 3) This, by the way, is the controversial "third use of the law" in the FC. However, if one keeps in mind the description of the human situation as *simul justus et peccator* it appears that this third use could easily be subsumed under the two uses as proposed by Luther. Luther's position has been the object of a number of significant studies since W. Elert rejected this "third use" as attributable to Luther.[1]

---

[1]*The Christian Ethos* (Philadelphia: Muhlenberg Press, 1957), pp. 294ff. Cf. Wilfried Joest, *Gesetz und Freiheit, das Problem des tertius usus legis bei Luther und die neutestamentliche Parunese* (Göttingen, 1951); Albrecht Peters, *Glaube und Werke* (Berlin/Hamburg, 1962); O. Modalsli, *Das Gericht nach den Werken* (Göttingen, 1963).

The significant result is not so much a precise number of "uses of the law" as the undeniable and profound relationship between faith and works in Luther's theology which was somewhat obscured by the more Kantian-idealistic interpretations. The fourfold use of the law suggested by later Lutheran dogmaticians (political, elenctic (manifestation and reproof), pedagogic, didactic, Hollazius, (1021))[1] is dubious not only as far as its biblical basis is concerned, but also tends to confuse the boundary lines between the law and the gospel.

For our discussion two insights of the Lutheran theologians ought to be retained. 1) The twofold use of the law, its political or civil use, conducive to a modicum of civil righteousness, and its theological use, driving us to Christ, basic for an understanding of the law. 2) *Lex semper accusat*—"The law always accuses and terrifies consciences."[2] Because and as long as men live in a broken relationship with God the law must always accuse them. Whenever this accusing demand of the law is obscured, the human situation is misunderstood and aggravated and the only remedy made unavailable.

The Nature of the Gospel in Theological Discourse

The gospel is the good news of God's saving deed in Jesus Christ. This is a personal deed reestablishing through the cross the relationship man has broken. It is anticipated in the Old Testament, recorded in the New Testament, and remembered and proclaimed in the Church.

1) Old Testament

The distinction between law and gospel is not identical with the distinction between Old and New Testament, for as the New Testament proclaims gospel and law, so the Old Testament proclaims law and gospel.

Covenant and Gospel—While the covenant is certainly and properly associated with the law, the same covenant is quite as properly associated with the gospel. It is God's gracious election which brings about the establishment of the covenant with Israel. This election is good news pointing in the direction of Jesus Christ, the author and finisher of our faith. For the Christian Church and according to its inner history, the Old Testament bears witness to the good news in Christ. The covenant must be seen in the context of the gospel as well as the law.

135

[1] H. Schmid, *The Doctrinal Theology of the Evangelical Lutheran Church*, Trans. Charles A. Hay and Henry E. Jacobs (3rd edition, revised, reprint; Minneapolis: Augsburg Publishing House, 1961), p. 515.
[2] Melanchthon, *Apology*, Cf. Theodore Tappert, ed., *Book of Concord* (Philadelphia: Muhlenberg, 1959), p. 112.

Universalism—But the gospel in the Old Testament points beyond the election of Israel to the saving deed of God for all men. "Behold, I make him a witness to the peoples, a leader and commander for the peoples. Behold, you shall call nations that you know not, and nations that knew you not shall run to you because of the Lord your God, and the Holy One of Israel." (Isa. 55:4-5). This is the message of Jonah: not only Israel but also Nineveh is within the realm of God's care. "God repented of the evil which he had said he would do to them; and he did not do it." (Jonah 3:10).

The Messianic Vision—The gospel appears clearly in the Old Testament in the anticipation of the Messiah, whether this Messiah be the Davidic king or of the apocalyptic Son of Man or the Suffering Servant of Deutero-Isaiah. All three anticipatory types—and there may actually be even more—are fulfilled and transcended in Jesus Christ.

2) New Testament

The New Testament proclaims this gospel as its central message.

Gospel and Covenant—The New Testament proclaims this gospel in continuity with the Old Testament, fulfilling, not rejecting, it. The New Testament is the new covenant, meaningful only in the context and against the background of the old covenant. Once separated from the Old Testament, the New Testament message deteriorates into religious gnosticism or philosophical idealism.

Gospel and Kerygma—The New Testament presents this gospel as a kerygma, i.e., a proclamation. It is not a series of logical propositions here recorded in a particularly brilliant or reliable manner; rather we are confronted by an urgent message which may appear illogical, even shocking, but which tells about God's deeds for men. Its value depends neither on the logical coherence of this message, nor on its incoherence (though it may appear to exhibit both); neither on its conformity to what could have been expected nor on its nonconformity; but rather on the deed which it proclaims, God's deed in Jesus Christ.

Gospel and Discipleship—This New Testament proclamation of the gospel does make a difference. It works a change. If God's deed in Jesus Christ is proclaimed and believed, something will happen. This is the new life in Christ, it is the discipleship which is always the result of faith in the deed of God in Christ. Where there is no new life there is no faith. This message, if believed, makes all the difference in life. To use Wingren's illustration of the check: "A person who receives a check in the mail certainly gains some knowledge when he takes the check and reads it. But if this is the main point, that before he read the check he lacked a certain knowledge which now has been given to him, he has a false conception of at least three realities. He has a false conception of his own situation before the check came, as if the absence of knowledge was the important part. He has a false conception of the function of a check, as if its primary function were to convey knowledge. And he has a false picture of the sender, as if he who was previously unknown now had made himself known."[1] If we carry this illustration a little bit further, if he accepts this check, if he believes that it is good, it will make all the difference in his life. If he acts as if nothing had happened, if he does not cash the check—frames it, worships it, but does not work with it—he does not really accept it. Discipleship means to work with what God has given, to take God at his word, the God who acts in Jesus Christ.

The Confusion of Law and Gospel

The present situation in theology is characterized by the confusion of law and gospel as distinguished in the discussion up to this point. The distinction is not being made, not even by Lutherans, and when they make it they do it in such a mechanical fashion that it contributes more to the confusion. The results of ignoring the distinction or making it inadequately results in certain detrimental tendencies in the life of the Church.

Theological Legalism—Theological legalism is the denial of God's love. The Christian message is homogenized into law, i.e., into demands ranging in their character from the sublime to the ridiculous. This law is understood as the message of the Christian Church and thus interpreted as the gospel. The difference between Christianity and other religions is then merely the difference in laws. One religion may demand one kind of behavior pattern; another religion may demand the exact opposite—but if religion is merely the demand of conformity to a certain pattern it is always legalism.

Another form in which this legalism may appear is that of reducing the very gospel into a law. Here the uniqueness of the gospel is formally recognized; the centrality of the person and work of Jesus Christ is emphasized. However, the relationship to this Christ is construed as a legal relationship. Christianity is now the acceptance of statements about this Jesus and his work. The good work which saves is not loving the enemy or wearing hooks instead of buttons, but rather accepting theological propositions about this Jesus Christ. The more these propositions run counter to logic and common sense, the more meritorious the

137

[1]Wingren, op. cit., p. 42 f.

faith. The sacrifice of the intellect is here the saving deed, and he who sacrifices his intellect with the greatest abandon is considered the most holy. This sacrifice of the intellect is then a substitute for all other good works which other legalists are prepared to do. Since these other good works, e.g., loving the enemy, giving alms, not getting drunk, etc., have definitely positive social aspects (civil use of the law), the intellectual legalism, which often disparages these deeds, is actually socially less useful than the other forms of legalism.

Theological Antinomianism—Another result of the confusion of law and gospel is an antinomianism which denies the relevance of the law for the Christian, either because of an unduly optimistic view of the human situation or because of a radical pessimism concerning man's predicament.

Since the time of the gnostic conflict which had threatened the survival of the early church there have always been some who claimed that Christians should sin so that grace might abound. Because of a peculiar metaphysics which resulted in an inability to associate the order of this world in any way with the God and Father of our Lord Jesus Christ, they felt that breaking this natural order was not only excusable but indeed advisable. Similar views have appeared again and again in the course of Christian history. They threatened the great Reformation of the Christian Church in the sixteenth century and were the reason for Luther's writings against the antinomians. Today there are also those who because of the superficial view of the nature of sin discard the significance of the law and speak and act as if obedience to the law were not part of the Christian life, indeed were beneath the dignity of the Christian.

Strangely enough, a complete pessimism concerning the human predicament leads to very similar conclusions to those of the contemporary optimistic antinomians. Some contemporaries see sin as so serious a deficiency and man so utterly perverted by it that the very effort to oppose it is considered vain glory and pride. The total depravity of man is made by the basic Christian assertion and the ambiguity of all human action so clearly discerned that all sensitivity to the shades of grey in human action has been lost. Here we find those whose advice in ethics to modern man is a counsel of desperation. It is not entirely comforting that Luther's *pecca fortiter* is their favorite saying, quoted frequently and always out of context.

Whether antinomianism has its roots in an unjustified optimism concerning the human situation or a radical pessimism, the denial of the law in either case results eventually in the denial of the gospel.

For the message of liberation cannot be taken seriously if either the slavery to sin and law is not understood radically enough or if the proclamation of this slavery usurps the place of the proclamation of the liberation. The gospel is not gospel if the law does not exist. But neither is the gospel good news if it cannot free us from the bondage of sin; if its proclamation makes absolutely no difference.

In contemporary Christian thought law and gospel are confused in so many and subtle ways that almost any corrective statement is in danger of aggravating the confusion by encouraging either legalism or antinomianism, the denial of God's love or the denial of God's justice.

The Contemporary Task

Within the framework of this presentation it is not possible to offer a solution to the problem, even if such a solution were available. Our task was to attempt a description and analysis of the problem. Yet a few hints indicating where the solution might possibly lie may be in order.

While the Lutheran distinction between law and gospel often appears hackneyed and has assumed the character of a theological panacea with which the Lutheran theologian can solve any and all problems, the basic concern expressed in this formulation is sound and must be recovered if the Christian message is not to be obscured and falsified.

It is the same God who deals with men through the law as well as the gospel, who confronts men as the God of justice and of love. The work of the law may indeed be God's strange work while the work of the gospel is his proper work, but both are God's. Thus the Church has a responsibility to both. Unless it responsibly proclaims law and gospel, demand and gift, the power of God's justice and the power of God's love, its message becomes inept and confused sentimentality or harsh and self-righteous condemnation. Both dangers are clear and present today. Both are the direct result of the theological confusion of law and gospel.

139

But law and gospel are not the same thing. If they are identified and one is made merely the appendix of the other, neither the seriousness of the human predicament nor the glory of the divine salvation is described with precision. It is the task of the Church to make this distinction in its proclamation in order not to jeopardize the truth of the message. Only if the law is proclaimed as law in all its demanding seriousness does it produce its beneficial results for the social life of man. Simultaneously, only if the law is thus proclaimed is there any chance that it will accomplish its pedagogical work as a task master driving men to Christ. A law not taken seriously contributes nothing to the preservation of society or to the growth of the body of Christ.

And only if the gospel is proclaimed as God's gracious deed for man does it free man from sin and death. A gospel which is merely a new and different law, a heavier burden for mankind, a greater demand, is not "gospel" at all. The fact that the message of the Church has become associated in the minds of most people with irrelevant restrictions often applicable only to other times and climes, seems a sad reflection of the fact that the good news of salvation has not been proclaimed with perception and passion.

This situation is not helped by those contemporary advocates of a "new morality" who act as if an ethic of love were a simple human possibility.

When the Bishop of Woolwich writes: "Love alone, as it were, because it has a built in moral compass, enabling it to 'home' intuitively upon the deepest need of the other, can allow itself to be directed completely by the situation . . . it is able to embrace an ethic of radical responsiveness, meeting every situation on its own merits, with no prescriptive laws,"[1] he is really begging the question. He and his more sophisticated associates in the call for a "new morality" never tell us how the man the Bible knows, the man contemporary literature knows, the man we know—you and I—become enabled to love. Indeed the much-touted new morality seems only to be a new romantic and sentimental legalism.

Law and gospel are a problem to contemporary theology, partly because both are misunderstood, partly because both are confused. If the distinction between law and gospel is as crucial as Luther and our fathers believed, it is high time that we address ourselves to the problem of defining them both more accurately, distinguishing them more clearly, and relating them more positively.

---

[1]John A. T. Robinson, *Honest to God* (Philadelphia: The Westminster Press, 1963), p. 115.

Chapter Ten

CREATION AND REDEMPTION; LAW AND GOSPEL IN THE THEOLOGY OF JOHN CALVIN

by John H. Leith

THERE are three reasons why this paper concentrates upon creation and redemption, law and gospel in the theology of John Calvin. First of all, historical theology should contribute to the repair and renewal of contemporary theology. Secondly, party lines and theological biases in the Reformed tradition frequently have their roots in Calvin. They can be recognized and in some measure understood by a study of their origin. Thirdly, the theology of Calvin will give a *concrete* and *specific* basis for discussion with those who see these problems from Lutheran emphases and perspectives.

Creation and Redemption

(a) A study of Calvin's doctrine of creation immediately confronts one with the positivistic character of his theology. Here Calvin insists, even more emphatically than elsewhere, that theology is a modest enterprise that must be content with the givenness of creation and revelation. No higher cause should be sought than the will of God; and the givenness of creation and revelation is sufficient evidence of that will. A host of questions that any discussion of creation must raise has to be left unanswered. The Christian has to be content that God willed that the world should be in its essential structure the way it is. Only an unwarrantable theological curiosity desires to go further.

The question must be raised as to the wisdom of this very strong positivistic emphasis and of this rejection of theological reflection. Is Calvin too modest in setting the limits of the theological task? Does this limitation of the theological enterprise have significant consequences for his entire theology? Do we see here *clearly* a methodology that is at work everywhere in his theology?

141

Calvin lived at a time when man's understanding of the world was beginning a very important shift. Copernicus published his *Revolutions of the Heavenly Bodies* in 1543. In all probability Calvin knew of Copernicus, but so far as any one knows, he never mentioned Copernicus in any of his writings. Ideally he drew a very clear and sane distinction between the theological task and the scientific task.

> Moses makes two great luminaries; but astronomers prove, by conclusive reasons, that the star of Saturn, which on account of its great distance, appears the least of all, is greater than the moon. Here lies the difference; Moses wrote in a popular style things which, without instruction, all ordinary persons, endued with common sense, are able to understand; but astronomers investigate with great labor whatever the sagacity of the human mind can comprehend. Nevertheless, this study is not to be reprobated, nor this science to be condemned, because some frantic persons are wont boldly to reject whatever is unknown to them. For astronomy is not only pleasant, but also very useful to be known: it cannot be denied that this art unfolds the admirable wisdom of God. Wherefore, as ingenious men are to be honoured who have expended useful labour on this subject, so they who have leisure and capacity ought not to neglect this kind of exercise. Nor did Moses truly wish to withdraw us from this pursuit in omitting such things as are peculiar to the art; but because he was ordained a teacher as well of the unlearned and rude as of the learned, he could not otherwise fulfill his office than by descending to this grosser method of instruction. Had he spoken of things generally unknown, the uneducated might have pleaded in excuse that such subjects were beyond their capacity.[1]

Calvin himself was not greatly interested in science, but this may mean nothing more than that he was absorbed in the more pressing theological task of his day. He feared that man's curiosity about the physical world might draw his attention from more significant matters. Certainly this attitude must be understood in the light of the theological situation in which Calvin worked, one that is radically different from ours today. Nevertheless, it is possible that this theological attitude, proper perhaps in his time, is at work in Calvin's descendants who do live in another situation. This is the problem of archaism in theology, a problem that is always present in a church with strong traditions.

This problem in Calvin's theological method and attitude is well illustrated in his use of a story that he had found in the writings of Augustine. According to the story a man once asked what God was doing before he created the world. The answer he received was that God was making hell for those who asked such questions. Augustine's comment had been:

> It is one thing to see the answer; it is another to laugh at the questioner —and for myself I do not answer these things thus. More willingly would I have answered, 'I do not know what I do not know,' than cause

[1] *Corpus Reformatorium: Joannis Calvini Opera* XXIII:22.

one who asked a deep question to be ridiculed—and by such tactics gain praise for a worthless answer.[1]

Calvin, on the other hand, rejoiced in the answer. In the introduction to his commentary on *Genesis* he regarded this as an answer of pious man to an impure dog who was in this manner pouring ridicule upon God. In the *Institutes* he regards such a question as a mocking question of a shameless man. While this particular incident is not typical of Calvin's theology as a whole, it does indicate a tendency that is significant.

(b) Calvin's doctrine of creation underscores the radical distinction, upon which he insisted, between Creator and creature. "Creation," he wrote, "is not inpouring, but the beginning of essence out of nothing."[2] Furthermore, "nothing is more characteristic of God than eternity and self-existence—that is, existence of himself."[3] This same emphasis is seen in Calvin's Christology in which he insisted that Jesus Christ in his divinity is *autotheos*. Creation, all things visible and invisible, exist simply by the power of the will of God. This radical doctrine of the transcendence of God in terms of self-existent and contingent being is the presupposition of Calvin's doctrine of the sovereignty of God.

A second important aspect of Calvin's doctrine of creation is his insistence that the created world is good. Sin and evil are accidental qualities. The malice of the devil comes not from his nature but from perversion of his nature.[4] Likewise, the vitiation of man's nature does not flow from nature itself. "It is an adventitious quality that comes upon man rather than a substantial property that has been implanted from the beginning."[5] Creation, as the work of God, is good. This Calvin said with emphasis.

While Calvin restricted what he considered unwarranted reflection upon creation, he did, within his limits, take a very positive attitude toward creation as God's work.

> . . . they have with true faith apprehended what it is for God to be Creator of heaven and earth, if they first of all follow the universal rule, not to pass over in ungrateful thoughtlessness of forgetfulness those conspicuous powers which God shows forth in his creatures, and then learn so to apply it to themselves that their very hearts are touched. The first part of the rule is exemplified when we reflect upon the

143

---

[1]Albert C. Outler, ed., *Augustine: Confessions and Enchiridion*, Vol. VIII of "The Library of Christian Classics" (Philadelphia: The Westminster Press, 1955), p. 253.
[2]*Institutes of the Christian Religion* I, xv, 5. Quotations from the *Institutes* "The Library of Christian Classics" edition.
[3]*Ibid.*, I, xiv, 3.
[4]*Ibid.*, I, xiv, 15.
[5]*Ibid.*, II, i, 11.

greatness of the Artificer who stationed, arranged, and fitted together the starry host in heaven in such wonderful order that nothing more beautiful in appearance can be imagined; who so set and fixed some in their stations that they can not move; who granted to others a freer course; but so as not to wander outside their appointed course; who so adjusted the motion of all that days and nights, months, years, and seasons of the year are measured off; who so proportioned the inequality of days, which we daily observe, that no confusion occurs. It is so too when we observe his power in sustaining so great a mass, in governing the swiftly revolving heavenly system, and the like. For these few examples make sufficiently clear what it is to recognize God's powers in the creation of the universe.[1]

Furthermore, Calvin intended that the enjoyment of the bounties of creation should be a part of the Christian life.

But it would be an immoderate strictness wholly to forbid neatness and elegance in clothing. If the material is said to be too sumptuous, the Lord has created it; and we know that skill in art has proceeded from him. Then Peter did not intend to condemn every sort of ornament, but the evil of vanity, to which women are subject. Two things are to be regarded in clothing, usefulness and decency; and what decency requires is moderation and modesty.[2]

But shall the Lord have endued flowers with such beauty, to present itself to our eyes, with such sweetness of smell, to impress our sense of smelling and shall it be unlawful for our eyes to be affected with the beautiful sight, or our olfactory nerves with the agreeable odor? . . . In a word, has he not made many things worthy of our estimation, independently of any necessary use?[3]

Should any one object, that a frugal use of food and drink is simply that which suffices for the nourishment of the body: I answer, although food is properly for the supply of our necessities, yet, the legitimate use of it may proceed further. For it is not in vain, that our food has savour as well as vital nutriment; but thus our heavenly Father sweetly delights us with his delicacies. And his benignity is not in vain commended in Psalm CIV, 15 where he is said to create wine that maketh glad the heart of man. Nevertheless, the more kindly he indulges us, the more solicitously ought we to restrict ourselves to a frugal use of his gifts.[4]

144

In these words we are taught, that God not only provides for men's necessity, and bestows upon them as much as is sufficient for the ordinary purposes of life, but that in his goodness he deals still more bountifully with them by cheering their hearts with wine and oil.

[1]*Institutes* I, xiv, 21.
[2]*Corpus Reformation* LV:255.
[3]*Institutes* III, x, 2.
[4]*Corpus Reformatorium* XXIII:545.

Nature would certainly be satisfied with water to drink and therefore
the addition of wine is owing to God's superabundant liberality.[1]

(c) Calvin's deliberate ordering of the doctrine of creation and
redemption in the structure of the *Institutes* indicates the mutual relation of the two doctrines. The most obvious structure of the *Institutes*
is Calvin's four-fold division of the Apostle's Creed. Within this structure there is another division that is of crucial importance. The significance of this division has been pointed out recently by Edward Dowey.

Calvin divides the *Institutes* into two sections on the basis of our
knowledge of God as Creator and our knowledge of him as Redeemer.

> I do not yet touch upon the sort of knowledge with which men in
> themselves lost and accursed, apprehend God the Redeemer in Christ
> the Mediator; but I speak only of the primal and simple knowledge
> to which the very order of nature would have led us if Adam had
> remained upright. In this ruin of mankind no one now experiences
> God either as Father or as Author of salvation, or favorable in any way,
> until Christ the Mediator comes forward to reconcile him to us.
> Nevertheless, it is one thing to feel that God as our Maker supports
> us by his power, governs us by his providence, nourishes us by his
> goodness, and attends us with all sorts of blessings—and another thing
> to embrace the grace of reconciliation offered to us in Christ. First,
> in the fashioning of the universe and in the general teaching of Scrip-
> ture the Lord shows himself to be the Creator. Then in the face of
> Christ [cf. II Cor. 4:6] he shows himself to be the Redeemer. Of the
> resulting two-fold knowledge of God we shall now discuss the first
> aspect; the second will be dealt with in its proper place.[2]

Knowledge of God as Creator and knowledge of God as Redeemer
belong together. God cannot be known either as Creator or Redeemer
alone. The same God creates and redeems. Redemption presupposes creation. The work of creation can now be known only through the work
of redemption.

Edward Dowey has summarized the dialectical relation between
knowledge of God as Creator and knowledge of God as Redeemer as
follows:

> Man owes his creation and his redemption to the gratuitous love of
> God. Yet he owes his need for redemption to his sinful rebellion against
> God's orderly rule in creation, and he discovers that salvation consists
> in Christ's obedience, justification, and sanctification, which accom-
> plish the removal of guilt and the re-establishment of that orderly rule.
> The two sides are inseparable: the special, gratuitous quality of God's
> mercy and the orderly universal inclusiveness of law. Dropping the

145

---

[1] *Ibid.*, XXXII:90.
[2] *Institutes* I, xi, 1.

first produces a radical kind of *sola gratia* that Calvin never envisioned. Calvin held both—for the Creator and the Redeemer are one. Because of sin, however, this remains a statement of faith, not a relation describable by either rational or moral-legal systems of unity. The believer can never build a continuous thought structure relating the creating and redeeming work of God, because of the mystery of gratuitous love that lies behind both and the noetic effects of sin. The relation of the knowledge of God the Creator to the knowledge of God the Redeemer remains a dialectic one, or, as we called it above, a double presupposition. Each presupposes the other, but in a different way: (1) The redemptive knowledge must be seen to have come from God, the Creator of heaven and earth, the same God to whom Scripture points in the natural order and the moral law, whom Scripture describes as the Triune Creator and Sustainer of the world. This is a logical or conceptual presupposition. It is not a propaedeutic or a first lesson in redemption, for, as we have seen, merely opposing a Christian interpretation of the Creator to a heathen one does not produce faith; we know the Creator only in the gratuitous promise of mercy in Christ —which is the other presupposition: (2) The knowledge of God the Creator comes only to those illuminated by the Spirit in faith, although the knowledge of faith, properly speaking, is not God as seen in his general creative activity, but as seen in the special work of redemption in Christ. Thus, the knowledge of the Redeemer is an epistemological presupposition of the knowledge of the Creator.[1]

(d) While it is clear that the God who creates redeems, and that redemption must be understood in the light of man's original creation, a further question can be asked. Does redemption in Jesus Christ have any broader context than the healing of man's sin and rebellion? Is the incarnation simply the remedy for sin or is it the crowning of creation? Is the work of Christ simply salvation from sin, or is it also the fulfillment of the purposes of God in creation? Calvin regarded it a vague speculation of the frivolous and seekers after novelty to raise the question whether Christ would still have become man if man had not sinned.[2] Even when allowance is made for rhetoric, the direction of Calvin's theology is clearly set.

146 Calvin was aware that Christ is properly called the "first-born of all creation." Yet he never really develops this theme. His attention is focused upon the problem of man's sin and his guilt. He is not concerned, as was Justin Martyr, to elaborate the thesis that all truth is contained in Jesus Christ or even, with Zwingli, to hope to meet the philosophers in heaven. For Calvin the problem is man's guilt, not his sense of meaninglessness.

[1] Edward A. Dowey, Jr., *The Knowledge of God in Calvin's Theology* (New York: Columbia University Press, 1952), pp. 238, 239.
[2] *Institutes* I, xii, 4.

Yet the case can be put too radically. No Reformer excelled Calvin in his appreciation for the liberal arts, for the skills and powers even of unredeemed man. Furthermore, no one was clearer than Calvin in affirming the universal revelation of God, and even the objective adequacy of that revelation. In his commentary on John 1:5 he wrote:

> For there are two distinct powers of the Son of God. The first appears in the architecture of the world and in the order of nature. By the second He renews and restores fallen nature. He is the eternal Word of God: and so by Him the world was made; by His power all things keep the life they once received; in particular, man was adorned with the unique gift of understanding, he still sees and understands, since what he naturally possesses from the grace of the Son of God is not entirely destroyed. But because of his dullness and perversity he darkens the light he still has, it remains for the Son of God to assume a new office, that of mediator, and re-form lost man by the Spirit of regeneration. Therefore, they put the cart before the horse who refer the light which the Evangelist mentions to the Gospel and the preaching of Salvation.[1]

Nevertheless, Calvin, for all practical purposes, relates the incarnation almost exclusively to the problem of sin and guilt. In this he set the pattern for subsequent Reformed theology.

Law and Gospel

The law for Calvin meant the "form of religion handed down by God through Moses.[2] It also meant more specifically the "moral law," a godly and righteous form of living, as well as the ceremonial, judicial and political laws of Israel. Here we shall be concerned with the law as the moral law or as "the eternal rule of a devout and holy life."

The law, in the moral sense, was written, even engraved, upon the hearts of all men by God. The importance of this fact for Calvin is clear from his frequent references to it. In the general conduct of life, men, as the creatures of God, know in some measure the right. Moreover, the law that is engraved on the heart of man is sufficient to condemn him and leave him without excuse. Nevertheless, the law that is engraved on the heart has been obscured by man's sin. Hence there is needed the clearer manifestation of the law that is given in the Ten Commandments and in the teachings of Jesus Christ. Calvin and the Reformed tradition after him gave major attention to the Ten Commandments as the Summary of the Law. Gordon Rupp contends that John Wesley in shifting the emphasis from the Ten Commandments to the law of Christ as the

147

---

[1]*Corpus Reformatorium,* XLVII:7.
[2]*Institutes* II, vii, 1.

definitive statement of the law made a major contribution to the development of Protestant theology.

1) The Significance of the Law

The significance of the law for Calvin is indicated in some measure by the systematic ordering of the doctrine in his theological works.

In the *Institutes* of 1536 the chapter on the law stands first, but it is doubtful that Calvin had at this point really thought through the architectonic problems of theology. It is clear, however, that he is aware that he enters upon the theological scene when one of the pressing questions was, "Can Protestantism produce an ethical man?"

In the *Instruction in Faith* (1537) he discusses the law before he discusses the Creed, but in the Catechism of 1545 he reverses the order and places the law after the Creed.

In the liturgy that Calvin prepared at Strasbourg the law is placed after the prayer of Confession and the Absolution.

In the *Institutes* of 1536, 1539, and 1543 the law precedes the Creed. In the *Institutes* of 1559 the law is included in the section on God the Redeemer, though there are some discussions of the law in all four books. Prior to his major discussion of the law he inserts the chapter entitled, "Fallen Man Ought to Seek Redemption in Christ."

The systematic placing of the law seems to indicate that Calvin progressively sought to underscore the importance of the law, not simply as a preliminary for the Christian life, but as part of the Christian life itself.

2) The Interpretation of the Law

Calvin understood the law not in an impersonal sense but as the personal presence and claim of God. The "true and pure religion was so revealed in the law, that God's face in a manner shone forth therein."[1]

Moreover, the principles that Calvin lays down for the interpretation of the law make it clear that at least in intention he understood the law in a more existential, universal, and inclusive sense than any legalism or moralism would allow. The law must be understood in the light of the character of the Law-giver. Specifically, this means, *first of all,* that the law involves inward and spiritual righteousness as well as outward conformity. *Secondly,* the commandments always contain more than is expressed in words. "In almost all the commandments there are such manifest synecdoches that he who would confine his understanding

148

---

[1] *Corpus Reformatorium,* **XXIV:262.**

of the law within the narrowness of the words deserves to be laughed at . . . I think this would be the best rule, if attention be directed to the reason of commandment; that is, in each commandment to ponder why it was given to us. For example, each precept either commands or forbids. The truth of each sort comes to mind at once, if we look into the reason or purpose.[1] *Thirdly,* it is necessary to ponder what the division of the divine law into Two Tables meant. "The worship of God is the beginning and foundation of righteousness."[2]

By these methods of interpretation Calvin sought to express the validity of the law for his day and every day. He leaves no doubt that in his judgment the law had a universal and permanent validity. It was no temporary dispensation but God's will for man as man.

3) The Law and the Gospel

The gospel, Calvin never wearied repeating, abrogates the rigor of the law but not the validity and claim of the law. The rigor of the law was the necessity of perfect obedience as a condition of salvation. However, Calvin is very clear that even in the matter of salvation the problem was not in the law but in man.

> . . . Since our carnal and corrupted nature contends violently against God's spiritual law and is in no way corrected by its discipline, it follows that the law which had been given for salvation, provided it met with suitable hearers, turns into an occasion for sin and death. For, since all of us are proved to be transgressors, the more clearly it reveals God's righteousness, conversely the more it uncovers our iniquity. The more surely it confirms the reward of life and salvation as dependent upon righteousness, the more certain it renders the destruction of the wicked.[3]

The grace of the gospel is the gift of salvation when men failed to obey the law.

The gospel, however, relieves only the rigor, not the claim, of the law. The gospel means that man's salvation does not depend upon obedience and that man now has an additional motive for obeying the law, namely, gratitude for the gift of the gospel. Gratitude becomes a frequent theme of Calvin, but never to the exclusion of the fact that man is obligated to obey the law as the creature of God.

149

The following paragraph from Calvin's tract against *Spiritual Libertines* is a very good summary of his viewpoint.

> There are two things to consider in the law: the first is to apprehend the doctrine which is the rule for a good life because our Lord shows

[1]*Institutes* II, vii, 8.
[2]*Ibid.,* II, viii, 2.
[3]*Ibid.,* II, vii, 7.

to us that which is pleasing to him and that which he approves. Thus the doctrine of the law is to show us how our life should be conformed to the will of God. The second point is the rigor: in as much as it denounces to us that whoever is lacking in a single point will be cursed and does not promise salvation except to those who will have perfectly observed all his commandments. . . . Thus that is why the world despairs, if the law with its implications has authority over us. Because it is not possible to satisfy its requirements. . . . We see clearly that this liberty is only in regard to the curse and to the rigor.[1]

4) The Three Uses of the Law

This understanding of the relation of law and gospel is illustrated in Calvin's development of the three uses of the law.

The first use of the law is that of a mirror that shows man his sin and convicts him of his guilt. "It shows God's righteousness . . . it warns, informs, convicts and lastly condemns, every man of his own unrighteousness."[2] This function of the law is exercised both in the redeemed and in the reprobate. The redeemed come to realize that they are upheld by the mercy of God alone and the reprobate "are so routed by the testimony of law and conscience, that they betray in themselves what they desire."[3]

The second use of the law restrains men for the sake of the "public community of men." The law serves as a halter to regulate the conduct of men who are not inwardly moved. Again, even the regenerate need the law not simply to prepare them to seek what they lack, but also to restrain them from slackening the reins on the lust of the flesh.

The third and principal use of the law serves believers as a guide and spur to righteousness.

> The third and principal use, which pertains more closely to the proper purpose of the law, finds its place among believers in whose hearts the Spirit of God already lives and reigns. For even though they have the law written and engraved upon their hearts by the finger of God [Jer. 31:33; Heb. 10:16], that is, have been so moved and quickened through the directing of the Spirit that they long to obey God, they still profit by the law in two ways.[4]

Calvin's emphasis on the third use of the law is in line not only with his positive view of the law but also with his emphasis on sanctification. The fact that he moves immediately from faith to repentance rather than to justification by faith indicates that he wanted to avoid

---

[1] *Corpus Reformatorium* VII:206-207.
[2] *Institutes* II, vii, 6.
[3] *Ibid.,* II, vii, 9.
[4] *Ibid.,* II, vii, 12.

any misunderstanding about the importance of renewal of life. His constant emphasis on progress in Christian living and his choice of metaphors from the military to describe the Christian life as a battle and a conquest likewise underscore the same emphasis.

The relation of justification and sanctification is very similar to the problem of law and gospel. For this reason Reinhold Niebuhr's evaluation of Calvin's theology at this point can serve as an appropriate summary:

> The definition of the Christian paradox of justification and sanctification is probably made more carefully in Calvin's *Institutes* than in any other system of thought. If he errs on the side of claiming too much in the end it is an error which is difficult to correct without committing the opposite error. But that Calvin committed an error, in feeling too secure in the sanctification of the Christian, is attested not only by his other writings, where he does not always make such careful qualifications and reservations, but also by his own actions.[1]

[1] Reinhold Niebuhr, *The Nature and Destiny of Man* (2 vols.; New York: Charles Scribner's Sons, 1943), p. 200.

SUMMARY STATEMENT

Creation and Redemption   *Law and Gospel*
Justification and Sanctification

1. The Reformed and Lutheran traditions are agreed that creation is the work of God, the Father, Son, and Holy Spirit, and that, therefore, the creation is essentially good in spite of the presence and power of evil.

151

2. The God who creates also redeems and for this reason the creation must be understood in the light of redemption and redemption in the context of creation.

3. Some in our traditions tend to relate redemption too narrowly to man as sinner. We, however, are agreed that we should also bear adequate witness to the significance of redemption for the whole created order, inasmuch as creation and redemption have an eschatological dimension pointing to a new heaven and a new earth.

4. We observe that with respect to law and gospel there are different emphasis in our traditions. In part these differences were and are semantic and arise out of different patterns of theological thought. For example, the Lutheran description of law as "always accusing" (*Apology IV*, 38) restricts the meaning of the term "law" more severely than is the case either in the totality of scripture or in the Calvinistic tradition.

5. We are agreed both that Jesus Christ is the fulfillment and end of the law, and that in the Christian life God continues to lay his claim upon the redeemed; but we are not agreed how to denominate that claim, whether law or gospel. Both Calvinists and Lutherans know themselves to be saved through the gospel and called to Christian obedience.

6. We are agreed that the doctrine of justification by faith is fundamental in both traditions. We recognize, however, that for Lutherans this doctrine has played a more formative role in the articulation of theology. This difference is due in part to the historical situations in which Luther and Calvin did their theological work.

7. We are agreed that each tradition has sought to preserve the wholeness of the gospel as including the forgiveness of sins and the renewal of life. Our discussions have revealed that justification and sanctification have been distinguished from each other and related to each other in rather different ways in our traditions.

8. Failure properly to interpret and relate justification and sanctification leads to the development of antinomian and legalistic distortions in both traditions.

In the light of these observations we acknowledge that differences exist between us, but we record our gratitude to God for the progress we have made toward mutual understanding and resolution of our differences. We also acknowledge the obligation laid upon us to submit ourselves to the guidance of the Word and Spirit in the further pursuit of these objectives.

Chapter Eleven

ETHICS AND ETHOS—A REFORMED VIEWPOINT

by Joseph C. McLelland

HOW should a series of conversations end? The decision of our Lutheran-Reformed group has been that the closing dialogue ought to consider not only certain key issues that have arisen between us, but also a specific area not yet explicitly handled, namely the "ethics and ethos" that divide and untie us. The two words are intended to indicate the moral codes that officially govern us and the social behavior that actually characterizes us. It is a distinction without separation, since our life together manifests a complex, consequent upon a long history of the mingling of both traditional codes and social pressures. We wish to speak about the relationship of theology and ethics, but will find ourselves forced to accept many insights of the new "social sciences" about the observable "image" which we present to the world.

Sociology and Ecclesiology

Whatever else the church may be, it is a human institution. The theological insistence on the "humanity" of the church finds itself wide open to the analysis of sociology, an analysis both helpful and irritating. The familiar critique of institutionalism involves key concepts such as image, corporation, group dynamics—including the dynamics of conversation groups such as this one. But more important for this paper is the fact that every group develops a certain character of its own, a style, even a "psychology." The entertaining approach of C. Northcote Parkinson has introduced the subject widely: his description of types of corporations, for instance, with their own sex and family life, their intermarriage and offspring, elaborates a theme that has its plausible and sober roots.

The fact is that the image of the group is what functions in social intercourse, an image held by others but also a self-image. To give two examples: let us suggest images that seem to be popular about Lutherans and Presbyterians. A typical image of "Lutheran" might include the following elements: someone of German descent, usually

153

evangelical but never teetotal, dogmatic about his faith but uncommitted or perhaps unrealistic about social issues. (John Updike has a brief caricature in *Rabbit, Run* which conforms to this image.) Behind this lurks the strange figure of Martin Luther, many things to many people but usually associated somewhat with the earthy peasant lately sketched in John Osborne's *Luther*. And one suspects that the film *Martin Luther* stopped at a good place—weren't his later years pretty nasty? A markedly different image presents itself with the name "Presbyterian." In North America the typical Presbyterian looks to the Church of Scotland as the "Mother Church," perhaps even calls his ruling congregational Court "the Kirk Session," remembers St. Andrew and Robert Burns with liturgical regularity, and supports the Orange Lodge and the Masonic Order. More serious is the "Puritan" element in the image: the old bourgeois virtues still form our orientation, as we master the world through hard work, yet shun "worldliness" as the gravest temptation. The classic type described by Max Weber as "this-worldly asceticism" is summed up by a recent text as follows: "The religious code, by denying indulgence in joyful revelry and dancing, in sexual gratifications, and even in sleeping (the ideal of the long hard day), left the puritan the concentration on work as his major ascetic technique."[1]

The point of such typology is not that it fits all cases, but that it is significant enough of the "ruling myth" or "dominant ideas" (to use sociological terms) that it illustrates the "master symbol" in a recognizable way. It shows a mixture of historical, theological and ideological elements which make a purely theological critique lopsided. This is the point that has been made clearly and powerfully in our own generation. Is it significant that some of the leading names in this respect are Lutheran? Think of Bonhoeffer's pioneer attempt in *Sanctorum Communio* (1927), and of the contemporary American writings of Peter Berger, Gibson Winter and Martin Marty. No doubt Bonhoeffer was wrong in his choice of social model (as Berger has charged in his contribution to *The Place of Bonhoeffer*),[2] since he accepted a formal and systematic concept of "collective person" from Simmel and Toennies; but he was entirely correct in noting the inescapability of sociological method for ecclesiology. The shape of community, of our "life together," is a shape open to empirical analysis and diagnosis.

154

[1]Hans H. Gerth, *Character and Social Structure: The Psychology of Social Institutions* (London: Rutledge and Kegan Paul, 1954), p. 235.
[2]"The Social Character of the Question Concerning Jesus Christ: Sociology and Ecclesiology," *The Place of Bonhoeffer*, ed. Martin Marty (New York: Association Press, 1962), pp. 53-80.

Later sociology has turned to just such empirical investigation of the relationship between religion and society, often with devastating result. The sociology of religion has shown various functions of religion that raise the deepest questions for theologians—an integrative function (Durkheim), a role providing "social theodices" that justify oppression (Weber), and ideological bulwarks for patriotism (Yinger). Such service of religion to its society suggests that the classic analysis of H. Richard Niebuhr in *Christ and Culture* remains a good starting point, and provides a warning that religion tends to be transformed by culture. This sociological datum suggests that groups as such are not entities with "ethics" but only with an "ethos," so that it is ethical individuals that alone supply the prophetic protest and the catalytic initiative to reform the group according to ethical norms.

A final point in this area of methodology is that today we continue to witness the dynamism of groups in terms of denominations and ecumenism. That is, just as there have been "social sources" of denominationalism,[1] so there are new social sources of church unity.[2] During the past thirty years there have been social forces at work of a unitive tendency—indigenization of ethnic groups, for instance, and denominational cooperation in comity arrangements, councils, and community services. Finally, the thrust of the ecumenical movement of the past years has effected virtually a new alignment. While it remains true that the denomination retains a certain character, a unitive power over all its members, it is now also true that within each denomination the spectrum of views tends to be more openly recognized, the attraction across denominational boundaries to likeminded Christians in other groups. Our divisions now tend to be vertical rather than horizontal, cutting through every denomination at right angles to the traditional loyalties.

In every conversation group this latter phenomenon is observable, and it has made us aware of the new complexity of our contemporary ecclesiology. To some extent it has tended to soften the ecumenical blow, since we realize that hasty action may well mean splitting denominations along "party" lines; many remain within their church not chiefly because of strong denominational feeling but rather from this pragmatic analysis of the dynamics of unity/disunity in our time. We know the general laws which have governed this dynamics in the past half-century, beginning with the early period of hesitant conversation,

155

---

[1] H. Richard Niebuhr, *The Social Sources of Denominationalism* (New York: Meridian Books, 1957).

[2] Robert Lee, *Social Sources of Church Unity* (Nashville: Abington Press, 1960).

in which each side wished to articulate its own position. This passed into a period of the strengthening of these very positions, the paradox of ecumenicity. Then—after Lund—the new time of "common study" in which at last we recognized that we must move together in theological research, so that the dialogue becomes more open not only to the other but to what Skydsgaard has termed "the third party" in our dialogue, the Truth itself. In the light of this should we not confess that these present conversations in which we are engaged have tended to revert to the second stage, with our historical bias and our anxiety to note the differences between Lutheran and Reformed types?

Lest we renew former divisive tendencies by our historical approach, therefore, it is well to begin always from this caveat concerning our new situation. It is too simple an interpretation to say that the Reformation was the beginning of the modern era; it is rather a better interpretation, as Hanns Rückert has pointed out,[1] to say that the Reformation delayed the break-up of medievalism by humanism for some two hundred years, while its genuinely modern or revolutionary insight was quickly lost by the return to scholasticism. The great Reformers themselves therefore represent an interlude in medieval history, their progressive tendency not properly grasped until the break-up of scholasticism in the nineteenth century. For instance, medieval ontologism formed the context of Protestant scholastic debates, with the Reformers' breakthrough into "historicism" reserved for the modern era. Again, is not the human-existential starting-point of modern theology (without endorsing its obvious aberrations) a sound reflection of Luther's *pro nobis?*

If such a thesis is true to some degree at least, then the images we have assumed from our respective traditions were formed largely in an age which had reverted to (or continued) pre-Reformation positions. In that case, our ecumenical rapprochment is more genuinely "Reformation" than our party-strife could ever be. With these remarks in mind, let us now proceed to a brief sketch of the distinctively Presbyterian-Reformed "ethics and ethos," and then conclude with a section on the contemporary involvement of our two denominations in what must be designated a radically new situation.

156

Calvinistic Styles of Life

The distinctive Calvinist ethic is usually summed up as "puritan." This term may be negative (abstainer, killjoy) or positive (hard worker, successful), used in praise or blame by historian, sociologist or

---

[1] "The Reformation—Medieval or Modern?" *Zeitschrift fur Theologie und Kirche,* 1955.

theologian; in fact, it is a stereotype or image. The famous thesis of Max Weber, *Die protestantische Ethik und der Geist des Kapitalismus* (1904-5) has fathered such a wealth and diversity of off-spring that it would be folly to enter the discussion in this paper.[1] Its crux was stated by R. H. Tawney: "Capitalism was the social counterpart of Calvinist theology."[2] Tawney accepts Weber's equation of the "economic virtues" of bourgeois capitalism with former acquisitive vices now reverenced by a new climate of thought produced by Calvinism's emphasis on secular works as a sign of election. The cluster of ideas involved here was accepted much too simply by Weber and his followers, especially the assumption of a pragmatic-secular philosophy of work (Benjamin Franklin in his "ideal type") as the legitimate child of Calvinism. Weber was correct, of course, in seeing that Calvin himself had accepted Luther's doctrine of the *beruf* and that this had become related to the notion of human signs of divine election. But he missed the heart of both Luther and Calvin, who stressed the secular because of a different premise—the Christian's response to the gospel, "faith active in love."

Yet something more remains to be said. Luther and Calvin agree on essentials but with a noticeably different accent. Luther has a bold and delightful approach to the question of worldly stations which bowls over the traditional clericalism of the church and brings dignity and purpose to the common life. His relating of one's *Stände* to service ("God gives you office that you may serve") introduced an ethical principle—a third use of the law!—consonant with his primary datum of justification by faith. Yet he remained medieval in his reliance on the concept of "just price" and prohibition of usury as sufficient guides for the new economy, and in his assumption that the problem of guilt was the essential and timeless question of man. No doubt he was a man of his time and place—fighting on two fronts, against Roman work-religion and against the radical Reformation's "Kingdom economy;" and no doubt also he was affected by his eschatological presentiments (we can only "repair and patch" the world, "and punish abuses and put bandages and ointments on its pocks"); but Lutheran social ethics ever since have tended to rely on his distinction between the two kingdoms, and his rejection of the third office of law, and to avoid precision and sometimes realism, as the case of the *Deutsche Christen* party illustrates (according to a Common Reformed charge, at least!)

157

---

[1]An excellent summary and commentary of this "scholarly melee" is provided in *Protestantism and Capitalism, The Weber Thesis and Its Critics,* ed. Robert W. Green (Austin: Heath, 1959).

[2]*Religion and the Rise of Capitalism, A Historical Study* (London: J. Murray, 1926), p. 2.

Calvin's accent fell on the upbuilding of the Christian life through discipline, the third use of law. It may be significant that to word and sacraments Luther (for some time at least) appended penance whereas Calvin appended discipline. This was not merely ecclesiastical domestic. discipline, but a broad concern for society. It is seen in Geneva, where the Church Ordinances include regulation of interest rates, and especially in Scotland, where Knox's *Book of Discipline* (1560) envisages a covenanted nation, whose care for the poor and provision for educating the young come under the rubric "discipline." It is this sense of divine purpose present in all right vocations, and the acknowledgement of "the crown rights of the Redeemer" as being present, albeit indirectly, in the worldly realm, that became characteristic of the Puritan spirit. What was its theological basis? I suggest that it was rooted in a distinctive understanding of sanctification.

When Calvin approached the idea of justification it was already an established Reformed article of faith thanks to Luther. And already there were certain suspicions that it could lead to antinomian errors. For instance, John Knox avoided reliance on the words "justified by faith alone" and preferred such expressions as "justified through the blood of Christ," a more concrete and objective emphasis. Now Calvin also sought to preserve the Lutheran doctrine from error. He noted that justification and sanctification are inseparably joined, in analogy with the *unio hypostatica* itself. And he opts for a new point of departure, choosing to begin with sanctification, with the positive regeneration, the new life in Christ, in order to prevent misunderstanding.[1] It is this change in method and its resulting tone which led Karl Barth to name Calvin "the theologian of sanctification" as Luther is of justification. Calvin's theme is "the inhabitation of Christ in our hearts . . . the mystical union by which we enjoy him." Calvin can speak of our "participation" in Christ's righteousness, while struggling against the "essential righteousness" taught by Osiander. This appears to be little different from Luther's similar words, even in the early *Galatians,* where he does not teach justification as a legal fiction but clearly states that it is an effect of the indwelling Christ, of our union with him as members of his body.[2] Considering this, and Luther's original context for the teaching of justification (the penitential system based on saintly merit, focused on All Saints' Day 1517) must we not conclude that Luther

158

---

[1] *Institutes* III, 1-12.
[2] Cf. Philip S. Watson, *Let God Be God, An Interpretation of the Theology of Martin Luther* (London: The Epworth Press, 1947), pp. 167 ff. for Luther's teaching on union with Christ through which his "true and substantial presence" is shown; moreover the Holy Spirit dwells in believers "not merely as to his gifts, but as to his substance."

too was struggling for "sanctification by faith alone?"

Yet for Luther sanctification remained a problem in forgiveness of sins—he sees everything in the light of a prevenient grace, including this sphere of vocation, as Einar Billing and Gustaf Wingren have shown. Luther seems to be a man always looking at a single point in the christological spectrum, the initial red zone, examining all else in its peculiar light. In Billing's famous words: "Whoever knows Luther, even partially, knows that his various thoughts do not lie alongside each other, like pearls on a string, held together only by common authority or perchance by a line of logical argument, but that they all, as tightly as the petals of a rosebud, adhere to a common center, and radiate out like the rays of the sun from one glowing core, namely, the gospel of the forgiveness of sins."[1] It is Calvin's intention not to depart from this heritage but to move along the spectrum. This change in figure suggests the false alternatives presented by Billing's metaphor, for continuous thought may be held together by more than "common authority or . . . logical argument," it can follow the interior logic demanded by historical event, which presents a richer and more complex facticity than perhaps Luther's concentration allows. This is to say that Calvin offers a certain complement to Luther, developing implications of the gospel set free by Luther's reformation. (This is the way the Reformed Church learns its sixteenth century history, beginning with a long and devoted look at Luther, then proceeding to Calvin as to a further stage in the same story; Lutherans, I suspect, have difficulty proceeding to Calvin except as a threat or originator of debating points. In this regard, perhaps Lutherans attribute to the man Luther too great a respect for theological balance, whereas Calvinists generally view Calvin in a series of reforming figures.)

For Calvin, then, sanctification seems a better focus for theological reflection: the new life moves into prominence, lacking something of the dialectical tension of Luther's thought of the two kingdoms, and therefore providing a more positive context for ethical decision and action. Here, Luther's doctrine of "vocation" unfolds into a new stress on "stewardship." It is tempting to generalize, to see Luther as holding a sort of interim-ethic, so that Bultmann in our day is the outworking of such existentialism, whereas Calvin's stress on structures of power would issue in the critical realism of Reinhold Niebuhr, for example. At the least we may discern with each an accent which is distinct but not necessarily separate from the other. Luther's doctrine

159

[1] *Our Calling,* trans. Conrad Bergendoff (Facet Books; Social Ethics Series, No. 1, ed. Franklin Sherman; Philadelphia: Fortress Press, n.d.), p. 4.

of *larvae dei* may express a more pessimistic or hesitant acceptance of worldly structures than Calvin attains. Luther, we may say, seems to restrict sanctification to an analytical process, drawing out the implications of justification, always with an eye on works-righteousness. Calvin is able—surely because of Luther's prior work!—to move confidently into sanctification as a more synthetic question, drawing on insights from outside the purely soteriological, for example the *triplex munus* of our Lord in which kingship plays a key role. This is why he appreciates a third use of law, which he discerns especially in the Psalms, as a mirror to the life of faith, the works proper to faithful living. The Calvinist knows he is always a sinner, but stresses the adjective "justified" and so achieves a freedom from the "always accusing" role to which Lutherans restrict the law.

The historical outworking of Calvin's positive stress, however, provided ground for the puritan stereotype. The book by Scotland's James Hogg, *The Private Memoirs and Confessions of a Justified Sinner* (1824), like the incisive portrait in Robert Burns' *Holy Willie's Prayer,* shows a hypocrisy and antinomianism which indicate a dreadful separation of grace and election from faith and sanctification. The threat of antinomianism is not a Lutheran preserve! The dynamics of Calvinism which could produce this type also produced the legalistic preoccupation of certain puritan ethics (probably it is basically a legalism, creating conditions for libertarianism under the guise of "legalistic" adherence to doctrinaire predestinarianism). Whatever be our estimate of this typology, it is better to learn from our histories the pattern of temptation and error, and then to turn to our contemporary situation to see whether new factors have emerged. I submit that the novelty of our time reduced much of the historical sketch to prelude or preparation for dialogue; it cannot be normative.

The New Situation

160   Ours is a new age not simply because historical conditions have changed, so that we face new ethical problems of industrial, urban, secular man; but also because exegetical and theological studies have enabled us to hear the word of God in new ways from those of our fathers. Thus we appreciate the fact that scripture has to do with persons and communities of persons, and with certain patterns or styles of life. Joseph Sittler has stated: "Christian ethics is *Christological* ethics, not in the sense that such ethics are correlates derived from propositions about Christ, but in the sense that they are faithful re-

enactments of that life."[1] The phrase "style of life" has been made familiar by Jacques Ellul, and to it corresponds Bonhoeffer's category of "conformation." Again, Paul Tillich has warned that there are "structures of evil" to which we must oppose "structures of good." This sounds much like Reinhold Niebuhr's insistence on the corporate nature of ethical issues, the power structures of our world. These theologians, by the way, suggest part of our new situation—three are Lutheran, two Reformed, yet their work and influence is never judged on such denominational lines. Rather one finds a different sort of debate— between existentialist and situation ethics, for instance. We recognize the social element in every moral decision—Kierkegaard helped us understand decision but did not himself understand the significance of *Gegenwart*. We live after the Social Gospel but we cannot pretend that it did not deepen our ethical understanding. And whether we like Karl Barth's "law as the form of the gospel" thesis, we have to admit his insight into the unity of theology and ethics, the moral commentary flowing from every theological statement.

Modern ethics could be said to have shifted the tension between the "two kingdoms"—which Luther interiorized to a marked degree— so that we must reckon not only with the difference between church and world, but with a further dimension intersecting the other, between private and public, personal and corporate. Niebuhr's "moral man and immoral society" expresses this idea, and more recently it is shown by sociology to be a question of "structure/power" alignment. Therefore we are facing moral issues with a new appreciation of their complexity, and with a new stress on the social dimension. The emphasis today is on "the area of man's collective behavior—his use and misuse of political and economic power, his action as a racial being, as a consumer and producer, and as a citizen."[2] It is no longer a matter of private morality, expressing well-intentioned motives through acts of loving service to the "neighbor." The old question "Who is my neighbor?" has lost its meaning, for now the neighbor is not open to me in personal ways—as a fellow member of our "employee society," he is a functionary in a manifold of mechanistic-cybernetic impersonalism which chokes the natural flow of love which Luther and Calvin took for granted. Another word of Max Weber's is to the point: "The idea of duty in one's calling prowls about in our lives like the ghost of dead religious be-

161

[1]*The Structure of Christian Ethics* (Baton Rouge: Louisiana State University Press, 1958), p. 48.
[2]Waldo Beach and H. Richard Niebuhr (ed.), *Christian Ethics, Sources of the Living Tradition* (New York: Ronald Press, 1955), p. 478.

liefs." It does not fit into our new pattern of the power elite, the corporate authority, the elusive point of decision, the context of an I-It world. Stimulus now is given by mass communication media, and response in terms of ideology. The emerging *ethos* and its quasi-ethical *mores* has a statistical basis (quantitative: what is "normal?") and issues in a practical existentialism. What is being called "the new morality" reflects our dilemma, a reductionist form of Augustine's "Love and do what you will."

In such a situation, our game of Lutheran-Reformed dialogue must soon expire and give place to a hearty cooperation in the task of theological ethics; otherwise we abdicate from the twentieth century. So far we provide support for Sidney Mead's diagnosis of the "schizophrenia" of American denominationalism: we draw our values (moral and social ideas and attitudes) from the modern world, but our doctrine from the medieval, pre-scientific world.[1] Mead's analysis includes four characteristics of American Protestantism: historylessness (the anti-traditional view overcame the earlier view of the Reformation as the proper tradition), voluntaryism (the church is a promotional group intent on its own preservation and spread), mission enterprise (activist and interdenominational), and revivalism (reacting against the ethos of the Enlightenment, "the bulk of American Protestantism was molded primarily by pietistic revivalism and scholastic orthodoxy"). These combine to continue the style of the "epic epoch" of the frontier period, so that individualism remains the touchstone, and "personal ethics" the norm. The social concern, in the United States perhaps more than in Canada, remains suspect through ideological nuances of "creeping socialism," threat to the American way of life, betrayal of the Founding Fathers, etc. (e.g., any issue of *Time!*).

In the light of this more complex and more unified ethical task in our day, it would seem clear that even our traditional disagreement on the gospel/law distinction and the relation of the two kingdoms is not so directly significant as we assumed even last year. That is, I believe that other forces shape us today more powerfully than denominational stereotypes—probably nineteenth century forces still working themselves out. A recent example is the suggestion in the Lutheran journal, *Dialog* that Tillich's difference from Barth is explicable as follows: "here we have a modern version of the fundamental conflict between Calvinists and Lutherans in christology, between the *extra-Calvinisticum* and the *infra-Lutheranum*—whether the finite is capable

162

[1]*The Lively Experiment, The Shaping of Christianity in America* (New York: Harper and Row, 1963), p. 128.

of the infinite. On this question hinges the decision whether Tillich's method of correlation as well as his friendly relations with mysticism and philosophy were at all justifiable."[1] Now I submit that this will not do; you cannot typify these men in such traditional categories. They are both modern men, with a profound feeling for historical theology, yet conscious of the lines from nineteenth century thought (cf. Tillich's early work on Schelling and Barth's book on that very century). Moreover, they are post-Kantian, wrestling with existential-phenomenological and linguistic-analytical challenges and insights; and where Barth takes the Reformation most seriously, it is often to Luther that he goes rather than Calvin.

Can sixteenth century distinction—or battle-cries—such as *extra-Calvinisticum* and *finitus non capax infiniti* grasp us today? I think not. I think they screen us from continuing the Reformation, that is from being true to its spirit and moving on in line but considerably in advance of where our fathers stood. They prevent us from taking seriously the new things that have changed the shape of the human condition, altered the context of faith and its loving activity. Such theses as are advanced by those who view the modern "technopolis" as a new creation, or those who speak of the "death of God" as an event in our time—we may want to argue with them but if so it cannot be on terms other than today's. Perhaps a third area of modern debate, unknown to our sixteenth century fathers, is that of the Eastern religions, with their non-Hellenistic philosophical basis and their striking parallels to justification by faith. Here too our dialogue cannot simply dredge up old formulae forged in other contexts as if God had providentially arranged sixteenth century Europe as the essential human condition. Luther's recovery of the gospel was not a recovery of the whole gospel— no man's is—but of the essential gospel for his day. So Luther and Calvin are speaking to us today from a kind of tangential situation, relevant at points but not correspondent in certain key areas. This is the insight about the humanity of the church with which this paper began.

163

We are left, then, with a genuine distinction between two kinds of Christian spirituality, Lutheran and Reformed. During the past four centuries certain stereotypes have developed—the Gemütlich Lutheran and the Puritan Calvinist, for instance—which have operated to reinforce and deepen the differences. If we say that Luther is beer and Calvin wine, does this have to do with a theological essential? Is it not

[1]"Paul J. Tillich: Lutheran and Catholic," (Vol. V, Winter 1966), p. 7.

rather a case of having to extend the adiaphorist struggle to these differences in culture, spirituality, style of life? Such an extension would help us measure the differences against the proper "rule of faith," to accept one another with our differences, and to express our unity in today's situation and today's language without the bondage to old forms. Is not a mere repetition even of "justification by faith alone" a kind of legalism?

Therefore we need a balanced acceptance of differing *ethoi*—that involves a sense of humor about our cultural origins!—in order to clear the way for dialogue on the critical ethical issues of our day. Perhaps we can overcome the deadlock about law/gospel by attacking contemporary moral problems on our common basis of "faith active in love" and the sanctification that is inseparable from justification. I judge that we should find it possible to take up new positions consonant with our fathers but not tied to their view of the choices. This is what we have found in other ecumenical dialogue—the liturgical breakthrough that could circumvent the old stalemate between Roman and Protestant eucharistic theories is the most striking example. How sad it would be if we, both children of the Reformation, sharpened our differences and entrenched our debates, instead of going forward into something new, reformers still!

Chapter Twelve

LUTHER'S "TWO KINGDOM ETHIC" RECONSIDERED[1]

by William H. Lazareth

PROMPTED by all the anguish of World War II, Karl Barth charged German Lutheranism with social ethical bankruptcy. Transcending the immediate political and military factors, this weakness was traced back to Luther's controversial doctrine of the "two kingdoms" of creation and redemption. It follows that Barth's attack is ultimately directed against the biblical and theological foundations of Articles XVI and XXVIII of the Augsburg Confession. From a Lutheran standpoint, no issue in Christian ethics is more sorely in need of an ecumenical reconciliation.

Lutheran Quietism under Fire

Karl Barth charged in a 1939 open letter to the French Protestants: "The German people suffer from the heritage of the greatest German Christian, from the error of Martin Luther with respect to the relationship of law and gospel, of worldly and spiritual order and power, by which its natural paganism has not been so much limited and restricted, as rather ideologically transfigured, confirmed and even strengthened. . . . Hitlerism is the present evil dream of the German pagan who first became Christianized in a Lutheran form."

Barth went still further in a 1940 wartime letter to the Dutch Protestants. He wrote: "To a certain extent, Lutheranism has provided a breathing space for German paganism, and has allotted it—with its separation of creation and law from the gospel—something like a sacral precinct. It is possible for the German pagan to use the Lutheran doctrine of the authority of the state as a Christian justification for National Socialism, and it is possible for the German Christian

165

[1]This paper was originally published in John C. Bennett, ed., *Christian Social Ethics in a Changing World* (New York: Association Press, 1966). Permission to reprint it here has been granted by the publisher.

to feel himself invited by the same doctrine to a recognition of National Socialism. Both have in fact occurred."[1]

Barth's position must be judged in the context of recent European theological developments. A theology of "orders of creation" (*Schöpfungsordnungen*) was promoted by some influential German Lutherans in the 1930's which badly corrupted a Christ-centered interpretation of Christian ethics. It moved in the direction of Idealistic philosophy, natural theology and an autonomous primal revelation of God in creation (cf. Althaus, Gogarten, Hirsch). At its worst it was twisted by the Nazified *Deutsche Christen* party to sanctify their heresies of *Blut und Boden*. They offered a pseudo-Lutheran view of orders of creation (e.g., the state) which would make them a "law unto themselves," sacrosanct sources of divine revelation parallel to and independent of God's normative self-revelation in Jesus Christ.

In order to salvage the realm of God's creation from such non-biblical perversions, Barth affirmed the *de facto* lordship of the cosmic Christ over the "outer circle" of the state as well as over the "inner circle" of the church. By fusing the reigning Christ of the New Testament with the theocratic ideal of the Old Testament, Barth emerged with a "Christocratic" ethic which seriously weakened the Pauline opposition between the law (work-righteousness) and the gospel (faith-righteousness) as competing ways of salvation.

Barth offered instead the novel hermeneutical principle: "the law is nothing else than the necessary form of the gospel, whose content is grace."[2] This conflation of the realms of justification and justice (*"Rechtfertigung und Recht"*) permitted him to suggest "examples of analogies and corollaries of that Kingdom of God in which the church believes and which it preaches, in the sphere of the external, relative and provisional problems of the civil community."[3] Employing language strangely reminiscent of the Liberal theology he originally set out to destroy, Barth justifies his approach on the ground that it is part of the church's mission "to set in motion the historical process whose aim and content are the moulding of the state into the likeness of the Kingdom of God."[4]

For most Lutherans, Barth's so-called "Christological monism" represents an understandable but indefensible reaction against the Nazi-

---

[1]The full texts of both letters are in Karl Barth, *Eine Schweizer Stimme, 1938-1945* (Zollikon-Zurich: Evangelischer Verlag, 1948).
[2]Karl Barth, *Community, State and Church; Three Essays* (New York: Doubleday Anchor, 1960), p. 80.
[3]*Ibid*, p. 179.
[4]*Ibid*, p. 171.

fied *Deutsche Christen* movement. Hermeneutically, his reversed sequence of gospel-law does not permit God's new covenant in Christ to purify as well as fulfill his old covenant with Israel. Theologically, this downgrades the unique work of God the Sanctifier in the church and works its way out in the direction of a "Christological" universalism. Ethically, this also downgrades the preserving work of God the Creator in society and works its way out in the direction of a "Christocratic" clericalism. In a noble attempt to check the godless autonomy of a modern secularized state, Barth seems to have substituted Christ's *de facto* rule over the world in a "theology of glory" for his *de jure* rule through the witness of the church in a "theology of the cross."

The basic fact remains, however, that Barth has properly exposed the "soft underbelly" of Lutheran social ethics in the realm of creation. Lutherans have been far more responsible in the realm of redemption. They have rightly stressed the redemptive significance of Christ, grace, scripture, faith and the gospel. But they have often neglected the crucial importance of the nonredemptive counterparts of Caesar, nature, tradition, reason and the law. Lutherans must quickly recapture and boldly champion the Reformer's appreciation of the "sacred secularity" of civil life which is at once free from church-rule and yet subject to God-rule.

In brief, there is nothing so sick about Lutheran ethics that a strong dose of Luther can not cure! Echoing the judgment of H. Richard Niebuhr: "More than any great Christian leader before him, Luther affirmed the life in culture as the sphere in which Christ could and ought to be followed. . . . Luther's answer to the Christ-and-culture question was that of a dynamic, dialectical thinker. Its reproductions by many who called themselves his followers were static and undialectical. They substituted two parallel moralities for his closely related ethics. As faith became a matter of belief rather than the fundamental, trustful orientation of the person in every moment before God, so the freedom of the Christian man became autonomy in all the spheres of culture.

"It is a great error to confuse the parallelistic dualism of separated spiritual and temporal life with the interactionism of Luther's gospel of faith working through love in the world of culture."[1]

Luther and the Augsburg Confession

The biblical message of salvation is for Luther a tension-filled unity which can be viewed from the perspective of any one of its constitutive elements. He can speak of "grace alone," "Christ alone," "scripture

---

[1] H. Richard Niebuhr, *Christ and Culture* (New York: Harper and Brothers, 1951), pp. 174, 179.

alone," or "faith alone" and mean thereby the same saving event in terms of its eternal source, historical expression, apostolic witness, or personal appropriation. In fidelity to this Christ-centered faith, Luther roundly condemned the moral and rational work-righteousness inherent in the philosophical theology of Rome in his day. Before God, reason must submit to scripture and works must bow to faith. In an evangelical "theology of the cross," men humbly confess that "the righteous shall live by faith" (Rom. 1:17).

With their salvation thus assured in the unmerited forgiveness of Christ, grateful Christians are free to redirect their reason and good works toward serving their neighbors' welfare. Luther grounds his ethic in the paradoxical nature of Christian freedom which accepts liberation from satanic bondage as the invitation for human service. All men act as their brother's keeper: willingly in faith, begrudgingly in rebellion. Since the Christian is at once righteous and sinful, his enforced service aids his self-discipline while his voluntary service meets his neighbor's needs. Against the presumption of Roman clericalism, Luther insists that all baptized Christians be permitted the beneficial exercise of their royal priesthood in loving service to their God-given neighbors.

In opposition to all unevangelical ethics of principles, "blue laws," ideals, or rules and regulations, Luther portrays the biblical pattern of a life of "faith working through love" (Gal. 5:6). A Christian ethic based on the "divine indicative" of God's grace (rather than the "divine imperative" of God's law) preserves the freedom of the believer under the guidance of the Holy Spirit through the Bible, the church, and prayer, to discover anew in each concrete situation what the will of God permits or requires of him then and there.

For the biblical foundation of his social ethic, Luther rooted his doctrine of the "two kingdoms" of creation and redemption in the Pauline eschatology of the "two ages" (*aeons*) in Adam and in Christ (Rom. 5). In the kingdom of God, the Redeemer rules all regenerate believers through Christ and the gospel in personal faith and love. In the kingdom of men, the Creator rules all sinful creatures through Caesar and the law in civil justice and order. As both Redeemer and Creator, God is at once the Lord of both kingdoms; as both righteous and sinful, the Christian is at once a subject of both kingdoms. Hence for an evangelical theology of society, the two kingdoms must always be properly distinguished, but never separated in secularism or equated in clericalism.

In this doctrine of the "two kingdoms" of creation and redemption, Luther reaffirmed the "sacred secularity" of the ordinary tasks of the common life as those which best serve our neighbors' needs to God's glory. Whether empowered by Christ in faith-activated love (Christian righteousness) or compelled by Caesar in law-abiding reason (civil righteousness), the Christian citizen lives not for himself but for the benefit of others.

Christian social action was a major concern in Luther's own life and thought. The profound effects of the Reformation in the area of religion is common knowledge to all. What is not so well known—or, at least, not so commonly acknowledged—is the impressive social reformation which Luther's theology envisioned and even partially brought about in the broad and inclusive expanse of the common life. Here again, Luther's contribution to a better world is incalculable.

This emancipation of the common life was not so popular a crusade as it might at first appear. Luther's understanding of the Christian ethical life compelled him to combat both extremes of clericalism and secularism as unevangelical. From the outset, he had to fight for the preservation of music, art, and sculpture in the worship life of the church (*Against the Heavenly Prophets*). Against Roman Catholics, he had to struggle for the opening of the monasteries and the freedom of all Christians to marry and to engage in secular pursuits without endangering their salvation (*On Monastic Vows: On Married Life*).

Against recalcitrant parents and lax public officials, he also fought for educational reforms and the establishment of community chests to replace the illiteracy and begging so prevalent in his day (*On Keeping Children in School; Preface to an Ordinance of a Common Chest*). Against irresponsible merchants, he attacked economic injustice and proposed government controls to halt unfair commercial and labor practices (*On Trading and Usury*). Against both the reckless mobs which confused their Christian freedom with their civil rights, and the arbitrary rulers who disregarded their responsibility under God for their subjects' economic and social welfare, Luther appealed for both civil obedience and—less strongly!—political justice in a community of law and order (*Admonition to Peace; Exposition of the Eighty-second Psalm*).

It is true, however, that Luther did not normally conceive of the Christian's social responsibility as transforming the existing structures of society. While persons can be transformed by the gospel in the kingdom of God, institutions can only be reformed by the law in the kingdom of men. Men are to accept the social structures for what they are (the Creator's dikes against sin), and try to act as responsible Christian citizens within them (as the Redeemer's channels of serving love). When our secular occupations among men are faithfully acknowledged to be part of our religious vocation under God, then love provides law with its ethical content and law provides love with its social form.

For example, against those who would spiritualize marriage into a Christian sacrament, Luther protests that marriage belongs essentially to the realm of creation and not redemption. It is therefore ruled by God's law and not his gospel, and, as such, is one of God's temporal remedies against sin and not a sanctifying means of grace.

On the other hand, against those who would interpret this liberating message as justification for carnal lust and licence, Luther is equally insistent that marriage is rooted firmly in the creative will of God as one of his own divine ordinances. Although it is not a sacrament of the church, there is nevertheless no higher social calling in which a Christian can exercise his faith in deeds of serving love for his family and neighbors. Hence, the ex-monk Luther eventually married himself as a public testimony of faith in witness to his restoration of the evangelical view of marriage and home life under God.

For Luther's social ethic, all offices and stations of life—ecclesiastical, domestic, economic, political—embody in institutional form a particular command of God's law. They are all integrated within the earthly kingdom of men as the Creator's divinely-ordained bulwarks in his ongoing struggles against Satan. There is no particularly "Christian" form of these "orders." Though corrupted by sin themselves, the "orders" are still the means by which the Creator graciously preserves his fallen world from even greater chaos, injustices, and suffering.

This is why the church can "Christianize" politicians and economists but not politics and economics. These "orders" are ordained by God to remain secular, enjoying a relative autonomy of their own under the sovereign law of the Creator. Hence not faith and love but reason and justice are normative for the temporal realm of life. At the same time, however, it cannot be emphasized too strongly—against the background of the *Deutsche Christen* tragedy—that faith can illumine reason and love can temper justice whenever Christians meet their civil responsibilities as part of their religious discipleship. Lutherans, above all, need to learn anew from Luther that it is only through the priestly service of Christian citizens and the prophetic judgment of Christian churches that the state's "sacred secularity" is saved from godless secularism.

To conclude this brief survey of the Lutheran Reformation heritage in the area of Christian ethics, we shall cite four articles from the Augsburg Confession in which Luther's restatement of the central thrust of Paul's ethic is afforded normative authority by the Lutheran Church.

On the personal level, Article IV rejects all moral work-righteousness by grounding man's salvation solely in his being justified before God for Christ's sake through faith alone. Then Article VI militates against any ethical quietism by affirming that this Christian faith—"a living, busy, active thing"—is bound to bring forth good fruits, and that it is also necessary for Christians to do those good works which are commanded by God for the neighbor's benefit.

On the social level, Article XVI guards against any secularism by insisting that Christians are not to espouse any rigorous dualism between the two kingdoms of creation and redemption, but are rather to permeate all of society with personal love and social justice in the exercise of their Christian social responsibility. Finally, Article XXVIII complements this stress with a rejection of clericalism by sharply distinguishing the valid functions of the church and the state in the two kingdoms, and by refusing to permit the church to make or prescribe civil laws which fall properly within the domain of the state.

It is thus relatively easy to demonstrate the ways in which the Nazified *Deutsche Christen* misinterpreted the social ethic of Luther and the Lutheran confessions. Far more crucial, however, is the corollary challenge which now confronts those Christians who believe that Luther's social doctrine, in its essential features, is a valid restatement of Paul's eschatology of the "two ages" of Adam and Christ (Rom. 5). Is this not a relevant biblical answer to both the false heteronomy of the *Corpus Christianum* and the equally false autonomy of *Nausea* and *No Exit?* Can this doctrine be "de-medievalized" and qualified sufficiently to help shape the daily lives of Christians and non-Christians alike in a world "come of age"? The remainder of this essay represents a halting first step in that direction.

Lutheran Social Ethics
Christocentric Depth and Trinitarian Breadth

Evangelical Christianity embraces within itself both a religious faith and an ethical way of life. Creed and deed may be distinguished but never separated as faith supplies the power and love the direction for a life committed to the lordship of Jesus Christ. Both are determined by the biblical gift and command of a righteous life dedicated to the love of God and neighbor. Religiously, the emphasis is placed on "the righteous who shall live by *faith*." Ethically, stress is given to "the righteous who by faith shall *live*." Either way, this interaction of man's God-given faith and life constitutes an organic unity in which the Christian religion and ethic complement each other as root and fruit of the same God-pleasing tree. Faith gives life its religious meaning, while life gives faith its ethical opportunities.

Conceived of in this dynamic fashion, Christian ethics may be defined as that branch of theology which is concerned with the social activity of men as "the co-workers of God," through whom he governs the common life of society. The Christian life is essentially man's faithful re-enactment of the loving shape of God's act in Christ. It is God's love channeled through man's faithful deeds meeting his neighbors' needs. That is Christian ethics: faithful deeds meeting neighbors' needs.

Furthermore, it is a central affirmation of Christian theology that God rules the whole of his creation through the power of his holy word. This includes both the demands of his law and the promises of his gospel. By the law God rules men as their Creator and Judge; by the gospel he rules them as their Redeemer and Sanctifier. This means that all of God's sinful creatures are subject to his law, while only Christians—as both righteous and sinful—are responsible under God's law and gospel alike.

This divine power-complex provides Christian ethics with its twofold task. On the one hand, it performs a prophetic mission by calling all of society to account for its conduct in keeping with the universal law of God (civil righteousness). On the other hand, it performs a priestly mission by empowering and guiding the ethical activity of Christians in their faithful practice of brotherly love and community service (Christian righteousness). By employing the double-edged sword of God's word in this dialectical fashion, Christian ethics remains faithful to the normative pattern of Christ's ministry by judging a rebellious society from without, while at the same time serving it from within.

172   The peculiar characteristics of an evangelical ethic are determined by its fidelity to the ongoing activity of the living Triune God. Men learn to do God's will once they are enlisted into his service against the forces of evil in this world. Created and in the process of being restored to God's holy and loving image, Christians can best determine what they should be doing by first learning what God is doing. The testimony of Holy Scripture is clear that God provides all the resources necessary for a life devoted to the faithful stewardship of his manifold gifts in keeping with his sovereign will. As Creator, God supplies the

Christian life with its theater of action; as Redeemer, he provides its pattern and style; as Sanctifier, he generates its motives and power.

1) *When incorporated into the divine work of God the Redeemer, the Christian ethic is seen first as an ethic of freedom.*

To be a Christian is to accept what God has done for man's salvation in the person and work of Jesus Christ. It is for man to receive Christ as his personal Lord and Savior, faithfully acknowledging that on the cross of Calvary the Son of God atoned for his sin in his stead. It is to share through faith in the blessed fruits of Christ's righteousness. These fruits center in reconciliation with man's sin-forgiving Father and in redemption from the civil forces of sin, death and the devil. The Christian is freed from rebellious slavery for a life of faithful, hopeful and loving service.

This is what it means for man to be "justified by grace through faith for Christ's sake unto good works." This is the glorious gospel message of the mighty act of God in Christ. This is the "divine indicative" of God's gracious action which always precedes the ethical actions (or better, responses) of Christian men.

This liberating power of Christian faith as a life-transforming commitment to a personal Savior—rather than to an impersonal ideology, system of thought or institutional structure—militates against any ethic which would subject men once again to the yoke of self-righteous legalism. Nevertheless, every Christian age and tradition has been tempted to betray men's Christian liberty by denying that "Christ has set us free for freedom" (Gal. 5:1). Work-righteousness is a perennial danger for evangelical ethics, whether in its moralistic form in types of Catholicism and Calvinism, or in its rationalistic version in types of Lutheranism and Anglicanism. Christians do not have "merits to earn," "principles to apply," "ideals to realize," or "rules to obey." They have rather a crucified and risen Lord "whose service is perfect freedom."

2) *When incorporated into the divine work of God the Sanctifier, the Christian ethic may also be viewed as an ethic of grace.*

173

It is God and not man who generates the unselfish love which Christians try to transmit to their neighbors. It is the living Lord himself who acts through the actions of Christians after they have dedicated their lives to become the willing instruments of his love. For being a Christian means not only to accept what Christ has once done for us and our religious salvation (justification). It also involves the acceptance of what he continually does in and through us for our ethical service (sanctification). Whomever God declares righteous by grace through faith he makes righteous by grace through love.

The Holy Spirit resides in the hearts of Christians and enables them to exercise his gifts of peace, love and joy as regenerated "little Christs" to their neighbors. Living within the community of grace we call the church, Christians are constantly nourished by God's word in sermon and sacrament to empower their growth in grace as new creatures in a new age. However tarnished by the forgiven sin which still remains in their hearts, the social action of Christians is acceptable to God as the "Christian righteousness" of faith active in love.

Certain of the righteousness of God through faith in Jesus Christ, Christians are free both personally and corporately to join with other men of good will—whatever their faith—in working together for more just civil approximations of the moral law of God. Such cooperation is possible in the temporal realm of "civil righteousness" because some form of God's law (however corrupted by sin) is to be found written on the hearts of all men created in God's image. Through the common insights of God's general witness apart from Holy Scripture, enlightened men of all faiths can agree on many key features of personal morality and public legality.

Fortunately justice among men is not dependent on justification before God. Non-Christians who may not fulfill the spirit of God's law in faith and love are still able to obey the law's letter in reason and justice (often to the shame and judgment of more apathetic Christians). Consequently, as we shall note more fully below, Christians will find it highly necessary and beneficial to cooperate with all conscientious "children of light" in the ongoing struggles for peace, justice and freedom in the world.

3) *When incorporated into the divine work of God the Creator, the Christian ethic may finally be considered a social ethic.*

This does not mean, of course, that the Christian does not have any personal responsibilities. What it does mean is that the man of faith views his personal responsibilities from the perspective and within the totality of the myriad of communal commitments and relationships in which he is inevitably and inextricably involved.

God never lets man "go it alone" as a non-related "rugged individual." Insofar as man is righteous, he is ruled by God's gospel as only one among many other members of the corporate body of Christ. It is his participation in this religious community which propels his ethical service. But insofar as he remains a sinful creature, that same man is ruled by God's law as he "renders to Caesar" all that is expected of him in the civil community as loyal citizen, industrious worker, and responsible husband, parent and neighbor. Whether at church or at home, in school or the factory, the Christian always finds himself living within God-preserved social structures in the midst of particular neighbors with concrete needs which await his personal love and social justice. Faith incorporates our earthly occupation into our heavenly vocation through the social action of the priesthood of all believers.

Christians have not always been faithful to their dual responsibilities as citizens of both kingdoms of redemption and creation. Instead of nurturing community-minded individuals and individual-minded communities, misguided Christians have often espoused a truncated ethic which has led them into either a false individualism or a false collectivism. Perhaps the former—individualism—is more common to Protestant piety, in which a man often limits his ethical concerns to his own immediate, personal contacts, and permits the more impersonal social structures of the community to become "a law unto themselves" in a godless ethos permeated by secularism. On the other hand, Roman Catholic piety has sometimes encouraged a collectivistic ethos in which the institutional church and its hierarchy are permitted to dominate the temporal affairs of men in political and economic life and thereby invite the equally dangerous evils of clericalism.

It is precisely at this concluding point that we should recall the Barthian critique of Lutheran ethical quietism. In attempting to translate Luther's theology into the twentieth century, we must never forget to shift the ethical accent since his chief enemy was clericalism whereas ours is secularism. Oversimply, Luther had to put the church back under the gospel; we must put the state and society back under God's law.

Let no one underestimate the difficulty of this mission. Yet many unnecessary obstacles might be prevented at the outset if Christians would properly distinguish the gospel as redemption from the law of creation, and then further differentiate the law's theological function to condemn sin from its political function to promote justice. Especially in our pluralistic culture, men and women who cannot worship together under the gospel are still going to have to find more ways in which they can work together under the law. In mapping out the terrain, Christian social ethicists have an incomparable service to perform at this point.

For example, is there not a "hard core" of non-redemptive morality in what Lutherans call "civil righteousness," and what Calvinists call "common grace," and what recent ecumenical statements call "middle axioms," and what Roman Catholics call "natural law," and what Jews call "social justice," and what secularists call "enlightened self-interest?" Even Karl Barth is compelled to admit, "It cannot be denied that in the lists of examples [of ethical guidelines] quoted, we have more than once made assertions which have been justified elsewhere on the basis of natural law."[1] Well, as Shakespeare said, "a rose by any other name . . ."

Lutherans must now be challenged to make their fair-share contribution to this mighty ecumenical effort. Their traditional concentration on the gospel has energized a sound evangelical personal ethic: "faith active in love." But the whole vast realm of corporate structures and institutional life has often thereby been deprived of the normative judgment and guidance of God's law by the church's neglect of any corresponding social ethic: "love seeking justice." Though responsible for the proclamation of the whole word of God, Lutherans have generally been much stronger on the personal appropriation of God's gospel (for politicians and economists) than on the social demands of God's law (for politics and economic life).

In short, what Lutherans need desperately today is a prophetic counterpart to the priesthood of all believers. Evangelical Christians will be reverent to God's Word as well as relevant to God's world by expressing both their priestly "yes" through faith active in love and their prophetic "no" through love seeking justice.

176

---

[1]Barth, op. cit., p. 180.

Summary Statement on Ethics and Ethos

CHRISTIAN SERVICE IN THE MODERN WORLD

1. We are agreed that there is a common evangelical basis for Christian ethics in the theology of the Reformers. Both the Lutheran and the Reformed traditions have emphasized the new obedience of Christians through faith active in love and the inseparability of justification and sanctification. Our dialogue leads us to conclude that differing formulations of the relation between law and gospel were prompted by a common concern to combat the errors of legalism on the one hand and antinomianism on the other. While there remains a difference among us as to the importance we attach to the need for the instruction of God's law in the Christian life, we do not regard this as a divisive issue. We affirm together that Christians are free from the bondage of the law in order to live in love under the direction of God's Word and Spirit to the end of good order and eternal life.

2. In attempting to translate Reformation theology into the twentieth century, however, we must take into account not only a clericalism that frustrates the ministry of the laity, but also a secularism which denies that the world is the creation of God and the object of His love. This world is the arena for Christian ethical service. The impersonal structures of power in modern society are morally ambiguous. While they tend to pervert the humanity of men and the proper use of things, they also offer untold possibilities for good. This situation compels us to search for new ways of loving our neighbors. Recent technological and sociological developments intensify the urgency for translating personal love into social justice.

3. We believe that faithful obedience in modern life involves renewed stress on the vital interaction of Christian righteousness and civil righteousness. In response to the gospel of Christ, we welcome the opportunity for a united witness through Christian social action in service to the world. Such responsible public action will also involve us in cooperation with men of good will who are likewise committed to peace, freedom and justice in society.

177

Supplementary Statements Formulated at Evaluation Session

At the final meeting of participants in these conversations at Princeton, New Jersey, February 24-27, 1966, most of the time was given over to a discussion of the summary statements drawn up at the first three meetings. This was deemed necessary because some of the issues discussed earlier had been left unresolved with the statement that further attention must be given them. Also it was felt that the participants should assess the progress made during the total course of the conversations and relate the consensus reached to the historic differences between the two theological traditions. Therefore the summary which appears in this section covers more fully some of the points previously discussed. At the request of the group Dr. Warren A. Quanbeck prepared an additional paper which interprets the findings of the participants in the perspective of intellectual change and theological development between the 16th and 20th centuries.

The final document is the text of the report of the participants to their two sponsoring groups. Although the conversations were sponsored officially, the representatives appointed by the sponsoring organizations could speak only for themselves and not for their respective church bodies. Therefore the reaping of the ultimate fruit of these conversations will depend upon the steps which these bodies choose to take in the years ahead.

179

CONFESSIONAL SUBSCRIPTION

1. We are agreed that the Summary statement of 1963 (pp. 37-38) may stand as an accurate representation of our consensus with respect to the nature and centrality of the gospel, the nature and authority of scripture, and the necessity, functions, and historical provenance of our respective confessions.

2. We recognized at the 1963 Consultation that "credal and confessional subscription is regarded seriously in both Lutheran and Reformed Churches." Further discussion and reflection have led us to look in a somewhat different way at the fact of diverse opinion as to the "meaning" of confessional subscription (see p. 37, #7). We offer the following statements in order to clarify our common understanding of both the purpose and the use of confessions.

3. We have come to see that the unity of the Lutheran confessions has given them a place of such importance in the interpretation of scripture and in the determination of a theological position, that at times they have dominated scripture and led Lutherans into a false confessionalism. On the other hand, the multiplicity of the Reformed confessions has tended to relativize all of them with respect to their role as exegetical and theological guides, and has in some cases led Reformed churches into a false biblicism.

4. We have also come to see that in actual practice the variations *between* the Lutheran and Reformed Churches with respect to formal pledges of subscription, as well as to the degree of theological uniformity brought about by the use of the confessions, are very much the same as those *within* each Church.

5. We wish to avoid the dangers of biblicism and confessionalism by focusing upon the gospel to which both the scriptures and the confessions bear witness. We are agreed that a confession serves as a doxology, a hermeneutical guide, and an expression of theological consensus. It is clear that in serving these purposes creeds and confessions are not ends in themselves, but are instrumental to the proclamation of the gospel, the ministry of pastoral care, and the identification of a particular church in a given time and place.

6. In the effort to understand the sense in which confessions have a "binding" character, we must have in mind the fact that they are historical documents. They give testimony to the catholic Christian faith and to the way in which the scriptures have been understood in certain specific periods in the life of the church. One who subscribes to a confession affirms that it faithfully interpreted scripture with reference to the issues in question at the time the confession was framed. Insofar as the issues are the same, and no new perspectives from which to deal with them have been found, the confessional position is still affirmed, not merely as a formality but in the sense that the subscriber identifies himself by an inner consent with the confessional statement.

7. A confession is authoritative and binding because it is acknowledged as a responsible and effective way of interpreting the gospel. As such it provides a bond of unity, a sense of identity and a frame of orientation for those who make it their own. The subordinate and historical character of a particular confession, however, prevents it from serving as a final and exhaustive interpretation of the gospel and requires openness to the testimony of other churches. Confessional subscription obligates us to join with others in seeking a better understanding of the scripture and the contemporary culture. The church must seek to relate its life and message to the expanding knowledge and the changing thought-forms of each new generation. Thus, a confessional statement allows for the tolerable diversity of theological conviction that is to be found within as well as between our churches.

8. We are agreed that the absence of confessional commitment is injurious to the integrity and effectiveness of a church and its ministry of proclamation and pastoral care.

THE PERSON AND WORK OF CHRIST

1. We recognize that in the New Testament there is a variety of witness to the person and work of Jesus the Christ. This variety finds its unity in witness to one saving event.

2. The concern for this soteriological reality was manifested in the development of the Trinitarian doctrine and the Chalcedonian Christology.

3. The work of salvation depends on the person of Jesus Christ being really God and really man. It was wrought in history when God condescended to identify himself with sinful man in the life, suffering, and death of Jesus for us, and exalted us with him when He raised him from the dead and made him Lord.

4. The event of salvation is the once and for all conquest of sin, death, and all hostile powers and the once and for all achievement for man of forgiveness and newness of life.

5. God's saving work in Christ is made effective for men by the caring of His Holy Spirit. Through Him they are led to participate by faith in the crucified, risen, and ascended Lord who comes in the gospel as proclaimed, heard, and received in the Spirit.

6. The God who suffered and won the victory in Jesus Christ is the God who is everywhere present and who becomes God-for-us in His proclaimed work.

7. Jesus Christ gives us victory over sin and death and the hope of life to come. He frees us for a truly human life in and for the world, which itself shall be brought to fulfillment in God's eternal purpose.

LORD'S SUPPER AND CHRISTOLOGY

After fuller discussion of the Summary Statement on pages 103-104, paragraph 10, we now wish to say the following:

1. We acknowledge the obligation of churches and Christians to manifest publicly the unity they have in Christ. Among other ways in which this obligation is fulfilled is the celebration of the Lord's Supper.

2. The mobility of population in our age and the anonymity of an increasingly urban society have often altered the context in which the Lord's Supper is observed.

3. Intercommunion between churches, which may give a mobile population readier access to the Lord's Table, is not only permissible but demanded wherever there is agreement in the gospel. Such agreement means proclamation of the same gospel as the good news of God's reconciling work in Christ rather than uniformity in theological formulation.

4. Where this gospel is denied, intercommunion becomes a false witness on the part of those who receive the Lord's Supper and at the same time supports the false witness of those who administer it. Under such circumstances non-participation becomes a demand of responsible love.

CONFESSIONAL INTEGRITY AND ECUMENICAL DIALOGUE

by Warren A. Quanbeck

CONVERSATIONS between denominational families always raise questions and sometimes also suspicions about the thoroughness and loyalty of the proceedings. If differences could not be resolved in the 16th and 17th centuries, when the very survival of the Reformation seemed to hang upon some kind of agreement, why should they be easier to resolve in the present day? When those taking part in the discussion announce that they see no insurmountable barrier separating Reformed and Lutheran churches, journalists rejoice at the prospect of a good story, but doctrinal loyalists on both sides harbor suspicions. They suspect that the real issues were not faced squarely, or that formulas have been devised which pretend agreement but which only conceal deep differences, or that one side in the discussion has simply given in to the other. Is it possible for Reformed and Lutheran theologians, in full loyalty to their respective traditions, to face the issues which have separated them for centuries and reach profound and genuine agreement?

It is important to recognize that this is a possibility in our day, not because theologians are willing to betray their confessional heritage, or because they are skillful in contriving deceptive formulas of agreement, but because the whole theological scenery has been transformed through a tremendous growth in knowledge and through changes in theological perspective which have developed in the last century and a half. The development of empirical method in the natural and historical sciences, which began in the Renaissance, has in modern times produced profound changes in the way we ask questions, in the way we experience reality and in the way we understand ourselves and our relation to the world. It has greatly expanded the amount of knowledge we have of the world and our past and at the same time given deeper insight into the complexity of human problems. Man's scientific horizon has been expanded outward in a remarkable way through the replacement of a Ptolemaic world view by the Copernican outlook. Our knowledge of the past has been enriched in a corresponding way through historical research. The sciences of anthropology, psychology, sociology and others have presented us with an immensely detailed knowledge of human life and culture in a great number of different settings. From this information we have come to recognize the fact of cultural differentiation: that different cultures view the world and human experience in different ways and express their apprehension of life in different conceptual frameworks. This has led to a deepened understanding of languages in human life and thought and the realization that there is not simply one human way of thinking and speaking, but that even within a single linguistic tradition there are multiple languages corresponding to man's different ways of apprehending and reacting to his environment.

These developments have immensely enriched and complicated the task of theological reflection but they have also provided perspectives from which traditional questions appear in a new light. This does not mean that we are automatically wiser than our forefathers, but only that we have the same task in a quite different situation. They attempted to make the gospel meaningful for their time; our task is to communicate the gospel in an age of science, secular humanism and universal culture. The gospel remains the same, and the missionary responsibility of the church is the same, but the change in situation imposes upon us the task of using our resources to confront our contemporaries with the gospel. Let us examine some of the ways in which the changes in our cultural situation affect the traditional differences between Reformed and Lutheran theologies.

1. The development of modern historical science has given us a new way of apprehending both past and present. Whereas an older way of thought saw the world and man himself as something given, complete and essentially unchanging, we today see our experience in developmental terms. We see the world not as a static essence, but as a process of development. We see man and human institutions as products of a past and processes of development in the present— growing, maturing, declining, dying. We can only understand man, an institution or an artifact, in relation to the culture in which it exists, and to ignore this social, historical and cultural situation is to forego understanding.

185

This has important consequences for our understanding of the bible. The exegete of the Middle Ages could treat the bible as though it has no historical context, and apply texts immediately to his problems without attempting to understand them in the situation out of which they developed. When this method involved him in interpretative difficulties, he could escape into spiritualizing interpretations, invoking the tropological, allegorical or analogical sense of the passage. Today we cannot profitably or honestly ignore the historical context from which the books of the bible have emerged, and when we cannot be sure of this context, as happens, for example, in certain psalms, we find ourselves in interpretative difficulties. We can only understand what a text says to us when we understand what it meant to its first readers. This does not mean that all older commentaries are useless, for the best interpreters of the bible, Augustine, Luther, Calvin and others, brought great theological insight to bear on the problems of interpretation, and frequently operate in historical categories. But their work must be critically examined, and it sometimes turns out that their theological insight was better than their exegesis. Luther's understanding of the Lord's Supper, for example, shows insight which anticipates much laboriously achieved modern understanding of scripture, although a modern exegete would have a difficult time defending some of the exegetical scaffolding by which he supports and defends his position. Or in examining a dogmatic treatise we may agree with the theological assertion which is made even though we conclude that many passages of scripture assembled to support it have nothing to do with the question.

The historical-critical approach to the scriptures is not something to be opposed, rejected, or merely tolerated; it is a necessity of modern biblical study, and without it, it is more difficult for us to hear the word of God in the scriptures. The wrong use of the method should not lead to condemnation of the method, but rather a correction of a poor methodology. The method itself is one of God's gifts to his church in modern times; many contemporary students have learned that its proper use enables them to hear God speaking in the bible.

The awareness of historical development also has important consequences for our understanding of the history of theology. In its light we can see clearly that the Nicene Creed uses the theological method and vocabulary of the 4th century to assert the truth about Jesus Christ and to reject misunderstandings of his person and mission which threatened the clarity and power of the gospel. The language of the creed is not biblical language, but that of fourth century philosophy. Those who drew up the creed were compelled to use non-biblical language to assert the truth of the biblical message. We grasp what was at issue at Nicea as we use historical scholarship to understand the terminology used by the contending parties, to comprehend the issues in dispute, and so to understand how the church defended the true proclamation of the gospel against perversions. When we become familiar with the methods of historical scholarship we recognize that no theological vocabulary can be absolutized; each vocabulary has arisen in a specific situation for a special task and can only be understood in its situation. The task of theology is not simply to repeat the words which have proven effective in proclaiming or defending the gospel in past situations, but to understand the gospel so that we can do in our day what other theologians have done in the past. In fact, the process of repeating theological formulas can communicate a wrong understanding of the gospel if the meaning of the words has changed or the situation is altered. To repeat theological expressions addressed to humanistic optimism in a situation of despair about human capacities may not produce a repentance leading to life but only deepen a sorrow leading to death. And to proclaim to incorrigible optimists the encouraging words properly addressed to those in despair may not lead them to the true evaluation of the human predicament.

The problem of man is also illuminated by an historically informed theology. The static, essentialist theology had great difficulty doing justice to the biblical understanding of man in society or to the eschatological dimensions of the gospel. It tended to speak of man in individualistic terms, overlooking the meaning of the biblical expression "in Adam" as a collective existence under judgment, and doing less than justice to the new life in Christ as life in the people of God, the body of Christ, the new humanity. Its static terminology was also inadequate to express the dynamic tension of the Christian life between the resurrection of Christ and his *parousia*. The recovery of dynamic and eschatological language has enabled theologians to relate more effectively to the view of man expressed by modern anthropologists, sociologists and psychologists and thus to enter into a real exchange of ideas and genuine discussion and not be imprisoned in an ecclesiastical monologue.

In brief, the historical-developmental way of thinking gives the theologian tools which enable him to understand the scriptures and the history of theology more effectively, and also give him a standpoint to enter into a real discussion with contemporary thinking about man and his problems. This does not mean that the theological work of earlier times is without value and must be discarded. The worth of the earlier work becomes especially clear when it is studied historically. In this way the purpose and religious concerns of earlier theologians become available to illuminate our theological tasks and to give us the benefit of their wisdom and insight, even though we must learn to express it in contemporary vocabulary if it is to be meaningful for us or others of our time. The love of God in Christ remains the same, human estrangement in sin continues to be a constant, but the specific shape of man's flight from God varies from culture to culture. It is this varying form of man's evasion of God which sets the theological task: to recognize what tactics contemporary man uses to hide from God and to find the language which can communicate the judgment and love of God to him in his hiding place. The problems of theology have a certain consistency from age to age, and yet the shift from substantialist, static thinking to developmental dynamic categories means that every problem appears in a new light and from a different perspective.

2. A second way in which the historical development of theology has altered the setting and treatment of traditional questions is in the immense amount of new knowledge at the disposal of contemporary thought. The last century has witnessed a kind of explosion of knowledge so that the amount of material to be mastered in every branch of theology has greatly increased. Both in our knowledge of the scriptures and of the history of theology new dimensions of material are now available. It now appears that the different positions taken by Calvinist and Lutheran theologies are not always at odds with each other, but often represent different but complementary accents, different approaches which are both needed for a grasp of the fulness of the problem.

One example can be seen in the differing confessional histories of the churches. They differ from each other not as two answers to the same problems in arithmetic, one of which can be shown to be right and the other wrong, but as two different methods or styles of writing confessions. The Augsburg Confession of 1530 shows the church of the Reformation relating herself to the ancient Catholic tradition, and concerned to assert that what the reformers teach is no innovation but the true Catholic heritage. It is confession in the primary biblical sense of the word, the praise of God in the heralding forth of his mighty saving deeds. It points to the great primal realities of the Christian tradition and calls attention to the way God has acted for human salvation in Christ, and how he continues to act in the life and witness of his church. The Reformed Confessions, on the other hand, come from a later period in the life of the Reformation, in which the break with Rome is now taken for granted, and the churches of the Reformation seek to identify themselves. They are not as doxological in character as the Augsburg Confession, but are more dogmatic. They reflect the changed situation in the second generation of the Reformation, where the concern is less identification with the Catholic tradition than with the differentiation of one theological position over against another.

The development of an ecumenical approach to theology has also been aided by the increased amount of historical information available. When theology is concerned with only one church tradition, it can easily become narrow, defensive, and apologetic. But where it is exposed to a wide range of traditions, and sees them in historical perspective, it can no longer limit itself to justification of a single tradition, but must deal responsibly with the entire range of Christian churches. To the extent that its reading of other traditions is sympathetic and imaginative it discovers theological concerns similar to its own and also emphases which complement and occasionally correct elements in its own tradition. As it develops self confidence it finds less necessity for defending every event in its own denominational history, can acknowledge that the gospel has not always been expounded in its fulness, and can recognize and appreciate the presence of Christ in other traditions as well.

This induces a new theological mood. The task of the theologian is seen not as that of attorney for his own ecclesiastical institution, who must at all costs score points for his side in the theological debate. It is rather seen as responsibility to the whole gospel, and the ability to recognize both the strengths and the weaknesses of one's own tradition. The theological discussion also changes, becoming more a joint search for the truth of the gospel than an attempt to justify one's own side. It lays heavy demands upon those who take part in such discussion. It requires that they know the scriptures, that they are informed about the history of the church, the development of theology, and the situation which the church confronts today. It demands maturity, poise and self-confidence to avoid the perils of defensiveness and self-righteousness. It presupposes openness to the truth, and a willingness to have one's understanding of the gospel deepened and enriched by encounter with representatives of other traditions.

The discussion of the doctrine of the Lord's Supper is an especially good illustration of the benefits of an historically informed study proceeding under ecumenical auspices. The historical study of the scriptures and of the development of eucharistic doctrine has shown how rich and complex the Christian tradition is at this point. Each of the great traditions has developed one aspect of the biblical witness and worked out its implications for the whole of Christian doctrine, for worship, and for service. Other elements have not usually been excluded, but have not been worked out with the same thoroughness.

When the traditions are set alongside each other and examined in a sympathetic way, it can be seen that one does not necessarily have to choose one doctrinal tradition to the exclusion of all others. To be a loyal Lutheran does not mean that one can see no value in the dogmatic or liturgical tradition of the Eastern Orthodox churches, or that one must condemn the total doctrinal statement of the Roman Catholic or Calvinist traditions. The New Testament witnesses to a rich variety of theological motifs in interpreting the Lord's Supper: memorial, communion, thanksgiving, sacrifice, mystery, anticipation. No tradition in the church has done justice to them all; each tradition has sought to develop one or more of them. What is seen in the study of the scriptures, and noted again in the development of the church's doctrine, becomes real and existential in ecumenical discussion. Here one can see how Thomas Aquinas and John Calvin strive to assert the same religious concerns, how Luther's profound sacramental realism can be complemented by Calvin's stress upon the Holy Spirit, how the entire Western tradition can learn from a study of Eastern Orthodox theology and spirituality. As we perceive the richness and diversity of the church's tradition rooted in the scriptures we begin to see the dimensions of our theological task. We need a more thorough knowledge of the scriptures, an ever deepened understanding of the development of doctrine, and a sensitivity growing out of experience which enables us to recognize the significance of doctrine for worship, fellowship, service and mission.

REPORT TO THE SPONSORING CONFESSIONAL ORGANIZATIONS

1. We believe that the work assigned to us, namely: "to explore the theological relations between the Lutheran and Reformed churches to discover to what extent differences which have divided these communions in the past still constitute obstacles to mutual understanding," has been completed, that the conversations have been fruitful, and that additional meetings of this group are not necessary.

2. We recommend that the several judicatories of our respective groups be encouraged to
   a. Sponsor a series of Lutheran-Reformed study groups in various strategic geographical areas, using the four publications growing out of our work as background information and guides, and involving members of the Lutheran-Reformed theological discussion group, and other selected theologians and pastors as resource persons.
   b. Make these four publications available to all the theological seminaries of our two traditions, urging them to make use of these materials in an appropriate course or courses.

3. We recommend that full publicity be given to the findings of these consultations and to their implications for the life of our churches today.

4. As a result of our studies and discussions we see no insuperable obstacles to pulpit and altar fellowship and, therefore, we recommend to our parent bodies that they encourage their constituent churches to enter into discussions looking forward to intercommunion and the fuller recognition of one another's ministries.

PARTICIPANTS

Representing the Lutheran tradition:

Dr. Conrad Bergendoff, President Emeritus, Augustana College, Rock Island, Illinois

Dr. Herbert J. A. Bouman, Concordia Seminary, St. Louis, Missouri

Dr. George W. Forell, State University of Iowa, Iowa City, Iowa

Dr. Martin H. Franzmann, Concordia Seminary, St. Louis, Missouri

Dr. Martin J. Heinecken, Lutheran Theological Seminary, Philadelphia, Pennsylvania

Dr. William H. Narum, St. Olaf College, Northfield, Minnesota

Dr. Warren A. Quanbeck, Luther Seminary, Saint Paul, Minnesota

Dr. Theodore G. Tappert, Lutheran Theological Seminary, Philadelphia, Pennsylvania

Alternates:

Dr. Paul M. Bretscher, Concordia Seminary, St. Louis, Missouri

Dr. Harold Ditmanson, St. Olaf College, Northfield, Minnesota

Dr. William H. Lazareth, Lutheran Theological Seminary, Philadelphia, Pennsylvania

Dr. Fred W. Meuser, Evangelical Lutheran Theological Seminary, Columbus, Ohio

Consultants:

Dr. Paul C. Empie, Executive Director, National Lutheran Council (U.S.A. National Committee, Lutheran World Federation), New York, New York

Dr. Virgil R. Westlund, Secretary, Department of Theological Cooperation, National Lutheran Council, New York, New York

192

Representing the Reformed tradition:

Dr. William Fennell, Emmanuel College, Toronto, Ontario, Canada

Dr. Howard G. Hageman, Minister, North Reformed Dutch Church, Newark, New Jersey

Dr. David Hay, Knox College, Toronto, Ontario, Canada

Dr. George S. Hendry, Princeton Theological Seminary, Princeton, New Jersey

Dr. John Leith, Union Theological Seminary, Richmond, Virginia
Dr. Henry Stob, Calvin College, Grand Rapids, Michigan
Dr. Bard Thompson, Drew University, Madison, New Jersey
Dr. Cornelius Van Til, Westminster Theological Seminary, Philadelphia, Pennsylvania

Alternates:

Prof. Robert C. Johnson, Yale Divinity School, New Haven, Connecticut
Prof. Joseph McLelland, McGill University, Montreal, Quebec, Canada

Consultant:

Dr. James I. McCord, North American Secretary, World Alliance of Reformed Churches/World Presbyterian Alliance, Princeton, New Jersey